The New Argument in Economics

The William Volker Fund Series in the Humane Studies

EPISTEMOLOGICAL PROBLEMS OF ECONOMICS
by Ludwig von Mises

THE ECONOMIC POINT OF VIEW
by Israel M. Kirzner

ESSAYS IN EUROPEAN ECONOMIC THOUGHT
Edited by Louise Sommer

SCIENTISM AND VALUES
Edited by Helmut Schoeck and James W. Wiggins

A SOCIALIST EMPIRE: THE INCAS OF PERU
by Louis Baudin

RELATIVISM AND THE STUDY OF MAN
Edited by Helmut Schoeck and James W. Wiggins

FREEDOM AND THE LAW
by Bruno Leoni

MAN, ECONOMY, AND STATE—2 vols.
by Murray N. Rothbard

THE ULTIMATE FOUNDATION OF ECONOMIC SCIENCE
by Ludwig von Mises

PSYCHIATRY AND RESPONSIBILITY
Edited by Helmut Schoeck and James W. Wiggins

THE FREE AND PROSPEROUS COMMONWEALTH
by Ludwig von Mises

SCIENCE AND HISTORY: A CRITIQUE OF POSITIVIST
EPISTEMOLOGY
by Heinrich Rickert

THE NECESSARY CONDITIONS FOR A FREE SOCIETY
Edited by Felix Morley

ESSENTIALS OF ECONOMICS: A BRIEF SURVEY OF
PRINCIPLES AND POLICIES
by Faustino Ballvé

THE NEW ARGUMENT IN ECONOMICS
Edited by Helmut Schoeck and James W. Wiggins

The New Argument in Economics

THE PUBLIC versus THE PRIVATE SECTOR

Edited by

HELMUT SCHOECK AND JAMES W. WIGGINS

Papers by

KARL BRANDT	ARTHUR A. SHENFIELD
LOWELL B. MASON	GEORGE J. STIGLER
JEROME WILSON MILLIMAN	WILLIAM S. STOKES
SYLVESTER PETRO	ERNEST VAN DEN HAAG
J. FRED RIPPY	ELISEO VIVAS
WILSON E. SCHMIDT	W. ALLEN WALLIS

D. VAN NOSTRAND COMPANY, INC.

PRINCETON, NEW JERSEY

TORONTO   LONDON

NEW YORK

D. VAN NOSTRAND COMPANY, INC.
120 Alexander St., Princeton, New Jersey *(Principal office)*
24 West 40 Street, New York 18, New York

D. VAN NOSTRAND COMPANY (Canada) LTD.
358, Kensington High Street, London, W.14, England

D. VAN NOSTRAND COMPANY, LTD.
25 Hollinger Road, Toronto 16, Canada

PRINTED IN THE UNITED STATES OF AMERICA

Contributors

KARL BRANDT, Professor of Economic Policy and Director of the Food Research Institute, Stanford University. He served as one of the three members of the President's Council of Economic Advisers from November 1, 1958, to January 20, 1961, and participated in the preparation of three of the President's Economic Reports. As a university professor and research director—before 1933 in Germany and since then in this country—he has served as a consultant to agencies of the Federal Government, foundations, international organizations, and foreign governments. He is the author of many books and articles on economic and agricultural policy issues.

LOWELL B. MASON, LL.B., LL.D., Attorney. He has been Assistant Corporation Counsel of the City of Chicago, a member of the Illinois State Senate, and counsel to two subcommittees of the United States Senate. In 1945 he was appointed by President Harry S. Truman to the Federal Trade Commission and was reappointed in 1949 for a seven-year term. Commissioner Mason is the author of *The Language of Dissent,* and is now a practicing attorney in Washington, D. C.

JEROME WILSON MILLIMAN, Associate Professor of Business Administration, Indiana University, on leave with Resources for the Future, Inc., during 1962–63. He is a former consultant on water resource economics to the National Planning Association and to the RAND Corporation; currently he is consultant to the Committee for Economic Development on area redevelopment. He has written a number of articles in professional journals and (with Jack Hirshleifer and James De Haven) *Water Supply: Economics, Technology, and Policy* (1960).

SYLVESTER PETRO, Professor of Law at the New York University School of Law and member of the Illinois bar. He is a specialist in labor and antitrust law, and a contributor to legal and other periodicals. Among his books are: *The Labor Policy of the Free Society* (1957), *Power Unlimited: The Corruption of Union Leadership* (1959), and *The Kohler Strike: Union Violence and Administrative Law* (1961).

J. FRED RIPPY, Professor Emeritus of American History, University of Chicago. He is the author of several books on the history and foreign relations of the Americas, including *Globe and Hemisphere* (1958), *Latin America: A Modern History* (1958), and *British Investments in Latin America* (1959).

WILSON E. SCHMIDT, Professor of Economics, The George Washington University, where he has been teaching since 1950. He has been a consultant to various organizations, including the Industrial College of the Armed Forces and the American Enterprise Institute for Public Policy Research. In addition to many articles, he has written (with J. N. Behrman) *International Economics: Theory, Practice, Policy* (1957).

ARTHUR A. SHENFIELD, Economic Director of the Federation of British Industries since 1955. He has served as assistant editor of the London and Cambridge Economic Service, lecturer in economics at the University of Birmingham, economic adviser to the government of Trinidad, chairman of commissions of enquiry, and chairman of the Finance Committee of the Imperial College of Tropical Agriculture, and was in active practice at the English bar. He has lectured on British economic affairs in various countries and is the author of numerous essays and articles on economic questions, and, in particular, reports on economic problems in the British Caribbean. He is Ford Foundation Visiting Professor in the University of Chicago Graduate School of Business for 1963.

GEORGE J. STIGLER, Walgreen Professor of American Institutions, University of Chicago, and President-elect of the American Economic Association. He is the author of six books, including *Theory of Price* and *Production and Distribution Theories*, and was chairman of the Price Statistics Review Committee, whose report was recently published by the Joint Economic Committee.

WILLIAM S. STOKES, Senior Professor of Comparative Political Institutions at Claremont Men's College and the Claremont Graduate School. He was chairman of the Latin American Affairs Committee of the American Political Science Association and has conducted research in all the Latin American countries, leading to over two hundred publications in English, Spanish, and Portuguese. Before accepting an endowed chair at Claremont Men's College, he was Professor of Political Science at the University of Wisconsin. Dr. Stokes has lectured at many Latin American institutions of higher learning. His books are: *Honduras: An Area Study in Government* (1950) and *Latin American Politics* (1959).

ERNEST VAN DEN HAAG, Professor of Social Philosophy at New York University and lecturer at the New School for Social Research. He is a Fellow of the Royal Economic Society and of the American Sociological Association. In addition to many articles, his books include *Education as an Industry, The Fabric of Society* (1957) (with Ralph Ross) and *Passion and Social Control* (1963).

ELISEO VIVAS, John Evans Professor of Moral and Intellectual Philosophy, Northwestern University. He is associate editor of *Modern Age: A Quarterly Review*. He has worked in the field of ethics and aesthetics and is now occupied with problems of philosophical anthropology or philosophy of culture. A contributor to technical journals and literary reviews, he has written *The Moral Life and the Ethical Life* (1950), *Creation and Discovery* (1955), and *D. H. Lawrence: The Failure and the Triumph of Art.*

W. ALLEN WALLIS, President of the University of Rochester and Professor of Economics and Statistics. He is Chairman of the Editorial and Advisory Board and of the Executive Committee of the new *Encyclopedia of the Social Sciences.* Formerly Dean of the Graduate School of Business and Professor of Statistics and Economics at the University of Chicago, he has served on the staffs of Yale University, Stanford University, Columbia University, the National Bureau of Economic Research, the National Resources Committee, and the Ford Foundation. He spent two years at the White House, where he was a special assistant to President Eisenhower. He has served as editor of the *Journal of the American Statistical Association,* is co-author of several books, including *Statistics: A New Approach,* and has published numerous technical articles on statistics and economics.

Preface

In September of 1961, at a place ideally suited for an undisturbed exchange of ideas, a group of fourteen men spent one week together considering critically the early drafts of the papers finally presented in this volume.

Including the editors, the group came from the following disciplines: economics, statistics, business administration, history, law, philosophy, political science, and sociology. In addition to their academic backgrounds, some of the participants in the symposium came from extensive experience in public service.

The title for the volume was chosen in irony, of course. The "new argument" in economics and public policy is, as anyone familiar with economic history knows, even older than pre-nineteenth-century socialism. Mercantilism and sumptuary laws, the latter even found in rather undeveloped tribal societies, anticipated many of the notions now revived in the present adoration of the "public sector."

Perhaps most of the participants in our symposium had feelings about our topic similar to those expressed by President Wallis in his theme-setting essay. The fashionable scolding of the "private sector," while imploring compassion for the allegedly starved "public sector," for political and emotional reasons, has not really produced a novel or intrinsically viable problem. There are more attractive and meaningful issues which realistically demand examination. But sometimes men must devote themselves reluctantly to a final inquest, especially when it is necessary to separate promising ideas from sterile and inhibiting principles.

Toward the later fifties, the intriguing dichotomy, the public sector vs. the private sector, appeared ever more frequently in

ix

economic, sociological, and journalistic writings. At times, it seemed to serve the same purpose (and have the same emotional connotation) as the favorite antithesis of the early and middle fifties, "developed" vs. "undeveloped" countries.

As the history of social theories shows, the pleaders and engineers of "social change" usually need a dichotomy, a "polarization" of social reality. Once it was proletariat and bourgeoisie, imperialist and colonial people, rural and urban areas, developed and underdeveloped; and now it is the private and the public sector. These semantic devices usually imply merely a preferred direction of change. "Social change," so the proponents of the dichotomy insist, must transfer power, prestige, income, influence, expenditures, etc., from one to the other. Depending on the viewpoint of the observer, the transfer is inexorable and progressive, or reactionary and wicked.

The authors who have contributed to this volume tend to disagree perhaps, either on pragmatic or philosophical grounds, in regard to the exact balance between the private and the public sectors for any particular area of life. But they do share, it would seem, an abiding distrust of the notion that history, that social change, is a one-way street.

THE EDITORS

Contents

	PAGE
Contributors	v
Preface	ix

CHAPTER

1 NEOMERCANTILISM AND THE UNMET SOCIAL NEED-ERS
by W. ALLEN WALLIS — 1

2 THE ECONOMIC ROLE OF THE STATE
by GEORGE J. STIGLER — 12

3 GROWTH OF THE "PUBLIC SECTOR" AS A BY-PRODUCT
OF PRICE-FIXING AND OF SEGREGATING COST-BEARING
FROM BENEFIT-SHARING
by KARL BRANDT — 24

4 PRIVATE AND PUBLIC EXPENDITURES: A REAPPRAISAL
by ERNEST VAN DEN HAAG — 51

5 CAN PEOPLE BE TRUSTED WITH NATURAL RESOURCES?
by J. W. MILLIMAN — 72

6 PUBLIC POLICY AND THE FOREIGN SECTOR
by WILSON E. SCHMIDT — 107

7 THE EXPANSION OF THE PUBLIC SECTOR THROUGH
FOREIGN POLICY
by J. FRED RIPPY — 131

8 THE *CONTRAPRODUCENTE* CONSEQUENCES OF THE
FOREIGN-AID PROGRAM IN BOLIVIA
by WILLIAM S. STOKES — 145

9 TRADE-UNIONISM AND THE "PUBLIC SECTOR"
   by SYLVESTER PETRO   185

10 THE UNAUTHORIZED GROWTH OF BUREAUCRATIC POWER
   by LOWELL BLAKE MASON   201

11 ART AND THE ARTIST'S "CITIZENSHIP"
   by ELISEO VIVAS   216

12 THE PUBLIC SECTOR VERSUS THE PRIVATE SECTOR
IN BRITAIN
   by A. A. SHENFIELD   232

INDEX OF NAMES   257

INDEX OF SUBJECTS   259

1

Neomercantilism[1] and the Unmet Social Need-ers

W. ALLEN WALLIS

That this symposium has as its subject "The Private versus the Public Sector" is a tribute to the power and pervasiveness of propaganda. For the phrase represents no specific substantive issues. Its frequent occurrence in discussions of economic and social policy reflects the susceptibility of intellectuals to hidden persuasion by phrasemakers who seek status and affluence in our society or aspire to overpower the elite through flamboyant, imaginative, entertaining, and "gliberal" glowering.[2]

When I say that no specific substantive issues are involved, I mean two things. First, the facts are not as they are portrayed. Second, even if the facts were as they are portrayed, the implications and significance of those facts would not be as represented. I could concede readily, of course, that attempts to discuss the phrase seriously should lead directly to age-old questions of great moment about relations between the individual and the state.

The discussions, written and oral, of the public versus the private sector that have drawn attention to this issue—or, rather, that have created the impression that there is a specific issue here—picture a society in which expenditures on schools, sanitation, care of the indigent, public health, highways, communication systems, churches, science, and the higher forms of art,

1

music, drama, and literature, are in squalid decline as a consequence of serious reductions in the funds available. The facts
are just the opposite. There has been tremendous acceleration
in the past decade in building schools, increasing teachers'
salaries, building superhighways, supporting science, aiding the
needy, conquering disease, clearing slums, constructing hospitals,
building churches, publishing books, performances by symphony
orchestras, attendance at art galleries, and innumerable other
worth-while public activities. The growth of public expenditures
since the Korean War has been great, and that growth has been
almost entirely in public services—in the "welfare state," not in
national security.

Part of the misrepresentation is achieved by statistical prestidigitation.

I will not comment on outright prevarication and downright
error, except to say that both are considerably more common
than prevailing canons of good taste permit one to recognize
publicly.

What is the distinction between a "public" service and a
"private" service? Included in the list that I have just given, of
areas in which spending is alleged to have declined but actually
has increased, are a number of items that those who argue about
the "public" versus "private" issue would ordinarily not class
as "public." The classification is generally made, not according
to whether the facilities are available to the public, but according to whether the costs are paid by the public through governmental agencies using money raised by compulsion. However,
the division between "public" and "private" ought to be made
on the basis of who has access to the facilities, not by reference
to who paid for them. Medical research supported by the Rocke-
feller Foundation is in the public sector just as much as medical
research supported by the National Institutes of Health. The
telephone system is just as much a public facility in the United
States as in England or as the post office in the United States.
Care of orphans is as much a public service when provided by
a private charity as when provided by a government agency.

Goods and services that are produced privately and provided

to the public on a sort of "common carrier" basis—that is, to anyone who pays an announced price—are, of course, not available to those without money or credit. This is not, however, a distinction between the public and private sectors. Many private services are available on the basis of need, without regard to ability to pay; National Merit Scholarships are an example. On the other hand, many public services are available only on an ability-to-pay basis; admission to Yellowstone Park, a room at Old Faithful Inn, or delivery of a letter are examples. Public provision of goods and services need not mean public production of those goods and services; college education under the GI Bill is an example.

Those who argue that the public sector should be increased often define the public sector implicitly, not even as everything that is paid for by the government, but as only that part that is provided directly by the government through government employees using government-owned facilities. They are thus arguing in effect that the provision of certain services should be transferred from private to public hands. Churches are a good example of a public facility that in this country is provided exclusively by private funds. Even the most ardent advocates of transferring the financing and control of public facilities from private to public hands stop short of advocating this transfer with respect to churches, presumably because of an ingrained belief in separation of church and state. Private institutions of higher learning are another case in point. In this instance, perhaps the principal reason that the "unmet social need-ers" usually stop short of advocating transfer to public control is that many of the most imaginative of them are employed by private universities, and their most valuable economic freedom is academic freedom. (It should be noted, however, that public financing of political parties is occasionally advocated; and this would be more dangerous to our political liberty than public financing of religion would be to religious liberty, or than public financing of higher education is to academic freedom.)

Indeed, the "public squalor argument is," as I have said on another occasion, "simply this decade's battle cry of socialism, which—intellectually bankrupt after more than a century of seeing one after another of its arguments for socializing the *means* of production demolished—now seeks to socialize the *results* of production."

The statistical prestidigitation used to misrepresent trends in the public and private sectors is sometimes a tribute to the authors' ingenuity—or perhaps only to the assiduity with which they have absorbed Darrell Huff's masterful little book telling *How to Lie with Statistics*. Their shifts from absolute numbers to per capita figures, to percentages of one base or another, and back again, sometimes involve footwork fancier than that of Eliza crossing the ice. A particularly meretricious device is to express some public expenditure as a percentage of gross national product—or of national income or of consumer income or of consumer expenditures on tail fins—and then interpret a decline in this percentage as a decline in the public sector. Some of the more pretentious statistical efforts project astronomical growth in needs over the next decade—or generation—and then project microscopic rates of expansion, and thus display an awesome portrait of an increasing gap and impending disaster.[3]

A last resort, when the more homely statistical contrivances fail, is Russia. Comparisons with the Russians can be made in absolute terms, in per capita terms, in absolute rates of change, in percentage rates of change, in lead and lag times, and in various other ways—most of which are spiced with a generous dash of imagination and speculation as to what the Russian data, and sometimes our own, really mean. A couple of summers ago the newspapers reported an impending lag in women's gymnastics. According to the reports, the proportion of Russian women engaging in organized gymnastics—gymnastics through the public sector, that is—is far greater than the proportion of American women. Worse still, the Russian lead is steadily widening. "A country that doesn't do better than we do [at training engineers, at foreign language training, at turning out steam engines, at research in entomology, at women's gymnastics, or whatever the subject may be] perhaps does not deserve to survive," is frequently the somber conclusion of these comparisons.

Another approach to the "public" versus "private" sector discussion makes little or no use of statistical or factual argument, but relies on an analysis through the apparatus of theoretical economics. This approach starts with the recognition that we have a "mixed" economy. That is, some economic functions are carried out through private enterprise, some through government, some through the family, and some through eleemosynary institutions. The proper proportions for this mix, it is implied, are to be determined on the principles of marginal analysis, just as are the proportions between the production of automobiles and the production of moving pictures. But governmental decisions are not the resultant of independent, voluntary decisions by individuals, and so are not amenable to marginal analysis. The decisions are, in fact, often of an all-or-none character, though they may be determined by the marginal voter.[4]

Even in the private sector, choices are not made among great aggregates like recreation and transportation. On the contrary, choices are made among comparatively small units that may contribute to a number of different kinds of service, as when a consumer's purchase of an automobile contributes both to his recreation and to his transportation to his work or even in his work. Furthermore, the ratios among various types of expenditures are not chosen for all people, but are simply the results of aggregating individual choices.

Another feature of analytical approaches to the public-sector vs. private-sector discussion is that they frequently profess, and apparently with pride, to be "pragmatic." It is seldom clear what "pragmatic" means in this context. Often it seems to mean not that the test of a policy is how it works, but whether it can be "put across." Also, the label "pragmatism" often seems to conceal neglect of long-run or indirect consequences, for analysis of these is necessarily theoretical.

De Tocqueville pointed out in 1840 that democracy in America seems to cause the pressures to solve a problem to mount as the problem itself dwindles. He applied this particularly to inequality:

The hatred which men bear to privilege increases in proportion as privileges become fewer and less considerable, so that democratic passions would seem to burn most fiercely just when they have least fuel. I have already given the reason of this phenomenon. When all conditions are unequal, no inequality is so great as to offend the eye; whereas the slightest dissimilarity is odious in the midst of general uniformity: the more complete this uniformity is, the more insupportable does the sight of such a difference become. Hence it is natural that the love of equality should constantly increase together with equality itself, and that it should grow by what it feeds on.[5]

This burning-most-fiercely-when-the-fuel-is-least seems to operate in much of our social spending on welfare measures. Only after substantial success was beginning to be achieved in providing retirement income, through individual insurance and private pension plans, did pressure for public provision of retirement income build up to the point of compulsory federal provision of funds for old age. As the problem of medical care for the aged has steadily diminished, partly because of improved health of the aged, partly because of higher per capita income, which has made it easier for people to provide their own resources for old age and to care for their aged relatives, and partly because of the wide increase in organized saving for retirement, pressure for some form of governmental program has increased. Similarly, in the case of race relations, only after rapid progress finally began to occur through private means did serious pressures grow for governmental compulsion. There are many other examples of the same kind.

De Tocqueville makes two other remarks that are particularly helpful in understanding the current pressures for expanding collective action and diminishing individual action:

As conditions of men become equal amongst a people, individuals seem of less, and society of greater importance; or rather, every citizen, being assimilated to all the rest, is lost in the crowd, and nothing stands conspicuous but the great and imposing image of the people at large. This naturally gives the men of democratic periods a lofty opinion of the privileges of society, and a very humble notion of the rights of individuals; they are ready to admit that the interests of the former are everything, and those of the latter nothing. They are willing to acknowledge that the power which represents the community has far more information and wisdom than any of the members of that community; and that it is the duty, as well as the right, of that power, to guide as well as govern each private citizen.[6]

Every central power, which follows its natural tendencies, courts and encourages the principle of equality; for equality singularly facilitates, extends, and secures the influence of a central power.

In like manner, it may be said that every central government worships uniformity: uniformity relieves it from inquiry into an infinity of details, which must be attended to if rules have to be adapted to different men, instead of indiscriminately subjecting all men to the same rule. . . . . The faults of the government are pardoned for the sake of its tastes; public confidence is only reluctantly withdrawn in the midst even of its excesses and its errors; and it is restored at the first call.[7]

In addition to the points made by De Tocqueville, two other factors seem to me to contribute to the growth of collective action.

The first of these is failure to diagnose a problem and failure to analyze the consequences of a proposed solution, or else wrong diagnosis and wrong analysis. The provision of retirement income through a federal social security program, for example, began shortly after the Great Depression, and it may well be that hardships of the aged that were in fact due to that depression were attributed to inadequate provision for old age. Similarly, since the Korean War, financial hardships entailed in medical care for the aged are in fact due largely to the transitory inflations of the Second World War and the Korean War which, in effect, confiscated large fractions of the savings of many who are now retired; but the hardships (or alleged hardships) are misdiagnosed as due to persistent forces that will continue to affect all retired people.

Instead of myself discussing the neglect of long-run consequences, I should like to quote from the Federal Reserve Bank of Chicago's *Business Conditions* bulletin of June, 1961. Under the title "Depressed Areas—Some Lessons from the Past," the bulletin says:

In the course of wide debate, economists and public policy makers have often overlooked the fact that depressed areas have been a recurring aspect of the economic development of this country. American history includes many accounts of the rise and fall of communities and whole regions owing to changes in technology, exploitation and exhaustion of natural resources, changes in demand and the migration of industry to other parts of the country in response to the pull of new markets—the same factors cited as contributing to chronic unemployment in today's depressed areas. . . . .

There is, of course, an inherent danger that some attempts at solving the problem may backfire and only prolong the process of readjustment as well as contribute to an inefficient allocation of the nation's resources. . . . .

Thus, the experience of economic readjustment to the decline of the lumbering industry in the northern counties of the Lake states has emphasized . . . . that there is always the risk that some attempts to solve the problem of depressed areas may not work at all and may only complicate and delay the adjustment process. Witness the collapse of the campaign to promote farming on the cutover lands despite vigorous backing from the state governments, the railroads, lumber companies, local businessmen and even "experts" from the agricultural colleges.

I have the impression that good examples could be drawn from European history of the great costs that may be incurred by neglecting long-run consequences when adopting policies that seem to provide some hope of temporary relief of symptoms. For the United States, it is probably not a great distortion to say that most of the worst economic problems that we face today have been created by the long-run ill effects of policies adopted in the past to deal with some much smaller problem.

The other force that I think must be added to De Tocqueville's in explaining the contemporary movement toward larger federal spending, for which the "unmet social needs" argument has provided buttressing, is a rather profound change in our political processes since his day. The expansion of the Federal Government's welfare activities has led to a great increase in the importance of pressure groups. Many of the programs for expansion of the public sector get their effective backing, not from those who would receive the service, but from those who would sell it to the government. While this is strikingly true in the case of education, medicine may seem to be a counterexample; but in the case of medicine, the opposition to expanded government activity comes from those who are now selling the service and who visualize others selling it or themselves selling it on less advantageous terms if the government expands its activity.

As a matter of fact, as government welfare programs have fallen more and more under the control of pressure groups, the real problems have tended to be neglected. The consideration of depressed-areas relief illustrates this. There is not *a* depressed-areas problem, but many different problems, with varied causes. Some of the most serious of these problems are in the so-called "hillbilly" areas—the mountain regions of certain Southern and border states. These groups for the most part lack sufficient voting strength to attract any substantial federal funds. Federal funds flow instead to areas where breakdown of law and order, lack of even justice in the courts and administrative agencies, demoralization of the labor force, and exploitation by state and local governments have driven industry away. Federal funds tend to subsidize and perpetuate the causes of the difficulty. In the "hillbilly" areas, on the other hand, there would be some prospect for success of efforts to improve the level of education and skills, knowledge about opportunities elsewhere, and mobility.

In conclusion, let me remark that it is perhaps a mistake to call the position of the "unmet social need-ers" socialism, even though their position represents, as I pointed out earlier, a gradual evolution from the socialist position of a century ago and is its contemporary counterpart in the United States. Socialism has traditionally been associated with government ownership of land and capital. The modern movement would continue a large measure of private ownership and private enterprise, but seeks to elaborate and to extend control of private activities and to confiscate a large and growing part of private products. This is carried on partly in the name of unmet social needs at home, and partly in the name of national security. It is in many respects on all fours with mercantilism, the economic policy followed by England and other European countries in the seventeenth and eighteenth centuries, which was a major cause of the American Revolution. Indeed, the movement to enlarge the "public sector" represents perhaps the most powerful re-actionary force that has arisen since the departure of mercantilism from this country with the adoption of the Constitution in 1789.

NOTES

1. W. H. Ferry, Vice President of The Fund for the Republic and Staff Director of its Center's Study of the Economic Order, wrote in the *Bulletin* (January, 1962) of the Center for the Study of Democratic In-stitutions under the title "Caught on the Horn of Plenty": "Abundance will enable a reversal of the old order of things. Modern mercantilism will remove the economic machine from the middle of the landscape to one side, where, under planning by inducement, its ever more efficient automata will provide the goods and services required by the general welfare. Humanity, with its politics and pastimes and poetry and con-versation, will then occupy the central place in the landscape. Manage-ment of machines for human ends, not management by them, is the true object of industrial civilization.

 "This is the promise of modern mercantilism, and if the time is not yet, it is yet a time worth striving for."

2. *See* Vance Packard, *The Hidden Persuaders, The Waste Makers,* and *The Status Seekers;* J. Kenneth Galbraith, *The Affluent Society* and *The Liberal Hour;* C. Wright Mills, *The Power Elite;* and almost any issue of such magazines as *Harper's, Atlantic, Saturday Review, Re-porter, New Republic, Nation,* etc.

3. Mark Twain anticipated some of our contemporaries nearly ninety years ago in his *Life on the Mississippi:* "In the space of one hundred and seventy-six years the Lower Missisippi has shortened itself two hundred and forty-two miles. That is an average of a trifle over one mile and a third per year. Therefore, any calm person, who is not blind or idiotic, can see that in the Old Oölitic Silurian Period, just a million years ago next November, the Lower Mississippi River was upward of one million three hundred thousand miles long, and stuck out over the Gulf of Mexico like a fishing rod. And by the same token any person can see that seven hundred and forty-two years from now the Lower Mississippi will be only a mile and three-quarters long, and Cairo and New Orleans will have joined their streets together, and be plodding comfortably

along under a single mayor and a mutual board of aldermen. There is something fascinating about science. One gets such wholesale returns of conjecture out of such a trifling investment of fact."

4. This is not to minimize the importance of Milliman's points about the relevance of marginal analysis to choices among various projects within the public sector. The point here is that the diversion of the national income between the public and the private sectors is not the sum of individual balances between the expenditures through the public and private sectors. The public-private division is political, not economic.

5. Mentor edition, p. 294.

6. *Ibid.*, p. 291.

7. *Ibid.*, p. 295.

2

The Economic Role of the State

GEORGE J. STIGLER

The proper role of the state in economic life is that which makes for the best attainable society of men. This statement has the pleasing property of reflecting accurately the views of both Thomas Jefferson and Karl Marx. It also has the more disturbing property of forcibly reminding one that there is no such thing as an economic theory of the role of the state in economic life—that only if the nature of the society of men one strives for is specified can one proceed to an economic or, for that matter, political analysis of the state in economic life.

Yet societies, at least democratic societies, do not have an explicit and coherent blueprint of the proper role of the state. Such blueprints are made only by the more ambitious political philosophers, and they never describe faithfully the ruling beliefs of any real society. To read the unwritten popular consensus, one must look at the past trends, the present status, and the momentum of actual policies of the state in dealing with economic affairs.

The direction of public policy is clear even to those who like it: the role of the state in economic life has expanded on a thousand fronts and contracted on none worthy of mention. Direct, if incomplete, measures such as the share of national income spent by governments or the share of the labor force employed by governments are unequivocal on this score.[1] The dense network of public controls over private economic activity is much more difficult to quantify, but no one can doubt its tendency to increase in scope and detail.

Why has this expansion occurred? There are a series of traditional answers, and I propose to examine them critically. Each answer will be subjected to the test: Was it a genuine historical force in bringing about an expansion of the state's activity? By a "genuine historical force" I mean one that was causally valid, even though in some deeper sense it might be false. To illustrate: Suppose a community abandoned a fertile valley because it feared repeated floods. This explanation could be valid even though it would have been more economical to build a dam (or even if there never was a flood). The separate question whether the forces that historically led to an enlarged economic role for the state should have had this effect will also be discussed.

1. *The Growth of Wealth*

A first explanation for the expansion of the state is essentially an application of the theory of consumer demand: as a community becomes wealthier, it consumes relatively more governmental services just as it consumes relatively more medical services and good food. The richer the society, the more it wishes of public education, of highways; the more it needs of national defense.

Adolph Wagner went so far as to enunciate this tendency as a "law" of increasing state activity. But neither he nor subsequent writers have transformed it from a naked historical description into a substantive generalization. They have not shown that the economic functions that are intrinsically (most efficiently?) conducted by the state have a larger comparative role in a richer society, nor—what we shall consider later—that economic progress creates vast new political duties.

Comparative studies yield no support for the view that there is a simple, positive association between the wealth of nations and their control over economic life. Many rich nations such as the United States, Canada, and Germany exercise a lesser role in economic life than many poorer nations such as Italy, Norway, and India.[2] In modern times the role of the state has generally expanded within a nation as its income has grown, but this association has not been characteristic of earlier times (for example, state control diminished in England and the United States from 1650 to 1825).

In any event, coincidence is not causation, and no one has presented a logical connection between greater wealth and increased political control. On the contrary, the natural expectation has been that a wealthier, better educated citizenry would have less need for political intervention in economic life. Let me give two examples.

The provision of public education has been one of the largest peacetime functions of government, and we can accept as indisputable the fact that a richer community wishes longer and more elaborate formal education for its children. But one would expect that richer persons would prefer education tailored to their tastes, not the relatively uniform instruction which our state boards of education prescribe. Budget studies indicate that a larger fraction of children of well-to-do families than of poorer families go to private colleges, and one would expect this tendency to extend through lower levels. One might expect the economics of scale to dictate public education in a sparsely settled rural region, but in the densely populated urban centers of today any cost advantages of public over private education must be trifling at best.

Again, we naturally expect the richer community to insist upon more generous care of the ill and the aged than a poorer community could afford, but we would also expect the typical citizen to be increasingly more competent to take precautions against such actuarially foreseeable events if the distribution of income has not become notably more unequal. If one assumed, as this literature often does, that only after a given absolute income is exceeded can a family save for future emergencies, then, with rising incomes, relatively more families can afford to save. Unless the population is steadily becoming more myopic in affairs economic, a rising fraction should be able to care for themselves.

2. *The Advancing Technology of Government*

A second explanation is that advances in the technology of political organization have made state control of economic activity feasible and efficient. The main advances that have been cited are the development of a professional civil service; statistical and accounting techniques that yield prompt and comprehensive information permitting effective central control over economic activities; and the emergence of a ubiquitous and rapid communications network. Just as scientific advances have made air flights and air conditioning possible, so they are believed to have made detailed and continuous supervision of economic life possible.

Of course this is an explanation of the growth of political control only in the sense of being a permissive factor, which released other forces previously lacking implementation.[3] Even within this severe limitation, it is an explanation that seems more relevant to the centralization of political control than to its expansion, for it argues chiefly that the optimum size of all enterprises has increased.

The improvement of political technology is presumably attested by the fact that political controls have become more efficient and in some sense more successful. And this claim of success in turn seems to derive support primarily from the observation that the economic role of the state has expanded without immediately disastrous consequences. The state controls the airlines, and planes have increased in speed and safety. The state inspects the kitchens in restaurants, and people are living longer. The state supervises the Indians, and scalping has dropped off.

There is a remarkable absence of criteria of efficiency or success of governmental controls. The absence of criteria is shown by the fact that the folklore says that state activity X was successful or unsuccessful—as if the outcome of a complex undertaking can be described by 0 or 1. There is ample argument on what the state should do, but very little precise information on what it has done. How different is the American transportation system because of the ICC? When did the regulatory system codify existing practices? When were its goals achieved, and when were they adapted to the state of affairs? Similar questions can be asked, but have not been answered, with respect to a hundred more instances of public control.

I am skeptical of the importance of advances in political technology in general, but in one task—the raising of tax revenues—the state has benefited greatly from the general centralization of economic activity in modern corporate enterprise. It is extremely doubtful that thirty per cent of the income of a community organized in small proprietorships (including family farm enterprises) can be taken in taxes, especially in peacetime. The financial records (which first came into general use as instruments of controls for larger enterprises) would be too poor to support the collection of heavy income taxes, and excises of a magnitude necessary to yield such revenues would simply be uncollectible. It is, in fact, notorious that even today the small proprietors are somewhat negligent taxpayers.

3. The Increasing Complexity of Social Life

A third basis for state action that is often proposed is the increasing interdependence of citizens in a complex urban civilization. A larger share of the effects of an individual's actions are believed to fall on others than in olden days. A drunken cowboy was a danger chiefly to himself, and perhaps to his sponsor; a drunken driver may kill innocent strangers. A disgruntled farmer will starve if he does not work; a disgruntled labor union may bring the economy to its knees.

I am not certain what interdependence actually means here. If it means that increasing specialization narrows the range of self-sufficiency of an individual or family, then one must agree that interdependence has increased. But specialization does not necessarily call for larger state activity; after all, the market is the prime center for the co-ordination of specialists.

As the allusion to labor unions suggests, sometimes this interdependence refers to the possession of monopoly power sufficient to wreck the economy. Aside from the inconvenient fact that the power of labor unions is largely a product of deliberate governmental policy, it seems sufficient to make two comments. The first and minor comment is that only the unions exercise the power of withdrawal from production; no entrepreneurial monopolist, however greedy and powerful, would want to do so.

The second, important point is that the growth of state economic activity agrees neither in time nor in locus with the control of powerful monopolies. There was some relationship between fear of monopoly and federal regulatory activity at the end of the last century, but in recent times the most important regulatory programs, such as those in housing, agriculture, motor trucking, financial markets, and the like, have essentially no relevance to questions of monopoly.

Often the doctrine of interdependence seems to be a sort of generalization of the doctrine of external economies and diseconomies. On this version, it is held to be a characteristic of modern times that a larger proportion of the effects of an individual's acts falls upon others. And this in turn seems most often to be attributed to the increased proximity of individuals: the smoke from the chimney—that Gibraltar of external diseconomies—falls on more people.

This is largely an empirical quesion, and again it is one to which little systematic analysis has been devoted. There is surely more need to regulate vehicular traffic, but not obviously more need to regulate education or housing or agriculture. There is more need to compel the use of fire-resistant building materials, but not to regulate labor markets, security markets, or the professions.

But this question of interdependence raises also another: Can we not, with our increasing incomes, afford individually to protect ourselves from our social as well as our physical environment?

Privacy is also a producible commodity. In fact we do produce it, and the vast increase in the individual's mobility has become a major resource in choosing his social environment. The major migration from the central city to the suburbs that is now taking place is one vivid instance of this increasing power of the individual to choose his environment. The privilege of eccentricity for which John Stuart Mill pleaded is in many respects more widely enjoyed now than ever before in our history.

4. The Incompetence of the Individual

The final explanation of the expansion of the state is that the individual, whether a consumer, laborer, investor, or what, is incompetent to conduct his affairs properly. This explanation is, of course, related to the foregoing arguments that scientific and economic advances have made social life more complex, but I believe that it goes well beyond this.

The decline of confidence in the competence of the individual has in fact been the basic reason for the vast extension of the state's regulatory activities. States license teachers because local school boards would be incompetent to hire good teachers. The FTC compels the labeling of fabrics because the consumer could not detect substitutions of inferior goods. The individual is compelled to pay Social Security taxes because he would not or could not make provision for his personal security. Airline pilots are certified by the CAB because the airlines would not insist upon well-qualified pilots. Elevators are inspected because owners of apartment and office buildings would let them become dangerous. Stock prospectuses must be approved by the SEC, for investors would be susceptible to fraudulent claims. And so it goes.

This decline in faith in the individual lurks behind the great majority of public controls. Let the reader ask of any such control: Is it necessary if men are informed and in comfortable economic circumstances? If the answer is no, the control assumes incompetence.

It might appear paradoxical that during a century in which average incomes have risen at least fourfold and formal education now takes up more than twelve years of the average man's life, his economic and intellectual competence has been steadily denigrated. If all this education does not equip him for life, and if all this income will not give him the power to care for himself, how could he possibly have survived in earlier days without the assistance of ubiquitous governmental guardians?

One answer is that the world has become much more complex and makes demands for specialized knowledge that was not needed in earlier days. Anyone can judge the competence of a stagecoach driver, but not of a pilot; anyone can tell bad potatoes, but not the existence of cancer-inducing sprays on cranberries.

There is an element of truth in this answer, but it is a tiny element. People are just as able to predict old age, or the benefits of education, as they ever were; they are just as able to judge the cleanliness of the kitchen in the inn, or the reliability of an advertisement, as they ever were.

The real answer to the paradox is that we are no longer satisfied with the level of performance of the average individual. He may be better informed, and he is certainly richer, than his grandfather, but he is not so well informed as that reformer down the street. This average man crowds into a Boston night club and is burned to death; so we must regulate night club capacity and exits. He buys stocks from Samuel Insull; so we must control the Insulls. He lost a hand in a sawmill; so we shall compel sawmills to have guards on their saws. What was good enough for his grandfather—who lost three fingers to a saw and a year's income to a swindler—is not good enough for him.

I hope I have chosen highly plausible cases of the need for state regulation, because I wish to emphasize how persuasive this kind of consideration has been in almost every area of state control of economic life. The public as a whole has been educated or brainwashed—or should one use the more neutral word, persuaded?—to believe that there are many more serious problems than our ancestors recognized, and that at least a significant fraction of the population cannot individually cope with them in a manner that society should demand.

Since there is no absolute standard of competence, there is no limit to the possible scope of this extension of public controls. It is at least as difficult for an ordinary person to tell whether his television set is properly constructed as it is to tell whether the surgeon is skillful; so why not regulate the production of television sets? It is at least as difficult for this person to judge which universities offer satisfactory training for a Ph.D. in economics as it is to judge whether a house has been built properly; so why not regulate the granting of advanced degrees?

It is all too evident that by a proper use of statistics—and what is proper in the area of public opinion and policy differs remarkably from what is proper in a college course in statistics—one can continuously enlarge the area of individual incompetence. What is not so evident to many is that the same philosophy and technique lends itself to areas other than economic life, and in particular to politics.

An individual who cannot choose a barber still chooses his Congressman, a choice many would have deemed more difficult. (Why then has there been a secular improvement in refrigerators, which we are told we cannot judge, but not in aldermen?) An individual who cannot understand the cost of installment credit when he buys an automobile (or so certain probable legislation assumes) is quite able to judge the costs and returns of the foreign-aid program, the farm program, and the highway program. An antidemocratic element is clearly immanent in the position of the critics of individual competence.

If we accept, as I do, the increasing distrust of the individual as the primary source of the growth of the state's control of economic and social life, we still face the questions: Is the distrust justified, and is the remedy of public control appropriate?

In a sense, the distrust of the individual is always justifiable. If we merely pose, as public policy has posed, the question: Do some people act foolishly or blindly in any area?—the answer will always be, "of course." Whatever standard of wise behavior we accept, some people will fail to meet it. Someone will always starve amidst plenty, maltreat children out of thoughtlessness or sadism, buy fraudulent wares, etc. And since the standard of wise conduct is both arbitrary and flexible upward, this will always be true.

The magnitude of the shortcomings of individuals, however, cannot be ascertained so simply. Would a large number of parents fail to send their children to school in the absence of compulsory school laws? The proponents of such legislation assert this to be the case, but they offer no evidence.[4] Would city land-use patterns be chaotic (whatever that means) in the absence of zoning? It is so asserted, but the evidence has not been published. The history of reform rests much more upon shockingly reported episodes than upon documented failures of numerous individuals.

Nor, in the reckoning, is any attention paid to possible shortcomings of the state in seeking to remedy the deficiencies of some individuals. These shortcomings may be illustrated by one state activity: the licensing of teachers. Local citizens and their school boards were deemed incapable of choosing competent teachers; so state licenses must be obtained. The states have largely eliminated the ability of local school boards to hire untrained teachers or nephews of school board members, but only at real cost:

—The imposition of a set of course requirements that have the effect of reducing the competence of teachers.
—The exclusion of a large number of highly qualified teachers (the liberal arts graduates).
—The imposition of tenure systems that make it virtually impossible to discharge incompetent teachers.

There is no need to reach here a decision on whether the state's control of teachers has led to a net improvement or deterioration of education; the point is that deficiencies are at least as inherent in the political process as in the behavior of individuals that it seeks to remedy.

The matter does not rest only on a reckoning of private and public shortcomings in the performance of certain activities, but also on a deeper ethical question. Let the control of (say) housing by the state lead to housing that is superior to what the individual would obtain. Is there no value in the free expression of man's imperfect judgment? Are not the trials and errors of a man valuable things in themselves?

Good things, in short, are never free: unless one is willing to pay a price in terms of individual failures, there is no possibility of maintaining the dignity of the individual. Crucial traits such as self-reliance, prudence, tenacity of purpose are not to be achieved in a society where independence of action and fallibility of judgment are forbidden by law. There can be no successes where there are no failures.

It is a remarkable and a depressing fact that the vast expansion of the economic activities of the state has not been based upon rational analysis. If a fault was found with individual action, it was not necessary to demonstrate that the fault was serious or frequent. If it was proposed to eliminate the fault by state action, voluntary methods (which present information but allow freedom of action) were usually ignored and certainly seldom analyzed to see if they were sufficient. When compulsory methods were invoked, their costs were seldom realized and never measured.

Perhaps political life is inherently irrational, and only a form of social psychiatry can illuminate its course. But to the extent that it is rational, it has been a poor piece of rationality, and for this economists share some of the blame. The opposition of Adam Smith to state economic enterprise was based upon a vast history of failure. A century later the opposition had become traditional: there was no extensive history of public economic activity to criticize, and the criticisms became doctrinaire and unpersuasive.

The main task of the liberal is to restore to vitality the critical analysis of economic problems and their comparative administration by individuals and the state. To identify social action with public interest is as stupid as to believe that all change is for the worse. Only by hard, rigorous analysis of concrete problems and solutions can we raise public opinion and therefore public policy to a responsible level.

NOTES

1. *See,* for example, S. Fabricant, *The Trend of Government Activity in the United States since 1900* (1952), M. Abramovitz (with V. Eliasberg), *The Growth of Public Employment in Great Britain* (1957), and A. T. Peacock and J. Wiseman, *The Growth of Public Expenditure in the United Kingdom* (1961).

2. The Economic Survey of Europe in 1959 (Economic Commission for Europe, 1960) presents data on per capita income and governmental expenditures as a share of national income in eighteen countries (*op. cit.,* chap. V, p. 5. The relationship between the two is weak; the rank correlation coefficient is .38. The inclusion of the regulatory activities of government, if a measure could be devised, would probably serve to diminish this relationship.

3. The advances in organization and communication that have made certain kinds of state control feasible—for example, daily supervision of the capital markets—have, in general, had similar effects in the private sector that have reduced the need for state activity. The individual investor's access to information relevant to the security markets, for example, has also benefited from the same advances.

4. Actually the evidence is that these laws have had little effect; see my *Employment and Compensation in Education,* Appendix D.

3

Growth of the "Public Sector" as a By-product of Price-fixing and of Segregating Cost-bearing from Benefit-sharing

KARL BRANDT

In his *Economic Report to the Congress* of January 18, 1961, in the preparation of which his Council of Economic Advisers assisted him in accordance with the Employment Act of 1946, the President of the United States stated:

In our free economy, economic growth and the improvement of living standards depend not primarily on what government does but mainly on what is done by individuals and groups acting in their private capacities. In this system of shared responsibility, the tempo of economic activity is especially sensitive, for example, to the plans and actions of large firms and powerful labor organizations whose operations are national and international in scope.

Government makes its basic economic contribution not through the volume of its own expenditures but by promoting conditions favorable to the exercise of individual initiative and private effort. Accordingly, a dominant purpose of government at every level must be the preservation and invigoration of institutions that favor and support enterprise. In particular, the Federal Government should encroach no more than necessary on the province of private action. Indeed, it

24

should expand as broadly as possible the opportunities for private decision-making; strengthen incentives for businessmen, workers, savers, and investors; and promote a vigorously competitive environment in domestic and international markets.[1]

This conception of the role of the state in the nation's economic affairs simply repeated forcefully not only the orientation of the Eisenhower Administration from its very beginning, but also the philosophy pervading the Employment Act of 1946, which the Congress had passed in that year, and which had become law over President Truman's signature.

The government's share in the United States' Gross National Expenditures had expanded most ominously from 10 per cent in 1929 to 27 per cent in 1952. While this share did not decline in 1960, it at least still stood at 27 per cent.[2] Thus, the struggle of eight years to curb the trend toward greater encroachment of the government's expenditures upon the nation's total gross expenditures had not been in vain. Yet there is no guarantee for the years ahead that public expenditures will not again eat more deeply into the national account, i.e., grow at the expense of the privately run part of the national economy—which is the basis for the noncoercive society, its freedom, as well as its consumer-oriented allocation of resources and the steady creation of substantive national wealth.

The enormously powerful drift toward an accelerated growth of the public "sector" in our times is illustrated by a recent warning of the German economist Dr. Karl Albrecht: From 1955 to 1960, the government of the Federal Republic of Germany further increased its share in the Gross National Product to 31 per cent. If the social security contributions and the taxes for equalization of war damages are included, the "public hand" in West Germany has taken, in 1960, 42 per cent of the Gross National Product.[3] These German data are particularly instructive because West Germany is internationally considered as having one of the leading private-enterprise economies in the world.

Considering these American and German figures, we may ask

whether there is somewhere a limit to the growth of the public sector that divides a private-enterprise economy from a socialist or state capitalist system. Moreover, this poses the even more pertinent question whether a national economy can retain the private-enterprise system once the public sector has reached a certain degree of absorption or control of the social product. Probably this may not be possible without a political revolution or a *coup d'état,* because the public sector entrenches itself ever more firmly as larger and larger parts of the electorate, in a democracy, develop a vested interest in a maximum of public services rendered by more and more publicly operated or publicly controlled enterprises.

Years ago Colin Clark dealt with the question how high taxation must be to be considered as being too high. Where lies the danger point? [4] He cited the French public expenditure in 1922 at a level of 34 per cent of the national income. The concurrent inflation then continued so long that, because of the lag in civil service salaries, by 1926 public expenditures absorbed only little more than 20 per cent of the national income. From 1927 on, prices in France were stabilized. By 1934, French public expenditures had climbed again to nearly 34 per cent, and another spurt of inflation lasting until 1938 reduced their share to 25 per cent. Colin Clark argued at length that 25 per cent is the limit of a tolerable proportion and quoted Lord Keynes as having supported his view in 1945, a time when the share in Britain had risen to 42 per cent, from 26 per cent at the beginning of the war.

A major traditional approach to containing the expansion of the public sector is to seek control of the budget expenditures of government at the federal, the state, and the local levels. The technicalities of this throttling for the purpose of stricter controls over expenditures have been the subject of the two Hoover Commissions on Organization of the Executive Branch of the Government and their task forces from 1947 to 1949 and from 1953 to 1955. This is an approach that is at present being explored with particular energy in England. [5] It is a method that relies largely on public resistance to high taxes, on the strict control of expenditures through appropriations by the legislature, and on vigilant auditing of the accounts of the executive branch of government. To be effective, this effort must be continuous and without relaxation. The greatest impact of this approach will be primarily on the expansionist forces inside the vast bureaucracies of the executive branch of the government itself at all levels—federal, state, and local.

However, efforts at containing the growth of government and its expanding encroachment upon the private economy can succeed only through education of the majority of the electorate about the serious consequences of the continued growth of the public sector. People must be brought to visualize the curtailment of freedom of the individual and the resulting gradual loss of sources for the creation of wealth in the noncoercive society. Any start toward such an education of the electorate must begin by destroying the popular, perfectly Utopian idea that the increase in free public services does not require additional tax revenues. This myth rests on the assumption that the operational efficiency of governmental agencies can be improved, and that the savings thereby achieved will pay for additional services. Real curtailment of public expenditures requires first a restraint in demanding new services. This again requires that people understand the rather complex affairs of the government's budget and its items: *(a)* transfers and subsidies; *(b)* goods and social, economic, and environmental services.

Let us now search for the major driving forces behind the drift into the expansion of the share of public expenditures in the social product. What is the motivation of large parts of the electorate for decisions at the ballot box that lead to a disproportionally larger public sector? What are the economic and political circumstances that lead to the political endorsement of higher taxes and more public employment?

Our open society from its beginning felt dedicated to and still adheres to a philosophy of freedom and a system of checks and balances against too much power of the state and its personnel. But in the midst of our society there are many people and groups who have a low or ambivalent appreciation of the private part of the nation's economy. With all sorts of mixed motives,

they entertain varying degrees of preference for public enterprises, public employment, and a maximum of public social
security services. Of course, not only do these sentiments and
motivations differ, but the effective pressure exerted by them
also varies greatly. Particularly among intellectuals, much of
their indifference to the rising power of the state, at the expense
of freedom of the individual, feeds on a basically Marxian or
neosocialist criticism of the private economy. They cast the suspicion of dubious morality on the profit motive as an incentive
of entrepreneurs; they deplore the distribution of foods of different preference rating and scarcity according to income, the
opportunity for monopoly power, and even the freedom of consumers to express their preferences. Others—particularly among
those untrained in or not conversant primarily with economics,
such as engineers, architects, natural scientists, anthropologists,
sociologists, political scientists, and artists—lack sympathy with
the private economy because the free market, with its trial and
error, its spontaneity and uncharted mobility, appears to them as
disorderly, irrational, and inferior to a more tidy, centrally
planned and directed system.

There are still many other critics who share some of the two
major types of arguments, but with a different note. They have
no sympathy with socialism and endorse private property, but
they are critical of free competition and the elimination of the
marginal producers under its impact. They lean either toward
guildlike arrangements of restraint of competition, or they see
in the nonprofit, tax-exempt, co-operative association a morally
more valuable, more charitable, or at least more democratic form
of enterprise.

However, in addition to all these critics of the private economy, there are still other people who profess to be the champions of free enterprise, loathe socialism in any form, and yet
make it easier for all those antagonists who favor expansion of
the public sector. I mean those commercial farmers and captains
of industry or commerce who are only "in principle" in favor
of a free-enterprise market economy. They clamor for protection
by the state, or they form organizations or use devices for

restraint of competition whenever their own enterprise or type of business faces rough competition, dynamic shifts in technology, or dislocations of prices. In their *ad hoc* efforts, these eclectics frequently select means of state intervention in the market that lead to the worst and most far-reaching distortions in the private sector of the economy. This shortsighted request for state remedies supports the drift into more business activity on the part of the government itself. Inevitably the government becomes a direct competitor with private enterprise and an increasingly powerful factor in allocating additional resources to the public purchase of goods and services. This in turn forces corporations into more lobbying and other political-pressure tactics on behalf of their business.

The enormous expansion of national-defense activities in the age of atomic warfare and giant rockets shifts an extraordinary amount of resources to the government as a partner in contract business. But it is not only the race with nuclear arms, missiles, and space exploration that feeds the public sector. Government support of education and research also tends to favor the public at the expense of the private sector.

As an illustration of this entry on the part of government into business by nobody's design or desire, but simply as an unintentional by-product of public correction of the market, we may take a few consequences of agricultural policy. In any economy, farming is the kind of work that, as a result of the division of labor, suffers inevitably the greatest proportional, and for prolonged periods even absolute, decline in employment capacity and therefore the greatest geographical and occupational mobility of labor. In the United States the share of agriculture in the employment of the national labor force has fallen from 90 per cent to less than 10 per cent in a span of 150 years. This shrinkage in the proportion of employment in agriculture coincides with economic development, urbanization, and industrialization. In all countries agriculture, horticulture, forestry, and fisheries represent a sphere within the economy where political attempts to brake dynamic change and development, to protect a status quo, are most frequent, vehement, and popular. And it is in agriculture where the coercive society—ranging from fascism to communistic state capitalism—is always determined to apply brute force to wipe out private property, private enterprise, and the competitive market. But this is usually only the end of a road previously prepared by state intervention and tampering with the market.

In 1928, when the prices of primary materials started their world-wide sharp decline, in Germany the government of the Weimar Republic began to "stabilize" the prices of sugar and bread grain. For sugar, this was done by a compulsory price-fixing cartel of the beet-sugar mills; but in the case of wheat and rye a new public grain corporation soon became the dominating factor in the domestic and foreign grain trade and the flour-milling business. Between 1929 and 1933, the control of the government spread—not by design, but by the necessity of keeping price supports effective—from bread grain to flour and bran, to various feed grains, then step by step to potatoes, fats and oils, milk and dairy products. When Hitler came to power, his government extended the system of price-fixing not only to all remaining agricultural commodities, but rapidly to all food-processing and farm-supply industries. In the center of the completely cartelized business stood large commodity corporations of public law, totally controlled and directed by the totalitarian state's agricultural and food agencies.

This gradual destruction of the consumer-oriented market economy with its decentralized adjustments was initiated, in its early stages, by the right-wing conservatives in the parliament and cabinets of the Weimar Republic, with the support of the Social Democrats and the socialistic labor unions. The conservatives believed the price supports and government stabilization corporations would function merely as a means to pay huge subsidies to large-scale commercial farmers. The Catholic centrist party, which was influential in the coalition governments toward the end of the Weimar Republic, had no special preference for the market economy either and interpreted the Papal Encyclical *Quadragesimo Anno* to mean endorsement of arrangements similar to those of the corporate state, with guildlike restriction of competition to bestow social security on families running medium-sized or small-sized farms. The Social Democrats and national labor unions, on the other hand, supported government control of agriculture. Their hope was that, via government monopoly corporations and compulsory cartels in farming, eventually nationalization of basic industries and a socialistically controlled world economy could be achieved.

These long-run speculations by believers in the planned economy had certainly helped the drift toward more and more state intervention and a cancerous growth of the public sector. However, the crucial act was the betrayal of the free economy by those who believed in the superiority of the private sector but compromised their principles for the sake of expediency. Until 1932, the public sector in Germany grew because the doctoring of all sorts of symptoms of disease by static palliatives happened to have the unexpected and unwanted result of totalitarian control. Of course, once Hitler's National Socialists had assumed governmental powers, the ensuing totalitarian revolution entrenched itself through a centralized economic machine that boosted the public sector. From the moment of gaining power, the National Socialists under Hitler deliberately subjected the entire economy to the dictates of the *Führer* for his sinister purposes.

In Italy, Spain, and Portugal the corporative state similarly took control of the economy for the protection of agriculture and here too impeded economic development, which would have required competition, freedom of enterprise, and freely responding prices. In the United States in 1929, shortly after Germany had started to slide toward the planned economy, the Congress began, under a Republican Administration, to attempt the "stabilization" of the depressed prices of farm products to support the declining cash income of the farmers. Leading businessmen, such as Mr. Legge, Chairman of the Board of the International Harvester Company, conducted the affairs of the Farm Board until it collapsed and lost its capital. Beginning in 1933, the United States Congress took more massive measures to support farm income by fixing the prices of farm products. This led to the formation of the totally government-owned and government-operated Commodity Credit Corporation by Executive Order 6340 of October 16, 1933. In 1962, it is still capitalized at $100 million, but has the authority to borrow "not in excess of" $14.5 billion. It buys the farm crop surpluses (caused by the fixing of the price above its market level) and thus paralyzes the automatic adjustment processes from the supply as well as the demand side. This monstrous public corporation, with its gigantic borrowing authority, by far exceeds the total net income of all private farm enterprises in the United States. In the second half of 1961 it had an "investment" in surplus commodities of about $8 billion. This massive intervention of the government in the market has changed the entire economic climate in the price-supported farm-commodity fields—domestically and internationally. It has driven the holding of stocks from private to government hands and has thus socialized the major part of this vast, once entirely private business, at the taxpayers' expense.

Without ever asking the American electorate or anybody else whether they were in favor of it, this corporation has socialized the business of holding the huge stocks of wheat, barley, corn, oats, millet, rice, cotton, and tobacco. Nobody in the major food- or feed-processing industries and the export trade has any longer an incentive for holding stocks of price-supported commodities at his expense or at his price risk, because the government pays all charges. Moreover, the risk of changes in prices due to sudden changes in government policy or merely by administrative action is too great to take, even for the largest private corporations. Besides, why should anybody be so foolish as to compete with the government in so costly a business, in which the government socializes the losses? Only public corporations can indulge in such folly because, so long as the legislators stick to the price-fixing farm policy and appropriate the funds, the United States Treasury fills up their capital out of tax revenues no matter how often they lose it. A private company ordinarily does not survive the loss of its capital.

This example of only one government-owned and government-operated corporation shows a very substantial replacement by public business of what would otherwise be private business. Amazingly enough, this happened without anybody's consciously pursuing such a goal. *The increase in the public sector occurred as a side effect of legislation that did not have any such purpose,* but simply chose innocently—we hope—from among a large number of available alternative means of state intervention on behalf of subsidizing farm income, exactly the one that established a gigantic, monopolistic government agency in business, where it competed with private business and drove out a large part of it. This agency has grown to such an extent that its business of commodity-price stabilization constitutes the third largest item in the federal budget. It represents not only a huge socialistic enclave within the domestic private economy, but distorts the entire world markets for grain, cotton, and several other commodities. It also offers an example for other countries and groups of countries, for instance, the European Economic Community, to set up similar public enterprises in their farm-commodity trade and thus to curb major interests in expansion of foreign trade and investment in deference to the imagined needs of commodity-price stabilization. *This sort of government action in the midst of a private economy yields private gains for all the beneficiaries and the socialization of losses. It does not strengthen the private-enterprise economy*—as some want to believe—*but corrodes and corrupts it.*

The Commodity Credit Corporation's surplus stocks of grain have a book value at 30 per cent above the world market price. To sell them would require, however, aside from adjusting the price downward by 30 per cent to the world market level at the expense of the United States Treasury, subsidizing transportation to the recipient countries and granting long-term soft-currency loans. In many instances the United States Treasury has to pay even for transportation and storage within the recipient countries. Competent experts estimate that no more than 15–20 per cent of the purchase price can be recovered eventually—in fifteen or twenty or many more years.[6]

The expansion of this single public corporation over a period of twenty-eight years has accustomed numerous people to windfall benefits. They are harvested year in and year out by accidental beneficiaries, not only by the farmers who were intended as the primary beneficiaries. In testing various plans for getting rid of the most gigantic stocks ever piled up in history and abolishing this system with its scandalous waste of economic resources, it has been found that the political resistance against such change would be enormously widespread. There are now too many beneficiaries who were never meant to get any, even indirect subsidies. Grain is a mass of living seeds, containing some moisture, inhaling oxygen and discharging carbon dioxide. Therefore, it must be moved while in dry storage. Stored grain also loses some weight and declines in quality. Our net surplus stocks amount to two parallel lines of freight trains, filled to the brim with grain, reaching from New York to San Francisco. Those stocks are transported by trucks and railroads at government expense, are stored and rotated, loaded on ships, transported overseas, unloaded from ships, and stored again—at the expense of the United States Government most of the way, if not all the way. There are endless numbers of trade, banking, insurance, transportation, and other agents occupied with moving this surplus, which, from the national and international points of view, is merely a misinvestment and a nuisance.

Inevitably all these parties, if they have anything to say about it, will try to stall and prevent any legislative move to stop this absurd waste. We can also expect the large corps of civil servants on the payrolls of the Commodity Credit Corporation in most states of the Union to throw their weight against any plans that would abolish their jobs.

We have seen how a policy with an entirely different purpose ends in a substantial increase in the public sector. Similar case histories can be found in innumerable business arrangements of the armed forces. Our main argument is that a great deal of growth in the public sector is either caused or at least not prevented by the public because it does not have sufficient knowledge and is not being properly informed about these unintended and detrimental results. It is difficult to bring the full extent of this cancerous growth inside the living body of the free-enterprise system into perspective for analysis because of a general apathy on the part of the American public about farm policies.[7]

It is a widely adopted, supposedly progressive and wise attitude of the American public that, when facing the alternative of having certain economic services performed either by private or by public enterprise, one should not be dogmatic in favor of either one form of enterprise, but should be open-minded and choose the one that can perform better. In reality the choice is seldom, if ever, made by this test. Compared with private enterprise, public enterprise has very decisive weaknesses. Even if these were generally recognized, they would probably not dissuade a part of the electorate from endorsing the choice of public enterprise, but in many instances they would prevent the majority decision in its favor.

Public enterprise operates usually as a monopoly, i.e., without the constant test of its performance by competition. In most instances it does not have to cover its full costs of operation because the public underwrites its losses. It has a minimum of incentives to improve its efficiency by innovation of equipment or procedure because such managerial decisions involve not only the opportunity of gain, but the risk of losses, which civil servants are not supposed to take unless they have received from superior officials, upon application, a full authorization to go ahead. This inhibition is worst where public enterprise is operated by civil servants with security of tenure, but even where the management is engaged by contract with a limited renewable term, the tendency is powerful to follow common traditional rules and standard procedures. The manager of a public enterprise is not, and therefore cannot—indeed must not—act like, a free, self-reliant entrepreneur, but must act as an employee who is dependent on the political approval of his superiors and, in the end, of the public itself.

On this subject a very independently minded and resourceful sociologist, Richard LaPiere, had this to say:

Any transfer of authority—religious, economic, or political—from small, local groups to a centralized representative of many such groups reduces by that much the possibility of deviation between such groups and the individuals composing them, increases by that much reliance upon fixed rule and regulation, and shifts by that much determination of group behavior from interpersonal give-and-take to impersonal bureaucratic operations. In such matters as highway construction, traffic control, and public sanitation, the advantages may all lie with centralization of authority and what stems from it. As more and more aspects of social life come under the jurisdiction of centralized authority, political or otherwise, there is, however, a progressive reduction in the scope of individual enterprise and in the social value placed upon initiative.[8]

Public enterprises have the tendency to perpetuate themselves even when the tasks for which they were established have long been solved, and even when the enterprises have been in the prolonged process of liquidation. This holds for public enterprises in general, but in particular for those thousands of governmental business units unknown to the general public. This latter situation prevails in the area of the armed forces, where literally thousands of business enterprises are being formed that are very hard to close down and to keep closed down. However, civilian agencies of the Federal Government tend to have just as indestructible a longevity as the military establishments.[9]

A typical example of the self-perpetuation of civilian public agencies is provided by the Rural Electrification Administration. Founded by executive order in 1935, and provided with statutory authority by act of Congress in 1936, its purpose was to give farmers and rural people in thinly populated regions the opportunity to have their farms connected with central-station electric-power service and telephones by subsidized loans at very low interest rates and with all administration expenses paid by the government. Several years ago it was recognized that this task had been fulfilled, and hence the agency could have gone into liquidation at once by transferring its obligations and assets to private banks. Of course, this was not done, and the large government-bank administration now extends subsidized credit to a majority of nonrural people and, since January, 1961, even has begun to expand its activity and staff. Naturally the provision of subsidized credit through a government-owned and government-operated bank drives any private agency out of this field of operation.

One of the fields of economic action where the danger of an expansion of the public sector is particularly great is the supply of energy and energy-bearing materials. For over four decades these basic industries have fascinated all the proponents of the planned economy. Hydroelectric power plants and power transmission have long been claimed for the domain of publicly owned and publicly operated enterprises. At present a new move is under way to nationalize electric power in the United States via huge regional and interregional grid systems of federal power transmission lines costing many billions of dollars. This may mean a new threat to private enterprise in electric-power generation and distribution, because expanded government control can drive private utilities out of business at any time by subsidized rates of public plants that pay no taxes and can attribute parts of their costs to various benefits, including intangible ones.

Economic theory generally offers no guidance for judging the differential performance of public and private enterprise. But we can point to certain crucial weaknesses of public economic action. The tax-fed public sector within the frame of political democracy is superimposed upon the supporting structure of the private economy while it is simultaneously interfering and competing with the enterprises that constitute the private economy.

The greatest weakness of a major part of the public sector lies in the segregation of the bearing of costs from the reaping of benefits, particularly at the federal and state levels of government. However, often this is true even at the local level of government. Since the economic activities of the public sector expand in relation to political control of votes, some groups of people are always tempted to try to get benefits without sharing in the costs. Because this requires little more than pressure-group tactics, it is a happy hunting ground for local and regional politicians. In the long run, of course, it is an illusion for beneficiaries to expect to escape entirely sharing the costs. But their successful political pressures frequently lead to substantial waste of the nation's resources and to unwarranted expenditures.

It is a general principle of government that—as a matter of social justice and equal opportunities for all—it will distribute the costs of many vital services according to the ability of individuals to pay. However, if the principle of equalization of the burden of costs is driven to the point that any sufficiently determined political-pressure group can help itself to large material benefits paid out of the federal treasury without sharing in the costs or with only symbolic contributions, obviously the results must be damaging to the national economy. This holds for insurance as well as interest rates on mortgages, and is particularly true for the federal financing of resource development. If crop insurance applied equal premium rates across the country, it would lead to intensification of farming in the areas with the greatest weather hazards at the expense of the areas with the most stable and safe yields. If the people in states with hardly any traffic can build six-lane highways financed out of federal revenues collected as taxes chiefly in other states, the national economy suffers from inappropriate allocation of scarce resources, which may create most serious traffic problems in those states that carry the burden of providing the tax revenues. Worse than this: if by such political waste the average national costs of production are lifted to such an extent that industries and commerce can no longer compete with prices of foreign producers in the world market, the nation will suffer severely in its economic well-being and face a crisis in its balance of payments and its currency.

Let us suppose that in a large community the inhabitants of one area insist on getting a new storm sewer. It would be a convenience but not a necessity, and a majority of the voters approve its financing through municipal bonds simply because they are people who do not own their homes but live in rented apartments. They will not pay the interest on and the amortization of the loan by an increase in the city property tax. Such action would involve again an expansion of the public sector as a result of the "something-for-nothing" illusion, because it would take only one or two years for the higher real-estate taxes to lead to an increase in rents. (Actually, local rents may be prevented from rising because of other factors, such as an oversupply of space for rent or competition from an adjacent area.)

The economic consequences of this "something-for-nothing game" in the modern political economy of a federal republic of a multitude of states are particularly felt in the development of natural resources. It is much cheaper to produce food and certain industrial products in humid areas with an abundance of fresh water. Aided by the "something-for-nothing game," arid regions sometimes succeed in developing scarce resources of fresh water at the expense of the humid areas in the nation. As a consequence, the national average costs of production will be raised above what they could be if the people were willing to obey costs rather than certain consumers' preferences for a desert climate. This side effect of the separation of cost-bearing from benefit-sharing is just as ominous in its impact on the economic and military strength of a nation as the general drift toward an expanded public sector.

To get something for nothing tempts even economically sophisticated people, since it has become more or less accepted that inflation is a built-in part of the American economy. They believe, therefore, that inflation will take care of a major part of the costs of public investment in all sorts of assets of public convenience. When public bonds are financed with terms of thirty, forty, or fifty years to maturity, this calculated reliance on evading real costs even has some speculative reasonableness to commend it. The real costs lie in the erosion of the faith of the people in the basic justice of the economic system as a whole.

Another corrupting influence that weakens the private sector is exerted by the cynical reasoning of a considerable number of people who deeply resent the growth of the public sector. They

persuade themselves to believe that since the Federal Government
has taken such a substantial share by progressive income taxes
and corporation taxes, they have actually already paid their
part of the funds to be made available from the treasury for
state and local public projects and therefore have no reason
to oppose state and local claims to federal appropriations for
water, power, or transport development; local sewage-treatment
plants; or similar facilities for strictly local benefits. I confine
myself to these few examples of the tendencies of citizens to
expand unwittingly the public sector, chiefly because of the
separation of benefit-sharing from cost-sharing.

There is another vast area in which on a world-wide scale
the public sector is invading with exorbitant power the private
sector of the economy and, like a parasite, either kills it or
drains its energy to gradual exhaustion. The public in the
United States, and probably also in Western Europe, does not
see either the extent or the pace of this process correctly. In so far
as the evaluation of the relative performance of public and
private enterprise is concerned, the most instructive and revealing sphere of the economy is throughout the world neither
water nor power nor transport, but agriculture. *Agriculture,* in
the broadest meaning of the term, including forestry as well
as horticulture, is one of the most hotly contested areas of
human action and sociopolitical ferment. This is far more
than an ideological debate, in view of the most gigantic experi-
ments of structural change in agriculture on large parts of the
surface of the earth by coercion under the dictate of the state
and with the iron rod of brutal penal codes. All this is done
to foster more rapid economic development or growth, meaning
primarily industrialization. In Soviet Russia, in the wake of the
Bolshevik Revolution of 1917, private property in land was
abolished. After 1930, millions of family farms were collectivized
by force into 235,000 *kolkhozes* at first, aside from several thousand *sovkhozes,* or large state farms. By 1958, the number of
kolkhozes had been reduced to 60,000 through amalgamation
into larger and larger operational units.[10] The socialized *kolkhozes* are operated under elected and politically approved and

controlled managers. On these collective large-scale farms all the manpower is reduced to manual labor, stripped of all managerial functions. These *kolkhoz* workers are paid out of the *kolkhoz* net income according to the work units credited.

In 1955, *kolkhozes* accounted for 80 per cent of the sown land area, and *sovkhozes* for 16 per cent. The remaining 4 per cent were in private family use of the individual *kolkhoz* members, or urban workers, or a few of the last surviving individual small holders. Yet in spite of twenty-five years of powerful pressure from the government, the *kolkhoz* members have concentrated all their interests and skills on this minute amount of private land and have increased its production so much that in 1956 they earned by sales of products over 37 billion rubles— not counting their own consumption—while their entire income and dividends from the common land yielded only 42.2 billion rubles.[11]

In 1959, these little private plots accounted for well over 46 per cent of the Soviet Union's production of potatoes and vegetables, 38 per cent of the output of beef and veal, 51 per cent of the output of pork, 50 per cent of the output of milk, and over 80 per cent of the output of eggs.[12]

How doggedly the small private enterprise continues to survive all the brutal coercion and persecution, and how it tries to fill the gap left by the inefficiency of collective enterprise is particularly well illustrated by the animal husbandry of meat- and milk-producing livestock and birds. In 1956, the Soviet Government passed a law severely limiting the ownership of livestock by city dwellers. In June, 1959, Khrushchev reminded the Soviets that in spite of that law there was only a small decrease in the number of farm animals kept by city dwellers and recommended a law prohibiting the ownership of such animals by urban people. Subsequently the Russian, Ukrainian, and Kazakh Republics decreed that the urban owners had to sell such animals to collective and state farms. Slaughter was put under heavy penalty, and noncompliance with the decree was punished with confiscation. Interestingly enough, it was not sanitation, public health, or the inconvenience of bad odors or unsightliness that banished goats and pigs, cows, calves, and chickens from the paradise of all proletarians; but the offensiveness of strong private initiative on the part of the workers and their wives.[13]

According to the latest data from the Soviet Union, the four per cent of privately operated land is responsible for 38 per cent of total agricultural production. American agricultural experts returning from trips through Russia report the conspicuously prolific growth of the intensively fertilized and cultivated crops on the individual family plots compared with the conspicuously hungry look of the crops on the *kolkhoz* fields.

The disastrous results of forcing over 120 million families, which operated as many family farms in Communist China, into some 24,000 rural communes with an average of 5,000 families have induced the Mao regime to recede from the "big jump forward" and to decentralize the operation of farm land into production brigades of 200 to 300 families, and to hand over to the farm families small plots for private exploitation. This does not prove anything about the future policy of the Chinese Soviets. All it does prove is the enormous resiliency and effective-production incentive of private initiative in family farming, where necessary adaptation to unique local, natural, and economic conditions defeats centralized decision-making by bureaucrats regardless of their scientific training and competence.

As the distinguished French agricultural economist Dr. De Lauwe shows in his thorough analysis, based on extensive travel in the Soviet Union in 1955 and 1960, the small family plots have been from the beginning of *kolkhoz* farming an enigma for the agricultural economy.[14] Potentially they always have been either a supporting institution for the productivity of the collective enterprise or a parasite that sucks it dry of its best human resources. This is why the government has, for thirty years, been continually seesawing between reducing the leeway for the residual private enterprise of the family plots and expanding it.

However, in order to grasp the genuine weakness of the collective farm system of the Soviet Union, as well as all sorts of so-called "co-operative" farm enterprises in other countries, we must look at the form of their management. It is obviously impossible to conduct the decision-making on a farm by democratic procedures. There are two kinds of the myriad of decisions to be made: first, those that determine the structure of the enterprise or its organization for the longer term of several years or for one crop year, such as the crop plan; and second, those that determine the operational or functional decisions from day to day and for certain seasons during the year, down to the hourly instruction of each worker.

Therefore, the *kolkhoz* statutes prescribe the method of participation of the members in the management of their farm enterprise. The general assembly, which according to the statute of 1935 "directs the affairs of the *kolkhoz*," elects the administrative council or board of directors and also elects the president nominated by the local Communist Party authorities. The election formula excludes secret ballots and instead provides for acceptance of the decisions of the general assembly of *kolkhoz* members by the raised hands of the majority, i.e., an open-standing vote.

This procedure reveals some of the most crucial defects of the collective system. Probably the selection of the powerful president and general manager of the large-scale farm enterprise is influenced primarily by his political standing in the judgment of the single party command, and secondly by his forensic vote-getting capacity, and to a much lesser degree by his genuine capacity to manage the enterprise with skill.

The results of thirty years of this gigantic experiment, still involving 45 per cent of the labor force of the U.S.S.R., show the weakness of the whole system. As Dr. De Lauwe reports, it is assumed in the Soviet Union that no more than perhaps 10 per cent of the *kolkhoz* presidents are performing satisfactorily. Khrushchev has said, "Nobody has calculated how much a bad president costs a *kolkhoz*. But he costs very dearly." [15] There is a heavy turnover in these presidencies.

However, this weakness of the management elected by ultimately political procedures is not the worst defect of the whole system. The much greater loss in this system probably stems from the fact that it condemns to idleness and total waste the vast potential inventiveness, ingenuity, and native abilities of almost one-half of the manpower of a country with 230 million people. They are reduced to manual gang-labor—the so-called "work brigades," which reduce the work output or its quality below the average of its potential. Aside from this reduction of output per worker, this whole coercive system has deprived the farm people of freedom and all its benefits—in production, consumption, and the development of their full human potential —for the individuals, the families, and society as a whole.

So far, more than thirty years of the Soviet Russian agricultural experiment have achieved only the confiscation of over 50 per cent of the gross income of the farm population and its transfer to investment in state-owned and state-operated industries, keeping the food supply of the Russian people at an anachronistically primitive level. This experiment has not proved at all the contention that the acceleration of the process of industrialization justifies the gruesome hardships imposed on the farm population for over forty years. On the contrary, the considerably faster growth of Japanese industries on the basis of much scantier agricultural resources is convincing proof of the opposite, because Japan has distributed private property rights in land in an agrarian reform—which is the diametrical opposite of collectivization of agriculture.

Several Latin American states such as Brazil, Argentina, and Uruguay have also squeezed half of the gross return out of agriculture by means of foreign-exchange control and by skimming off the amount of private revenues that is wanted for subsidization of new industries. In other words, a collective farm system is only the most radical sledge-hammer method of aiming at these highly dubious results of forced industrialization. While collectivization is the most destructive method in so far as growth of productivity is concerned, the other more concealed methods also generate a decided drift into more and more public enterprise.

With reference to agriculture, certain ideas are very popular outside of the Sino-Soviet bloc. They try to combine the nationalization of agricultural land, particularly in order to displace "absentee landlords," and the transfer of a limited non-negotiable title to such publicly owned land in small units to farm laborers or tenants, or the leasing of the publicly owned land to them. The stigma of being absent is used to indicate that the landowner has no function and hence collects unearned income as a parasite. If this were not vicious propaganda, it would reveal utter ignorance of the division of labor and the partnership of the owner and the operator of an enterprise. Moreover, if absenteeism were damnable, then bankers, brokers, commission merchants, architects, all would have to be damned too.

Both arrangements have serious defects. If the land is "owned" but cannot be encumbered, leased, or sold, a considerable part of it will be poorly utilized. The necessary gradual movement of the land and water resources into the use of the most competent and efficient managers, inherent in private property, is now blocked by law. Since no elimination of the unfit operators of such resources takes place by the competitive market process and eventual foreclosure in case of a lack of liquidity on the part of the owner, the government itself must establish procedures to deprive the unfit of their privilege, i.e., evict them and replace them with more competent farm operators. This is, of course, a procedure that gives public administration exorbitant power. Such power may at any time be used arbitrarily and with considerable bias—political, racial, religious, or economic. It brings the danger of corruption, if only as the result of self-defense on the part of the victims against the worst outrages. However, if the other choice should be made —namely, to lease state-owned farms by open bidding—the land may move into the hands of those who offer the highest rent and later default. The centralized administration of the leases, the supervision of the maintenance of all fixed capital by the state as an institutional absentee landlord, has far less economic efficiency and far more opportunity for bureaucratic and overbearing treatment of tenants than a totally decentralized system of private landlord-tenant contracts, with courts and the legislature as the guardians of the rights of both parties. The despair of the people in different countries who suffer from the inhumane operation of vast centralized bureaucratic administrations of government-operated business enterprises was best expressed by an employee of the French railroads who said to me: "Sir, one cannot talk intelligently with a machine. But it is our destiny to have to work under giant machines."

My excursion into agricultural policy was not contemplated as an evasion of the subject because of my interest in these problems, but it was motivated by several observations. I believe that in highly advanced industrial countries, as well as in countries at various earlier stages of economic development, the greatest aggregate of social and political pressures that operate toward the expansion of the public sector is active in the part of the political economy that comprises the farm population. Agriculture is the sphere within a national economy where economic development requires and brings about the most profound structural changes and therefore causes serious hardships connected with the necessary mobility of human resources.

There is another dimension of human action where, in the most advanced countries of the world, a massive assault on the private sector is under way on the broadest front and at all levels of government—local, state, and federal. This dimension is education in all its phases and forms, including research. Today, in the English system of higher education, 68 per cent of all expenditures of universities and colleges are paid out of the treasury, and nearly 80 per cent of all students have publicly financed fellowships or other public aid. In countries on the European continent, including Germany, Switzerland, and Austria, the situation is not much different. And in the United States, where privately financed and operated higher education is still very healthy and vigorous, the distinguished and initial former Chairman of the Council of Economic Advisers, Dr. Edwin G. Nourse, has appraised the situation as follows: "It is my belief as an economist that, in a country as rich and innately productive as ours, practical men will find that national growth and stability over future years will be promoted by channeling a somewhat larger proportion of the national income through public treasuries. This is to say simply that, as we have a larger productive surplus above basic bread-and-butter wants, we move deeper into an expanding area of public health, universal education, and national welfare that can be most fully activated and most equitably guided by our agencies of public enterprise. This does not imply socialism, communism, or autocracy; but that we the people shall be living up to our basic traditions of vigorous enterprise and enriched opportunities." [16]

This regrettably correct and all too realistic diagnosis of our drift into a further expansion of the public sector gives not only the kind of testimony of *Realpolitik* that drives this country rapidly into an increasing system of centralized government controls and reciprocal loss of individual freedom; this statement also contains a demonstrably erroneous view of the sources from which wealth flows, the causes why it flows, and the crucial differences between private and public enterprise. Nourse implies that private enterprise has served to produce the more primitive "bread-and-butter wants," but that public enterprise is more productive when a larger proportion of the high-quality services is wanted. This is indeed a strangely slanted summary judgment, which can be contradicted by an overwhelming array of hard and incorruptible evidence.

Unfortunately, as the academic discipline of economics is organized, taught, and practiced in nearly all American institutions of higher learning, it leaves most members of the economic profession remarkably weak in laws of relevance and in the logical analysis of what constitutes valid evidence.

Nowhere in this world is there, so far, any valid evidence, let alone any proof, that the decentralized organization of economic activity under the severe test of competition and a flexible price system has been outperformed or even been faintly approached in its achievements of economic progress by centralized government-directed systems. Yet, paradoxically, in nearly all countries the private economy must continually be defended against the all-pervasive ferment in public opinion that depreciates the private economy and simply assumes the superiority of those systems that depend on an expansion of the public sector.

Among the intellectual leadership in countries with a market economy there are too many people who see some transcendental values in collective forms of economic action and are prone to criticize the ordinary people for their stubborn insistence on their freedom as workers and as consumers. The defense against all those who seek the solution of most social and economic problems in more public and less private control of affairs requires first of all an understanding of the humane ends of the open society and the inalienable rights of individuals, and next, a better knowledge of the comparative strength and weakness of private and public ownership and management of enterprise as alternative means toward those ends. Beyond such basic education the defense of civil liberty requires, particularly in a democracy, better information of the public about these crucial differences.

Ultimately the wide divergence of views on these matters of policy derives from differences in values and the resulting divergent goals. If agreement were reached on these, much of the controversy about means would end. Therefore, the discussion must chiefly be on the grounds of philosophy, and not over minor points in various more or less technical disciplines. I consider economics a scientific discipline that deals with the pursuit of happiness by human beings, endowed by their Creator with an immortal soul, who are not simply members of a somewhat advanced animal species. The individuals are the essence of a human society worthy of the name, and they make decisions and express their preferences with the full responsibility for decisions and acts. Freedom and human dignity and their vital role in man's capacity to create and use wealth for graceful living, assisting his fellow man, and building a humane and open society, must orient the discussion of the private versus the public sector.

NOTES

1. *Economic Report of the President* (Washington, D.C., 1961), p. 57.
2. *Ibid.,* p. 135:
   Total Government Expenditures, 1929 = $10.2 billion;
   1960 = $137.0 billion. Gross National Expenditures,
   1929 = $104.4 billion; 1960 = $503.2 billion.
3. Karl Albrecht, "Gegenwartsaufgaben langfristiger Wirtschaftspolitik." Paper presented before the Industrie und Handelskammer, Duesseldorf, July 4, 1961.
4. Colin Clark, "Public Finance and Changes in the Value of Money," *The Economic Journal* (London, December, 1945), pp. 371–389. *Idem,* "The Danger Point in Taxes," *Harper's Magazine* (December, 1950), pp. 67–69; reprinted in P. A. Samuelson, R. L. Bishop and J. R. Coleman, eds., *Readings in Economics* (New York, Toronto, London, 1952), pp. 74–78.
5. Cf. the article by A. T. Peacock and Jack Wiseman, "The Past and Future of Public Spending," *Lloyd's Bank Review* (London, April, 1961), pp. 1–20; and the article by Ursula K. Hicks, "The Control of Public Expenditures," *ibid.,* pp. 21–36.
6. Cf. Karl Brandt, "Guidelines for a Constructive Revision of Agricultural Policy in the Coming Decade," *Journal of Farm Economics* (February, 1961), pp. 1–12.
7. Cf. Karl Brandt, "Agricultural Productivity, Economic Growth, and the Farm Policy Motivation of Urban Electorates," *Food Research Institute Studies* (May, 1961), pp. 83–93.
8. Richard LaPiere, *The Freudian Ethic* (New York: Duell, Sloan and Pearce, 1959), p. 264.
9. The (Hoover) Commission on Organization of the Executive Branch of the Government, *Business Enterprises* (Washington, D.C.), 1955; *A Report to the Congress* (May, 1955), listed (pp. 1 and 2) 47 different types of enterprise with over 2,500 separate industrial or commercial facilities owned by the armed services with a government investment of over $15 billion. A Special Committee of the House of Representatives found in 1933 that 232 government-owned business enterprises started during World War I were still in existence fourteen years later. (H.R. 1985, 72nd Cong., 2d Sess.)
10. At the XI International Conference of Agricultural Economists at Cuernavaca, August, 1961, Professor I. S. Kouvshinov of the Timiriazev Agricultural Academy of Moscow gave the official figure for 1959 as 54,600.
11. United Nations, *Economic Survey of Europe in 1957* (Geneva, 1958), chap. I, p. 25.
12. *Economic Survey of Europe in 1959* (Geneva, 1960), chap. II, p. 14; *Economic Survey of Europe in 1960* (Geneva, 1961), chap. IV, p. 13.

13. Cf. U.S. Dept. Agr., For. Agr. Serv., *The World Agricultural Situation, 1960* (Washington, D.C., December, 1959), p. 29.
14. Jean Chombart de Lauwe, *Les Paysans Sovietiques* (Paris, 1961).
15. De Lauwe, *op. cit.*, p. 147.
16. Edwin G. Nourse, "1960: Hinge between Two Decades," *The Virginia Quarterly Review*, Winter 1961, pp. 1–14. Cf. also Max Ways, "A New Mask for Big Government," *Fortune Magazine*, April 1960, pp. 112–284.

4

Private and Public Expenditures: A Reappraisal

ERNEST VAN DEN HAAG

In *The Affluent Society,* John Kenneth Galbraith persuasively refurbishes the arguments in favor of widening the public and narrowing the private sector of our economy. Let me examine some of his major ideas.[1]

I

Galbraith argues foremost that there is an "imbalance" between the public and the private sector. Economists have overlooked that "imbalance" because their obsolete "conventional wisdom" leads them to focus on "scarcity," whereas we have "affluence."

Galbraith's argument here rests on his confusion or equivocation between the technical meaning of "scarcity"—i.e., need for allocation—and the colloquial meaning—i.e., insufficiency, or poverty. If the two meanings of "scarcity" are separated, his argument is seen to be without merit.

Economists are aware that our affluence has increased (colloquial meaning); but affluence does not make rational allocation obsolete (technical meaning). Allocation, the subject matter of economics—the problem: how can we make the best use of our resources?—becomes "obsolete" only with the millennium. For, though we can and do produce a great deal in temporal society, we cannot produce enough to satisfy all desires; thus it remains rational to allocate—i.e., to choose between alternative satisfactions, and to economize—i.e., to satisfy desires with the least expenditure of resources.

Indeed, Galbraith himself advocates forcible reallocation of resources from the private to the public sector, thus implying that the scarcity, which makes allocation (choice) necessary, and which he is at pains to deny, is still with us. In his equivocation between the technical and colloquial meanings of "scarcity," Galbraith is not altogether original. He follows the "conventional wisdom" of millenarians, utopians, and Marxians. However, the chiliastic sects realized that there is scarcity in temporal society; and the Marxists realized that there is scarcity in non-Communist society. The discovery that scarcity is "obsolete" in *our* society is original with Galbraith, but no improvement on "conventional wisdom." (The supposed disappearance of scarcity leads Galbraith to conclude that we need no longer emphasize productivity—a consistent conclusion, as dangerous as it is wrong.)

Galbraith's "imbalance" itself turns out to be a rhetorical device disguised as an argument. No indication is given—let alone substantiated—as to where a "balance" could be found, or by what means one might locate it. Hence the word "imbalance" does no more than denote Galbraith's dissatisfaction with the present allocation of resources between the public and the private sector; his conclusion merely restates that premise; and his reasoning but affirms what it is supposed to prove, namely, that the public sector should be expanded.

(Galbraith suggests, often with striking illustrations, that specific public services are lagging. He takes it for granted that the lag is caused by insufficient financing. The term "imbalance" helps to evade analysis of the distribution and of the effectiveness of the use of money within the public sector—the actual problems causing most of the "deficiencies" Galbraith mentions. More money is not likely to improve matters and may make them worse. Reorganization is called for.)

Economists took the idea of balance from mechanics to describe a state without an endogeneous tendency to change (equilibrium). Galbraith gives it a laudatory sense—balance becomes an unspecified but ideal distribution between public and private sectors—and proceeds to use the descriptive term prescriptively. By this device, he retains the authority the term derived from its objective reference, though he has surreptitiously cut it adrift. This public relations stratagem has worked well; in defense of reason, I suggest that from now on, unless an author tells us how he determines "imbalance" in the economy, we ought to grant only that it exists in his mind.

Colin Clark has tried to prove that we suffer from the opposite imbalance, that the public sector is overexpanded whenever it uses (or, better, attempts to use) more than 25 per cent of the national income. When that happens, he thinks, the ostensive welfare goals are defeated, and the economy generally suffers. At least Clark tells us how to locate his imbalance and its effects. He tries to prove a meaningful proposition. I do not think he succeeds, but Galbraith does not even try—and for good reason: he does not have a genuine proposition to which evidence could be relevant.

In Galbraith's defense, one may argue that some public expenditures are directly complementary to private ones. Without roads, cars are of no use. But even here, "imbalance" is misleading. The proper quantitative relationship between road and car expenditures has not been worked out with any precision, and it may be impossible to do so in any way that would permit us to speak of a general "balance."

Here Galbraith follows convention, but would have done better to abandon it: we usually treat public expenditures as a dependent variable and the private expenditures to be complemented by them as an independent one. Yet this is certainly wrong. Both must be treated as dependent variables. They are functionally interdependent. The problem is not: how much road space is needed for automobile traffic growing at a given rate? but: how much automobile traffic should be supported, induced or balked, in view of public costs and various alternative expenditures and means of transportation? Roads invite automobile traffic as much as they accommodate it. (The undeveloped countries illustrate very well that automobile traffic is as much a function of road-building as vice versa.) Other factors—taxation, public transport, etc.—also influence automobile traffic. When roads are built with public funds, surely we must base decisions on the comparative desirability of fostering and accommodating automobile traffic, and not exclusively on the desires of actual and prospective automobile users. (In the case of toll roads, this problem differs—although toll roads do involve costs in addition to those paid for by users.)

To treat public expenditure as a dependent variable complementing independent private expenditures is about as reasonable as it would be to say, "Since many people want to drive at a speed of 100 miles per hour, injuring more pedestrians than we now can take care of, we must multiply hospitals and cemeteries." Should we not instead, or as well, discourage speed and other hazards, and perhaps automobile traffic?

Whenever possible, the cost of the public complement to private expenditure should be defrayed by the most direct and main beneficiaries. A fuller application of this ancient rule of fiscal equity might, apart from its intrinsic merit, greatly reduce public expenditures: the private expenditures that are now subsidized by complementary public ones might be reduced if the complementary public costs are borne by the direct private beneficiaries through taxes.[2]

Though easily abused, the attempt to determine theoretically complementarities between specific public and private expenditures can be fruitful when the relationship between the interdependent variables is treated as independent, and *both* variables are regarded as dependent. I doubt, however, that the attempt to find a general balance between public and private expenditure is fruitful. I can conceive of situations where 70 per cent of the national income might well be spent publicly even in peacetime and of others where ten per cent is too much. So many variables are involved—e.g., size and distribution of the national income, type of expenditure, tax structure—that I do not think a general

rule can do justice to concrete situations unless it be interpreted
as a warning to pay heed to the undesired and possibly self-
defeating effects of very high general levels of taxation. Clark's
attempt to weigh diminishing returns of taxation certainly has
this merit.

II

Galbraith next offers a value judgment: consumers spend
too much on trivialities. I share his judgment; but he miscon-
ceives the problem and proposes irrelevant and indefensible
solutions, likely to make matters worse.

Galbraith argues as though the problem were simply that
there are not so good (i.e., private) and good (i.e., public) expenditures; and he calls on all right-thinking citizens to make sure
that the "good guys" (government) get more money and the
"bad guys" (consumers) less. This will do for a Western; but
is it economic analysis? It replaces the all-too-real problem:
What values are we to live by, or how can people be free *and*
wise? with a pseudo problem: How can we keep people right-
thinking and buying? and then offers a pseudo solution: by
letting the government spend more of their income for them.

Thoughtful men have always agreed that consumers prefer
trivialities and vulgarities to the satisfaction of their real needs;
but they have never agreed on the real needs that ought to be
satisfied, or on how to make consumers do what is good for
them. This is not a new problem arising from affluence and
advertising, as Galbraith suggests. Nor is Galbraith's solution
new. It ignores what makes the problem problematic: neither
an objective nor an agreed-upon standard by which purchases
could be judged more or less trivial in general is available. (I
am making a factual statement: such a standard is not *available*.
Nothing is implied about its existence; and should it exist, about
its nature, applicability or imposition.)

Since Plato, those who in the past proposed what Galbraith
proposes—let the government decide (and spend) more, consumers less—were more consistent than he: they did not believe

in individual freedom; and they felt that right values can be objectively ascertained and collectively imposed. If Galbraith held these views, his theory would be consistent, however unacceptable to me. But though they are implied in much of *The Affluent Society*, I think he would repudiate such views when stated explicitly. One of the major defects of that book is that it disguises inchoate and chaotic philosophical ideas as economic analysis.

Trivialities and vulgarities now constitute a greater proportion of our total output than in the past, not because taste has deteriorated—it probably was always bad—but because it is satisfied more often. Affluence changes the ability to satisfy taste rather than the taste: whereas in the past only the rich had the privilege to indulge their taste, now the poor can too. I do not see why transferring expenditures to a government no wiser than the voters who elect it and less able to satisfy *individual* tastes would solve this problem. It would probably replace private folly with official silliness. *Si monumentum quaeris, circumspice.* And it would make harder the satisfaction of the minority tastes (including Galbraith's), which are usually more interesting than those of the majority.

I see one advantage of democracy in making reasonably certain, not that the government is better than the voters in general, but that it is not much worse; without democracy, this last happens quite easily. Still, in a democracy, if the government is likely to be not worse than the average voter, it is also likely to be worse than some voters. Therefore, the transfer of the power to decide from the individual to even a democratic government is justifiable only where the object is so indivisible, or indiscriminate, as to make collective decisions imperative.

The argument in favor of expansion of the public sector need not be based on the demerits of private expenditure alone. It can be based also on the merits of public expenditure. But these can never be general. Each expenditure must be considered on its own merits: Will benefits exceed costs by more than the benefits of alternative expenditures, public or private? How are benefits and costs distributed? The admitted triviality of many private expenditures and the "imbalance"—whatever it means —are utterly irrelevant unless the general superiority of public expenditures can be shown. By pointing to the triviality of private expenditures—which each consumer is likely to admit in regard to the expenditures of all other consumers—Galbraith suggests that the government would restrain those other consumers, and that, anyway, it could not do worse. But it always can and usually does. (These two fallacies are perennial assertions in the appeals for dictatorship: [1] followers of would-be dictators usually think that matters can only improve; and [2] that the dictator would frustrate the [trivial] wishes of others, but not their own [untrivial] ones.)

III

Though reproaching consumers for their silliness, Galbraith does not hold them responsible for it: according to the principles of ritualistic liberalism, the people always have their heart (or is it their stomach?) in the right place; when they err, it is because they have misread their heart's prompting, owing to some wicked seducer. This theory is popular all around: it enables people to eat their cake and profess that they did not really want it; and it enables the theorist to have his cake (people are good) and eat it (people act badly). In the past, the seducers were devils, capitalists, or Jews. Madison Avenue is fast replacing them in the folklore of our society. Yet recent myths are less convenient than the ancient ones. Jews and capitalists suffer from them, whereas in the past the devils were the main sufferers. Let me note that Galbraith's myth, though structurally analogous to those mentioned, if more urbane, is functionally quite different: Galbraith does not urge liquidation of Jews, capitalists, or advertising men. His theoretical mountain gives birth to a quite modest, practical mouse: a general sales tax. But then mice can be quite voracious, and they multiply fast. (The general sales tax may have technical merits as such. But Galbraith wants it because he believes it to be the best means to achieve his basic end of increasing the general level of taxation, of decreasing private and increasing public expenditure. I object to this end, rather than to a sales as compared to an income tax.)

Galbraith argues that consumers no longer satisfy endogeneous desires, but exogeneous ones "contrived" by advertising. Industry thus first produces the desires it then satisfies, whereas before *The Affluent Society,* the needs satisfied arose independently. Now to the extent to which we grant the truth and undesirability of this "dependence effect," it might argue against advertising. Surprisingly, Galbraith seems to think of it as an argument for reducing the purchasing power of consumers and increasing that of the government by means of a general sales tax. His not entirely explicit train of thought seems to be: consumers' purchases are trivial; they satisfy a demand "contrived" by advertising; therefore we should transfer purchasing power from consumers to the government; public expenditures will be less contrived and less trivial. There is no logical connection among the various parts of this argument.

Why should the government not do worse than consumers? Why are public expenditures less (rather than differently) contrived than private ones? Is the political process that spontaneous? Why is "contrived," i.e., influenced demand better or worse (more or less trivial) than uncontrived, i.e., uninfluenced (if that is conceivable) demand? Is the "contrived" demand for education, books, and soap worse than uncontrived spontaneous dirt and ignorance? One may spontaneously desire trivial things —as any child knows and does. Culture is contrivance, i.e., social influence, and there is no society without it. There is no less contrivance in primitive, or for that matter, in Soviet society than in ours. The problem is not that there is influence ("contrivance"), but its quality, source and direction, above all, whether influence is monopolized or whether it comes from many competing sources. The high taxes Galbraith proposes obviously would not affect these problems except by reducing the power of individuals and adding to the power of the government. Influence would not be eliminated; it would be centralized.

Galbraith's argument is irrelevant then. Is it true? Are consumers hapless victims of Madison Avenue? One would expect that they bought Ford's Edsel car in droves and not small foreign cars; or that the political party that spends most on advertising always wins. Presidents Thomas Dewey and Richard Nixon, and the Republican Congressional majority would testify to these beliefs were they true. They are not. But believers are unshaken by evidence.

Advertising is only one influence among others in political or purchasing decisions and is frequently offset by competing advertising. Yet advertising men as well as their opponents (for different reasons) cherish the belief that advertising is always the decisive influence. Advertising agencies want to impress prospective clients with the importance of what they may do for them. The motivation of opponents is more complex, though their faith is as strong. Some are looking for scapegoats; others are mildly paranoid; still others want to convince people that they lose nothing in getting government "protection" from their own use of freedom, since advertising mysteriously has deprived them of that freedom anyway.

Many consumers spend their money in ways many other consumers disapprove of. The first group of consumers assumes that the second cannot possibly have freely decided to spend its money as it does. The disapproved expenditure pattern is taken for evidence of their lack of freedom, just as apologists for dictatorship have always presented the election of a less than perfect democratic government, or of one they disapproved of, as evidence of a lack of political freedom. If you do not "really" have it, what can you lose in giving it up?

The moral connection between sumptuary and political freedom is anything but tenuous: if consumers are incapable of freely choosing among advertised products, why should they be deemed capable of freely choosing among propagandizing political parties? What is freedom if not the right to choose among competing influences? If these influences are considered coercion, or if people are deemed too incompetent to choose among them, freedom can never be more than sham, and we might just as well install a dictatorship. It would not follow that dictatorship will lead to better results; but there would be no reason to expect worse ones. We would give up something we never had, or were never able to use competently. But I like freedom because it allows me to make and judge my own choices, however foolish.

We might well oppose and seek to restrain seduction. But we cannot (unless it be practiced on the legally incompetent) treat it as though it were rape, precisely because it gives choice (and therewith part of the responsibility) to all parties concerned: it requires consent. Democracy does so no less than the "dependence effect": with freedom there always are competing influences. And advertisements for detergents no more hypnotize or coerce than advertisements for political candidates. If people are competent as citizens to choose among candidates, why should they not be competent as consumers to choose among goods? (I find it hard to believe that those who confuse influence with coercion can be sincere, but I may overestimate both their intelligence and their malevolence.)

Has the influence of advertising increased? The proportion of the population affected certainly has. Not, however, because Madison Avenue has discovered new tricks—there seems to have been little basic progress in propaganda techniques since Roman times—but because literacy and other communications media have spread; and because many people who did not in the past, do now have enough disposable income to follow fashions in purchasing. However, even the fixed purchasing patterns of the past were socially influenced. The peasant's dress, food, and housing were no more individual creations than the wigs of noblemen, or their extravagant garments. Nor were these things less trivial than the things advertised in *Vogue* today. Versailles, a medieval cathedral, or Vanderbilt's yacht were neither more of a necessity or more spontaneous than our tail-finned cars, or a copy of *The Affluent Society*—though perhaps of more lasting value.

The actual change that has occurred is not any new "dependence effect," but a general change from a pre-industrial, tradition-directed to an industrial, consumer-directed society with its concomitant mass culture.[3] This means that social influences are more changeable, that they come more often from below, that people are more attuned to them (more outer-directed). Rather than coming mainly from the nobility, the king, and the church, or having been internalized, influences currently come from a greater variety of sources; the advertising industry is among them, though perhaps it transmits more than it creates.

Characteristically, advertising agencies are not in the permanent service of a class, ideology, or church, but of whoever hires their services. Mostly private firms try to increase or maintain their profits by doing so. But firms are as interested in producing what people want as they are in making people want what they produce. The former is more profitable and more certain of success. In this sense, advertising probably is less engaged in "contriving" needs than the church was, or than Harvard University is when it raises funds. Indeed, the bad taste Mr. Galbraith deplores is indulged in largely because of the absence of the ancient contriving agencies—church and court. We are now catering to the taste of the masses, whereas before it could be ignored. There is no evidence to indicate that people would buy fewer or better things without advertising. They might buy slightly different things from slightly different people.

IV

The public expenditures Galbraith advocates to replace private expenditures—more public works, education, welfare services—are neither new nor supported by new arguments. This part of *The Affluent Society* amounts to tiresome exhortation. Yet a discussion of the specifics of public expenditures might have been fruitful. I am convinced that we need public services not now undertaken, and that many public services presently offered at high cost to taxpayers are "contrived": they become necessary because the government prevents private industry from rendering them or makes it excessively costly to do so, or finally, because they offset noxious government activities elsewhere. A classical illustration is the case of farm subsidies.

Through price support the government raises farm prices, i.e., the cost of living, mainly the price of food, but also of cotton, tobacco, etc. Taxpayers, via the government, spend more than $5 billion annually for the privilege of buying food at prices higher than those of a free market. This money is spent to buy supplies that would depress the market price, or to pay farmers for not producing them. No way to dispose of most of the supplies purchased has been found; they are stored at huge additional cost until they spoil. Some are sold at a loss abroad or given away. The subsidy, of course, perpetuates the misallocation of resources between agriculture and the rest of the economy that it is supposed to correct, and also within agriculture. More is produced of what is needed less, and less of what is needed more, *ad infinitum,* and subsidies are required *ad infinitum* to keep it that way.

There is no respectable argument known to economists for these subsidies. The argument usually heard is that without them the income of farmers would be lower than that of workers, or lower than it was in some past period. But most of the subsidy does not go to low-income farmers; their farms are so small and unproductive that higher prices or payments for noncultivation of their property add little to their income. Most of the subsidy goes to big-scale producers of unneeded farm products. (50 per cent of our farmers produce less than 10 per cent of the agricultural output.)

If we wanted to help low-income farmers, we could do so without raising food prices and fostering misallocation, and without subsidizing farmers whose income far exceeds the income of the taxpayers who must pay the subsidy. Without changing the whole complex structure of present legislation—a task that should not be neglected, but that requires time—the government could do so simply by purchasing only from farmers whose net income from all sources in any given year does not exceed, say, $7,000. (Surely farmers with higher incomes need no subsidies.) Any amount paid to farmers whose income exceeds $7,000 must be returned—and the government can return what it purchased from them. In time the government might limit itself to purchases from progressively older farmers. This ultimately would solve the problem; only those would remain or go into farming who can make an income that satisfies them by selling their crops at unsubsidized market prices. This, of course, would correct the allocation of resources and make further subsidies unnecessary.

I have outlined elsewhere how this proposal could be carried out and what the effects would be.[4] I have received heartening letters from economists. But nothing else. The mood of our times is such that if a problem can be perpetuated and made worse by high subsidies and brought nearer solution by low ones, we prefer high subsidies. I deliberately speak of the mood of the times. For in terms of their economic interests, the farmers who would not lose under the proposal—let alone consumers—constitute an overwhelming majority. But our general tendency is to make individual efforts less and less dependent on the value placed by the market on one's products or services, and more and more on political considerations: on the political power exercised by the selling group, or the power that politicians can gain by catering to it. Above all, the nature of the subsidy is carefully hidden. We speak of price supports when we make relief payments to some farmers who need them (and who should be trained for a different occupation rather than kept farming and receiving relief) and to many who do not.

By now the farm program has become a classical case. Some newer but equally dubious programs seem more complicated. For instance, the government feels it necessary to subsidize low- and middle-rent apartment-house building in many cities. It is contended that low- and middle-income families, although more affluent than ever before, cannot afford the rent for unsubsidized housing. But if their income is too small, we should subsidize them, not housing. Why a subsidy in kind, which deprives them of choice? Is it feared that they would make a choice that appears wrong to the government? What evidence is there to show that they are wrong and the government right?

As soon as we turn from vacuous generalizations about the affluent private and the starved public sector of our economy to an actual scrutiny of public expenditures, we find that, though it is true that some needed services are not performed, or not performed well, it is also true that many unneeded services are performed at immense cost. Often they serve as pretexts to perform still other services or pay subsidies to offset the effect they have. Increasing public expenditure is unlikely to remedy this state of affairs; it will make it worse.

V

Is additional public expenditure on education necessary, sufficient, or at least favorable to additional learning? The impression that the more we spend for education, the more education we get, is widely held but sadly mistaken. It derives, of course, from individual experience in purchasing items of elastic supply and easily measured quality. Unfortunately, education does not have these characteristics.

The supply both of educable students and of capable educators is limited, particularly in the short run. Given a minimum that we have long exceeded, the size of expenditure for education plays a comparatively small part in determining whether this supply is productively utilized and increased in the long run. Since neither teaching and research ability nor educability is measurable except in crude and arbitrary probability terms, immense amounts of money can be easily wasted without anybody's being the wiser. (Note, particularly, that most measurements tend to include, or altogether to rest on, the interpretative scheme they are supposed to validate.) The available resources, including money, are used badly now. Simple increases of total expenditure are more likely to hinder the necessary changes than to foster them.

Much of the clamor for more expenditure on "education" stems from a confusion. The solution of the world's problems by philosophy, religion, or psychology certainly is more important than chewing gum. But people spend more money on gum than on philosophers, ministers, or psychologists. Food is more important than sartorial elegance, but many people spend more on clothing. Health is more important than beer, but it does not follow that more should, or could, usefully be spent on medicine than on beer. The point is simple, but the confusion ubiquitous: how often are we told that more is spent on something less essential than on education—as though this were evidence that too little is spent on education! Yet expenditure need not and cannot be proportional to importance, moral or material. It must pay for the cost of whatever can be produced and used of the important thing or service. Any expenditure beyond that is waste—no matter how much more money be spent on less important things.

The returns on educational expenditure have been diminishing. To increase educational expenditure now is like giving sugar to diabetics who crave it no less than educational lobbies crave money, and for the same reason: improper utilization. Unfortunately, the lobbies are supported by many well-meaning people who have been assured that the money will result in better nutrition. But the trouble is that the patient cannot actually absorb it. Education is weak, but not undernourished. It is weak partly from obesity, partly from the faulty diet, and, above all, from lack of exercise. More money may assuage our guilt feelings, but it will do nothing else. Let us look at some of the specifics.

The "classroom shortage" is often cited as evidence for too little expenditure. At present about 70,000 new classrooms are built per year. At the usual 28 pupils per classroom, the need (compounded of the backlog owing to overcrowding and deterioration, and increased enrollment) is for about 60,000 new classrooms per year.[5] There are, of course, local shortages and surpluses—owing both to shifts of population and to local mistakes—but no general shortage and certainly no need for an overall federally financed building program.

This calculation does not take into account three obvious measures which, singly or in combination, could relieve any foreseeable shortage if it were to occur, and which might well make it possible to reduce the present high rate of school building. They are: lengthening the school year by one month; teaching on Saturday; double shifts. (By teaching on Saturday, and/or teaching a month longer per year, schools could make up any loss of time through double shifts.)

The five-day week most adults enjoy was the result of increased productivity and of a decreased need for production. But the need for education has not decreased, nor has its productivity increased. The long summer vacations (which adults are not usually granted) derive from the original need for summer child labor in an agricultural economy. This need no longer exists. And reduction of vacation time by one month leaves plenty for students and teachers. Finally, why should schools not be kept open, say, from 8:00 a.m. to 6:00 p.m.? By proper utilization of gymnastic and other special facilities, this span, with double shifts, could amount to six hours of schooling per day per child. If desired, this arrangement might also make it easier to dispense with expensive and elaborate cafeterias. The total, or the yearly school work of students or teachers, need not be increased. Utilization of school buildings by greater numbers of children and teachers is thus possible without requiring additional classrooms. The children and teachers who attend on Saturday may take off on other days.

A second reason frequently offered for greater public expenditure on education is "the teacher shortage" and the "need to raise teachers' salaries." There was a teacher shortage in the early 1950's owing not so much to "underpayment" as to sharp increases in enrollment. Since that time, the increase in the number of teachers has regularly exceeded the increase in the number of pupils, so that the National Education Association itself admits that by 1962 enough new fully certified teachers will be available to fill all the new positions and those left by teachers who have quit. This certainly does not indicate that salaries must be raised to get *more* teachers.

Teachers themselves, though they complain, apparently feel that they could not earn as much as gratifyingly in other occupations. About nine per cent of all classroom teachers quit their jobs every year. One-third of these do so to get married; it is unlikely that a higher salary would prevent this. Another twenty per cent just change jobs within the teaching profession. Fifteen per cent retire for old age or disability. Only about thirteen per cent of those who leave quit teaching for other occupations. This is about one per cent of all classroom teachers. The figure does not indicate economic pressure to leave. An unknown number of those who have quit return; and we do not know how many among this one per cent of the total take other jobs because they pay better, and how many prefer them for non-financial reasons. Moreover, every year the number of those entering teaching from other gainful employments exceeds the number of those leaving for nonteaching employments.

Something of the nature of the shortage is revealed by the *New York Times*, reporting, under the front-page headline (9/18/53) "200 New City Teachers Missing," that 200 newly appointed teachers had failed to show up because of low salaries. On 9/22/53, the same *New York Times* reported—this time on page 33 and without an editorial deploring the financial plight of teachers—"2,000 Flock to Get City Teachers' Jobs." According to the *Daily News*, there were 3,000—and the jobs were those very 200 underpaid jobs.[6] (As do all newspapers, the *Times* selects news and its prominence according to reader interest and expectations. Readers sensitized to a "teacher shortage" and "underpayment" are likely to be more interested in the first rather than in the second story. The *Times* does not seem to be worse than other papers, possibly better, certainly more dignified and comprehensive. How useful or ethical this news selection is, lies beyond my scope here to discuss.)

This is not to say that there is no shortage; there is in some fields, just as in others there is a surplus. Nor can we conclude that teachers' pay is satisfactory. Some teachers are underpaid—as others are overpaid. But the comparative income of teachers has improved. In 1909, the yearly salary of teachers was about the same as that of workers in manufacturing. Today, teachers make about $500 more than workers in manufacturing (including only the total time worked on the average: fifty weeks for workers, forty for teachers). Teachers' salaries also have risen more than those of government workers, dentists, and lawyers.

All these data depend on the periods selected for comparison. But the trend suggested is unmistakable. Of course, the educational requirements—or, better, the degree requirements—which teachers must fulfill have risen. Sixteen to seventeen years of formal education are now required for all teachers in almost all states. (Abroad, twelve years is the norm for elementary school teachers.)

Would higher salaries attract more able teachers? In occupations such as art, politics, literature, scholarship, judicial administration, and teaching, the average quality of the personnel attracted depends on the income offered only in the sense that a comparative minimum must be exceeded (even this is largely conjectural). There is no evidence that the quality is improved by raising incomes, particularly average incomes, beyond this minimum. The attractiveness of these occupations depends on the inherent satisfaction of pursuing them, and on such matters as prestige and intraoccupational advancement opportunity.

The interoccupational mobility between white-collar and blue-collar occupations is small. The student who considers teaching as a career compares it only with other white-collar occupations. No possible salary scale is likely to attract those whose major ambition is to become rich; they will go into business or an independent profession. On the other hand, the girl who eventually wants to raise a family but who has some intellectual interests as well, and who likes children in general, may find teaching attractive. Whether she becomes a teacher will not be greatly influenced by salary—provided her income compares favorably with white-collar occupations as easily open to her and not much less attractive. Exceptional teachers, who are certainly needed, must be attracted by exceptional advancement possibilities in prestige and money within the occupation, though these cannot be expected to compare with those in business and the professions. Increases in the average salary will not attract these teachers: they are not distinctive and cannot be great enough. An across-the-board raise will have no positive effects whatever in intensifying the attraction teaching holds for those actually talented for it, or in fostering a better utilization of the talent already available in the schools. To make teaching attractive for the talented, we must raise the standards of teacher education. We need not prolong the years of study, but we can make them more demanding and less silly by eliminating "education" courses and substituting subject-matter courses. The idea that more money is an all-powerful remedy is abetted by generosity and by the strong guilt feelings Americans seem to have toward their young: people realize that all is not well with education. And yet there is an unwillingness among teachers and parents to scrutinize the difficulties that have brought about the present state of affairs.

If we look at the matter in comparative terms—and there are no absolute standards—we find that our expenditure on education is extraordinarily high, and that our troubles are clearly related to the way these expenditures and, indeed, all our educational resources have been utilized. Less may be more here. The proportion of the national income spent by the United States on public education compares favorably with that of other advanced nations,[7] and the per capita expenditure is higher than that of any other country. As a percentage of our expenditures on consumption, expenditures on public education have risen— contrary to Galbraith's unsupported surmise—from 3.1 per cent in 1929 to 4.3 per cent in 1956; this despite the immense increase in consumption expenditure. Per capita expenditure for public education (calculated in constant dollars) has risen steadily in the United States; so has expenditure for private education; so has the percentage of the national income spent on public education and that spent on private education. Average expenditure *per pupil* per year, in *constant dollars,* has increased by more than 600 per cent since 1900. We spend, in real terms, six times as much for each pupil than we did sixty years ago—hardly a sign of financial neglect. On the contrary, one may suspect that the cost of education has risen by more than is justified by its accomplishments.

In terms of formal schooling, our expenditures have assured our pre-eminence. Thus, in the United States, 66.2 per cent of the 15- to 19-year-olds are in school, versus 17 per cent in

Europe and 48.6 per cent in the Soviet Union; and 12 per cent of the 20- to 24-year-olds, versus 3.7 per cent in Europe and 8.2 per cent in the Soviet Union. The number of school days per year has increased as well (though abroad it often remains greater). The size of classes, i.e., the teacher-student ratio has been consistently declining. (Incidentally, there are mountains of research but no conclusive evidence linking class size to learning rates; after kindergarten it seems to matter little.) Our school buildings and our auxiliary personnel and apparatus are far more opulent and costly than those of any other nation.

We are still advancing fast, perhaps too fast, in statistical terms. According to the United States Office of Education, of 1,000 fifth-grade pupils in 1924, 612 were in high school four years later, whereas of 1,000 fifth-grade pupils in 1952, 904 were in high school in 1960 (nearly 50 per cent more); of the first 1,000, 30 per cent graduated; of the second, 60 per cent (i.e., 100 per cent more). And, whereas only 118 out of 1,000 fifth-grade pupils in 1924 entered college (in the depression year 1932), 319 out of 1,000 in the fifth grade entered college in 1960. The difference leaves no doubt about the enormous increase of our expense on education, and about the statistical effect it had: an increased proportion of the population is subjected to increased amounts of schooling. Doubts start when we consider the return on this investment.

We spent, and are spending, a great deal of money and, in purely statistical terms, the results are excellent. Our trouble is that students do not learn much in school, and, in particular, not enough of what they need to learn. It is difficult to see how still better buildings, more highly paid teachers, or greater expenditures would solve a problem that has been created largely by emphasis on total expenditures and neglect of their use, of education.

NOTES

1. Most of Galbraith's arguments, were they correct, would not be necessary, and altogether they are not sufficient, for the conclusions he draws. (I have discussed *The Affluent Society* as a whole in *Commentary,* September, 1960, and January, 1961.)
2. The general sales tax proposed by Galbraith in place of the excise taxes here suggested would have the opposite effect.
3. *See* Ralph Ross and Ernest van den Haag, *The Fabric of Society, passim,* particularly chap. XV.
4. *See* "A Modest Farm Proposal," *The New Leader,* February 27, 1961.
5. The most reasonable analysis of the incredibly confused issue is found in Roger A. Freeman's *School Needs in the Decade Ahead* (Washington, D.C.: The Institute for Social Science Research, 1958; 3rd ed., 1960). His projections have since been abundantly confirmed.
6. Quoted by Freeman, *op. cit.,* p. 67.
7. This proportion is mentioned here because frequently quoted, and usually wrongly. It is not very significant, because (*a*) with a high national income, a smaller percentage is needed; (*b*) demographic factors distort the picture; (*c*) much depends on how much education is publicly financed. Much depends finally on how "education" is defined and how expenditure is calculated.

5

Can People Be Trusted with Natural Resources?[1]

J. W. MILLIMAN

It is the clear duty of government, which is the trustee for unborn generations as well as for its present citizens, to watch over, and if need be, by legislative enactment, to defend the exhaustible natural resources from rash and reckless exploitation.

—A. C. Pigou

There are a great many people in favor of conservation no matter what it means.

—W. H. Taft

If the resource problem is serious, then the price of a wide choice now is a sharply restricted choice later on. Surely even those who adhere to the biggest supermarket theory of liberty would agree that their concept has a time dimension.

—John Kenneth Galbraith

I

Throughout history most of the scrutiny given to policy for the use and development of natural resources[2] has been the province of tribal medicine men, religious thinkers, philosophers, poets, novelists, as well as physical and natural scientists. Only in the last century, and indeed only in the last few decades, have economists and other social scientists given much attention to the normative principles that should govern the exploitation (why are natural resources always "exploited"?) of natural resources. This newly found interest in natural-resource policy is in an embryonic state, however, and much current thinking is still enmeshed and clothed with the traditional moralistic and honorific trappings concerning the irrationality of man in dealing with the bounties of Nature.

In few other fields of analysis is there such a widespread feeling that private and individual decisions are to be deplored. Time and time again we are told that the innate selfishness of man causes him to take a myopic view of the future and thus to deplete "our precious hoard" of natural resources. The result is the standard old refrain that "future, unborn generations are being deprived of their just heritage." We shall explore this question at greater length in the body of the paper, but it is crucial at this point to ask: Which future generation? To infinity? Can we know what future generations will require? Who is society? Why does society know better? What is the proper distribution of wealth between generations, even assuming we know the quantity of wealth over time? Are men myopic and selfish only in the private sector of the economy?

Apparently, conservation of natural resources has achieved widespread, indeed universal, support largely on the basis of a guilt complex concerning the rapaciousness, induced by the profit motive and by individual self-interest, of men in using the "God-given" natural-resource heritage. On this score, some writers go so far as to deny the proposition that the ultimate end of policy is human welfare. Rather, they often imply that it is desirable to conserve natural resources in themselves apart from human ends and activity. In any event, this feeling that private decision-making is suspect when it deals with natural resources is widespread, not only by many twentieth-century liberals and progressives, but also by groups and individuals normally opposed to infringements upon private property and a "free" economy. In fact, if I sense the current scene correctly, there is very little acceptance of the thesis that the market system and private property can be used to deal effectively with many, perhaps most, of our natural-resource problems.

I do not wish to suggest that public control over natural resources is abhorrent; indeed, it is extremely necessary in some cases. As I read popular and academic sentiment, however, I find very little support for an appreciation of the large part the price system can play in the development of natural resources. Some conservatives, on the other hand, refuse to admit that governmental action and control have a role to perform in situations where private property and the price system cannot exist or perform satisfactorily. Of course, neither public nor private decision-making is free of blemish and imperfection.

A summary of popular thinking on natural-resource use seems to run as follows:

1) Natural resources are disappearing rapidly.
2) This disappearance is totally undesirable.
3) The major reason for this disappearance is the greed of individuals pursuing selfish and profit motives.
4) The result is that the well-being of posterity is being sacrificed for the satisfaction of the whims of present generations.

In this essay I wish to comment first upon the question of the adequacy of the supply of natural resources. Second, I want to examine some of the premises upon which one might base a choice of public versus private decision-making for natural-resource use and development.

II

It is often asserted that the natural-resource base of the United States economy is the basic ingredient of our industrial and military power. This hypothesis is usually coupled with the notion that natural resources are becoming increasingly scarce. The usual pessimistic forecast is that this scarcity will lead, possibly even in the next few decades, to an impairment in the rate of economic growth, to a weakening of our power position in the world, and to a decline in the welfare of future generations. A recent example of this point of view is found in the opening remarks of President John F. Kennedy's message on natural resources to the Congress:

> From the beginning of civilization, every nation's basic wealth and progress has stemmed in large measure from its natural resources. This nation has been, and is now, especially fortunate in the blessings we have inherited. Our entire society rests upon—and is dependent upon—our water, our land, our forests, and our minerals. How we use these resources influences our health, security, economy, and well-being.
>
> But if we fail to chart a proper course of conservation and development—if we fail to use these blessings prudently—we will be in trouble in a short time. In the resource field, predictions of future use have been consistently understated. But even under conservative projections, we face a future of critical shortage and handicaps.[3]

More fearful views are to be found in the writings of Samuel H. Ordway, Fairfield Osborn, William Vogt, Robert C. Cook, Harrison Brown, Charles Galton Darwin, Hyman Rickover, and Palmer Putnam.

At first blush this position seems so obvious, alarming, and critical that to express doubt or skepticism would brand one either as a fool or as a blind, unthinking optimist. It is the purpose of this section to demonstrate that it is not at all obvious that our basic strength lies in our supplies of natural resources or that these supplies are necessarily becoming increasingly scarce. And it is even less evident, perhaps, what an increase in the scarcity of resources might mean with regard to the rate of economic growth and to the welfare of future generations. I should caution, however, that this discussion is far too brief and cursory to do more than pose the questions in such a way that historical evidence and growth projections can be used to highlight the basic policy considerations.

FALSE NOTIONS CONCERNING NATURAL SCARCITY

It is not at all clear to me that "any diminution in the re-source base involves a potential reduction in output over-all." [4] The important question (from the standpoint of the economy as a whole) is not so much a concern of our natural resource base per se but rather with our *total* capital base and with all the forces that make for economic growth.[5] I would argue that natural resources are only part of the total stock of capital and that there is no a priori reason for believing that natural-resource capital is any more productive than other types of capital. It is not the *origin* of capital that is important, man-made or natural, but rather its total amount and the relative productivity at the margin of alternative forms of capital. According to this line of reason-ing, a decline in a country's resource base may be offset by an increase in other types of capital, and indeed would be if invest-ment in natural resources were less productive than alternative kinds of capital formation. Should our attention be focused upon natural resources as such, as many writers seem to urge, or should it be concerned with the maintenance and expansion of our total capital base? From this point of view, it is true that a diminu-tion of our stock of total capital may lead to reduction in total output, but the emphasis is then directed to the over-all prob-lems of consumption, savings, and investment rather than to natural resources as such.

The careful reader will note, however, that the preceding argument on whether or not natural resources—particularly land and energy resources—should be treated as a special category apart from other forms of capital depends upon two major as-sumptions. The first has to do with the question of the sub-stitutability of other forms of capital for natural resources. Could it be argued that substitution is not always possible and that beyond a certain point substitution becomes prohibitively costly? The second condition is concerned with the risk factor involved in projected future "requirements" for "key" natural resources such as land and water. Could it not be that mistakes of judg-ment and estimation of certain resources might have irreparable or irreversible consequences for the future well-being of society and that such consequences may not apply with comparable seri-ousness to other forms of capital? If either or both of these two conditions were present, one might well argue that preservation of natural-resource capital should receive special consideration.

Let us examine each of these two points in turn. Despite com-mon belief, it is quite clear that there is no such thing as a fixed, inflexible requirement for individual natural resources that is impossible of variation. That is to say, there is *some degree* of substitutability for each and every kind or class of input! It may be helpful, nevertheless, to admit that there are problems of easy substitutability between various kinds of capital, but it is difficult for me to see how this really constitutes an argument for special treatment of natural resources. First of all, it is not a question of "all or none," but a question of a little more versus a little less. In other words, we are concerned with marginal adjustments, i.e., marginal rates of substitution. And at the margin it is doubtful if the difficulties of substitution are of special concern.

I know of no important policy decisions that are of this "all or none" variety. Even though it is quite true that a particular resource—say water—is necessary to human life and thus has in-finite value, the question is never posed in these terms. Rather, policy questions are concerned, for the most part, with whether or not a certain incremental supply is justified; this is to ask what the value and the cost of water is at the margin. And at the margin, the value of extra water may be very low, particularly if it is to be used for the irrigation of low-valued crops already in surplus! For example, the Missouri River Basin Project is being constructed at a cost approaching three billion dollars. Approximately thirty per cent of the estimated benefits from the irrigation of an additional five million acres are attached to the production of sugar beets. Yet every acre of sugar beets will probably have to be protected by an acreage allotment, import restrictions on foreign sugar, and a government subsidy. This new production will constitute a seventy-five per cent increase in total United States sugar-beet output.[6]

It is also clear, moreover, that so-called "needs" or "requirements" computed purely on the basis of the physical possibilities for substitution are relatively meaningless in an economic context. Time and time again we study projections for the future based purely upon crude extrapolations of present usage without any consideration of the possibilities of changes in the combinations of inputs in the light of their changing economic feasibility. Economic demands must consider relative prices and costs, and the degree of substitution of various inputs will reflect these relationships. An example of this failing is found in a recent United States report on water resources. This report is now being widely quoted as the authoritative study of the prospective demand for and supply of water in the United States in 1980 and 2000. Although the report was prepared by an economist, these projections of demand and supply were developed without reference to such basic factors as prices, costs, alternative uses of water, interregional shifts, and most of the factors affecting the elasticities of demand and supply.[7]

Second, the fact that the cost of substitution increases the more it is extended is true for all capital inputs and does not appear to be a special attribute of natural-resource capital. That is to say, beyond a certain point substitution may become prohibitively costly for all forms of capital. It seems likely that the productivity of capital at the margin will tend to reflect the relative difficulties of substitution of all kinds of capital for one another and that conceptually it is possible to say that the cost of substitution has already been taken into account.

Of course, there may be special problems of imperfection in the functioning of capital markets, and this may be true of natural-resource markets in particular. For example, I have argued elsewhere that water law tends to hinder the transfer of water resources between competing uses.[8] And many other institutional and technological roadblocks for natural-resource allocation can be cited. This general question will be discussed in section III.

Proper policy here would seem to call for attempts to mitigate the imperfections directly, but it does not seem to call for a special capital theory for natural resources as such. In other words, the current opportunity cost of resources at the margin may not be optimum in a strict welfare sense, but it still reflects the current marginal productivity of capital. And to neglect the marginal productivity of capital when one is concerned with investment policy for natural resources is certainly incorrect.

In regard to the problems of risk and uncertainty in the use of natural-resource capital, it is difficult to understand why risk and uncertainty may be greater here than they are in the case of general capital investment. Risk and uncertainty are pervasive, but we never jump suddenly from 1963 to the year 2000. Rather, the future is approached day by day. We can continually alter our decisions in the light of new information and changed expectations.

This is not to say that the market as it presently functions is optimal or to deny that long-run commitments sometimes have to be made. I do suggest, however, that there is much greater flexibility with regard to future "needs" than is often considered. I know of no examples throughout history where any civilization suddenly "ran out" of this or that mineral. The "one-horse shay" concept of natural-resource deterioration must be discarded. Deterioration in the quality or quantity of natural resources does not come about suddenly, but rather gradually.

All of this implies that we should distinguish rather carefully between economic scarcity as opposed to physical scarcity. Resource limits, assuming we know what they are, refer to physical quantities and qualities of resources in a given form or state. Economic scarcity, on the other hand, must depend upon the general determinants of demand, i.e., the marginal rates of substitution. Economic scarcity is sociotechnological in character. It cannot be deduced from data on physical supplies; rather, economic scarcity can be judged only in the light of *all* the forces that influence demand.[9]

Economic scarcity is reflected in increasing *relative* costs. It encourages economizing and the search for substitutes and new techniques of production. The search for lower-cost substitutes is always present and, indeed, may actually take place before cost increases resulting from prospective shortages occur. The record of aluminum in replacing copper in several important uses is illustrative of this activity. Other common reactions to a prospective economic shortage include increased concern on the part of producers to be more efficient in methods of production, to turn to lower-quality sources, and to increase the intensity of exploration efforts. For individual countries the attractiveness of imports from sources abroad increases. Therefore, a whole host of market reactions will be induced by the rising prices accompanying a current or prospective shortage, tending to offset the decline in supplies, on the one hand, and also to redirect economic demands, on the other hand.[10] I shall explore the qualifications to these procedures in section III.

SOME NEW EVIDENCE ON RESOURCE SCARCITY

Within the last ten years, mainly under the sponsorship of Resources for the Future, Inc., a number of economists have begun to examine in careful fashion the question of the adequacy of our natural-resource base and the role natural resources play in economic development. Although these studies are not fully completed, and although they have not yet been subjected to widespread review, it is clear that the conclusions of the studies are not in accord with the popular views of resource scarcity. A summary of these findings seems to indicate that there are a number of resource problems and difficulties, but there *appears to be no significant danger of a general resource shortage in this country within the next thirty to forty years and perhaps longer.* Furthermore, the historical evidence *does not lend support to the hypothesis that the United States economy has been subject to diminishing returns from its natural-resource base.*

I hope that some readers can find time to examine a number of these studies. It is important that they be given widespread circulation among students of natural resources and among framers of public policy.[11] I should hasten to add, however, that each of these studies qualifies its optimism; each admits that, at best, the future can be seen only dimly, and that we cannot always be sure what the past means. It is also true that there are some apparently competent earlier studies which come to more pessimistic conclusions.[12]

Even though one may not accept most of the conclusions of these recent studies as I tend to do, it is evident that there are solid grounds for doubting that the general resource position of the United States is really critical. It is important to stress, however, that the arguments against special treatment of natural resources do not hinge upon the relative optimism or pessimism of the future outlook. *Actually, if the more pessimistic views about future supplies are correct, it is even more important that the correct principles of resource use and development be followed!*

I now wish to summarize and analyze some of these newer studies. First, I shall look briefly at the historical background of resource use in the United States, and next I shall turn to the question of the adequacy of the resource base for the future.[13] Major reliance for historical findings will be placed upon the work of Herfindahl, Fisher and Boorstein, and Barnett.

Herfindahl attempts to discover what has happened to the long-run cost of minerals in the United States. Has there been any persistent drift in prices up or down to indicate changes in relative costs? All of his data were deflated by the BLS Wholesale Price Index in an attempt to rule out changes in the general price level. Herfindahl is quite careful to point out the deficiencies in his data and the difficulties of his techniques. Also, each class or kind of mineral has had a somewhat different history, so that it is not easy to generalize. He finds that long-run price levels for the major classes of minerals do not show sharp or persistent upward trends. Apparently, any deterioration in the quality of natural resources has been offset by cost reduction within the mineral industries as compared with other industries. He also feels that:

So far as major metals are concerned—and on the basis of other information, coal and oil could just as well be added, although there are some difficulties in interpreting their price records—*difficulties in supply at or near present prices do not appear imminent.*[14]

The Fisher and Boorstein paper was prepared for the well-known study by the Joint Economic Committee dealing with employment, growth, and the price levels. Their paper deals with the adequacy of natural resources for economic growth. I shall refer to this paper again when we shift our attention to the future outlook. Here I shall summarize some of their historical findings: [15]

1) The rapid rate of economic growth in the United States has resulted from an interplay of forces and cannot be ascribed to any single cause (p. 39).
2) Since the beginning of this century, the resource base has been playing a smaller role in economic growth. Growth is less closely tied with abundant natural resources than before (p. 42).
3) Relative costs of some resources have fallen while others have risen, depending upon a complex of factors. The decline in importance of natural resources does not seem to have resulted from any general rise in the cost of resources or from a slow-down in over-all growth (p. 42).
4) Foreign-trade statistics show a general tendency to rely more on imports of resources from abroad. Although this tendency may present problems for military defense, it does not mean necessarily that American sources have become scarce [in a physical sense], but rather that foreign sources have often become even more abundant or inexpensive (p. 45).
5) Relative price movements are important indicators of long-run trends. The picture here is mixed, with no easily discernible general trend (p. 45).
6) The economy is securing more output from its resource base than it used to, and with fewer workers (p. 47).

Professor Barnett is intrigued with the possibility that resources are not becoming increasingly scarce after all. He attempts to test for national-resource scarcity in a model that exhibits general increasing returns in a dynamic sense. In Barnett's formulation an increase in resource scarcity would produce:

1) an increasing trend of labor input per unit of output in extractive sectors relative to the whole economy and

2) an increasing trend of unit prices of extractive goods relative to all goods.[16]

Relying on data prepared by Potter and Christy [17] covering the period from 1870 to 1956, Barnett finds that the scarcity hypothesis is unambiguously supported only in the case of timber. Here is a summary of his quantitative findings: [18]

RESOURCE	RELATIVE PRICE INDICATOR	RELATIVE LABOR PRODUCTIVITY INDICATOR
All extraction	Does not support hypothesis	Adverse to hypothesis
Agriculture	Does not support hypothesis	Adverse to hypothesis
Minerals	Supports hypothesis ambiguously	Adverse to hypothesis
Timber	Supports hypothesis	Supports hypothesis

Now let us turn to the future resource outlook. The tentative findings of Herfindahl, Fisher-Boorstein, and Barnett are helpful in questioning the dogma of historical resource scarcity. In themselves, however, they are not conclusive as to the future. The attempt to look into the future is full of speculation and pitfalls. What will be the rate of population increase? Can we rely on technology to develop substitutes and to open up new avenues of growth? A myriad of such questions blunt the attempt to make such estimates. Actually, I shall do no more than stress the general nature of the conclusions of three studies presenting a future orientation for normal resource use. These studies are authored by Fisher and Boorstein; Clawson, Held, and Stoddard; and Schurr and Netschert.

My purpose here is not to develop a comprehensive set of

future projections. Rather, I merely want to show that there appears to be no cause for panic or alarm, at least within the next three or four decades, with regard to our general resource base. The relatively favorable short-run outlook is, of course, no cause for complacency. There are certainly enough specific short-run problems to keep us occupied, even if the long-run future outlook were to turn out to be equally promising. The important thing, however, is that:

> We need not foresee everything in exact detail. There will be ample opportunity for restudy and for new adjustments in later decades. One advantage of long-range planning is that it affords general guides as to potential change and problems, but leaves to the future some, perhaps most, of the necessary adjustments.[19]

Fisher and Boorstein present a series of projections for the United States for 1980 and 2000. The projections cover such variables as size of population, work force, labor productivity, and Gross National Product. Along with these projections are given "estimated demands" for 1980 and 2000 for such materials as timber, wheat, cotton, feed grains, oil, coal, iron ore, aluminum, copper and fresh water.[20] After making allowances for the use of foreign, as well as domestic, sources of supply and for the likelihood of some technological responses to higher costs of particular materials, Fisher and Boorstein conclude that:

> The upshot of all this seems to be that, despite the prospects for very rapid population increase during the next two or three decades, the outlook for resources supplies at reasonable prices is favorable for this country. Even with this generally optimistic picture, difficult problems of increase in cost and shortage for particular resources materials and services undoubtedly will be encountered—for example, ground water in many places, a number of alloy and other metals, high-grade saw timber, and desirable outdoor recreation areas.[21]

Clawson, Held, and Stoddard develop a series of projections for changes in land use from 1950 to 2000. They examine uses of land for urban purposes, public recreation, agriculture, forestry, grazing, transportation, watershed management, and mineral production. In general, they find that use of labor, capital, and new technology will combine to prevent an increase in the demand for land as an input despite a large increase in the products from land. Changes *within* each type of land use will be more important than the allocation of land *between* uses. Major changes in land uses will tend to be localized. The greatest difficulties ahead appear to be land-use adjustments in urban use of land and in lands devoted to public outdoor recreation.

Schurr and Netschert almost overwhelm the reader with a lengthy survey of energy use by all major classes of fuels and power sources for the American economy from 1850 to the present. In addition, projections are presented for the energy supply-demand balance outlook through 1975. Their conclusion is that the United States can supply its demands for all energy through 1975 at no significant increase in costs from the conventional domestic sources. This finding places Schurr and Netschert across the street from the earlier pessimistic findings of Ayres and Scarlott and Putnam.[22] Beyond 1975, Schurr and Netschert foresee a possibility for an increase in the cost threshold of fossil fuels. There is a strong possibility, however, that improvements in nuclear power technology can set a relatively low ceiling on the cost increase.

Apparently, the next three or four decades will not bring a general shortage of natural resources, but what about the far-off future? Will the forces of rapid population growth prove inexorable and place an impossible burden upon the resource base leading to a destruction of the human race? Perhaps so. Why is it that compound rates of growth in regard to population always produce fright and gloom? Population experts seem to startle people by asserting that a rate of population increase of one and one-half per cent a year means that the United States population will double in approximately forty-seven years! Yet a three per cent annual rate of increase in national production or in productive capacity, providing for a doubling every twenty-four years, seems to excite no one. Indeed, we are concerned that the rate of growth is not higher.

My own feeling is that extreme pessimism is unjustified. The far-off future will present problems, but future generations will approach the future gradually, and human institutions can be modified to exhibit viability in the face of changing problems. Whether this will in fact happen is beyond the power of present generations to forecast or to determine. In this regard, I agree with Professor Edward S. Mason, who writes in similar fashion:

Perhaps because I am merely a pedestrian economist, these alternative visions of the future do not greatly stir me. There is really no need to assume that population will increase indefinitely at exponential rates, since human institutions and values have shown in the past some capacity for adaptation to changing situations. And while science and technology are wonderful, they show no signs yet of exorcising the persistent fact of scarcity. To undertake a serious discussion of conservation, the period of time under consideration has to be limited to that within which one can perceive, at least dimly, the approximate magnitude of the relevant variables.[23]

III

In this section I intend to examine two kinds of choice processes for determining the direction and the rate of natural-resource investment and consumption: the political allocation process and the market allocation process. I shall analyze each process in somewhat general terms within the natural-resource framework.

INDIVIDUALISM VERSUS THE GENERAL WILL

Any discussion of the market versus political processes must begin with some assumption about the nature of society. I will assume here that it is desirable to have a democratic society based upon individual choice. This means that the goal of society is to satisfy or carry out individual preferences. These preferences can be expressed or "polled" through informal devices such as mores, habits, and customs, or by the more formal devices of the market place and the ballot box. In the latter, the voter is the sovereign agent; in the market place we have the principle of consumer sovereignty. Both devices are individualistic in orientation.

An alternative view of society is that individuals exist to serve the state. This view assumes that the state somehow gets direction from sources other than the individuals that compose the group —perhaps from their leaders, from "divine" inspiration, or from the group "as a whole." The writings of Hegel, Rousseau, Green, and others express aspects of this view. Individual preferences are subordinate to the "general will." For Hegel, the state represented the highest possible ethical value; individual choices were to be subordinated to the national state. In similar fashion, Rousseau asserted that:

The social order is a sacred right which serves as a foundation for all other rights.
Each of us contributes to the group his person and the powers which he wields as a person under the supreme direction of the general will, and we receive into the body politic each individual as forming an indivisible part of the whole.[24]

According to Rousseau, individual preferences, expressed *either* in the market place *or* at the polls, should not govern. Instead, direction of resources would be above and beyond individual whims and desires. Perhaps some of this point of view is present in Pigou's admonition quoted at the beginning of this paper.

It is futile to debate the organic versus the individualistic view of society. My preference is with the latter. Frankly, I have never been comforted by the idea of an all-wise, all-knowing "general will." What is the supreme destiny of society? How can it be expedited? How does one know the desires of persons not yet born?

Assume for the moment, however, that Rousseau is correct and that we have a "general will." Does it follow that particular preference should be given to natural resources? Would the organic decision-maker necessarily want to hoard "exhaustible" natural resources or to "plant more trees" as opposed to alternative kinds of investment? All investment involves provision for the future. Natural-resource investment should be undertaken only if it is more productive than alternative types of investment.

It would follow also that the centralized or "organic" decision-maker would not necessarily wish to construct long-run projects as opposed to short-run projects. Durable forms of investment may provide less return over time and be less productive than less durable types. A series of reinvestment cycles, each with a high return, would contribute more to future generations than investment in a very long-lived project yielding a low return. How productivity is to be measured, of course, depends upon whose and what preferences are to count.

The individualistic theory of value does not deny that men are social beings influenced by the entire physical-social environment in which they live. Certainly, individual wants and preferences are socially conditioned. Collective wants and desires are also possible. Individuals can and do evaluate social wants. In fact, collective activity can be viewed as a form of individual behavior.[25] It is also possible (though it is fashionable to assert the contrary) that individuals, either in the market place or in the polling booth, are not necessarily grasping, greedy monsters. Individualism does allow for the expression of social, even altruistic, patterns of preference. Individuals and households do make provision for generations yet to be born.

THE SOCIAL RATE OF INTEREST

Perhaps this is the appropriate point to analyze the often stated need for a social rate of interest and for social planning periods for natural-resource investment. Again, why is natural-resource investment so singled out as opposed to other types of investment? A rather common argument in the conservation literature runs somewhat as follows:

Society's interest in conservation of natural resources is greater than that of individuals. Individuals generally have high time-preference rates and short planning periods. Society, on the other hand, tends to use a longer planning period and also a lower discount rate because of its interest in the welfare of future generations and also because of its ability to borrow money at low interest rates.[26]

I have trouble understanding the logic of this position. The fact that a government can borrow funds at low rates of interest does not reduce the *real* costs of any particular investment. Real costs must encompass the riskiness of the particular project, which may be much greater than the risk involved in general government borrowing. Second, real costs must reflect the output of alternative projects forgone, i.e., the marginal productivity of capital. This would seem to follow *regardless* of whether the total amount of investment were determined by consumer sovereignty, voter sovereignty, or by centralized planning. Society, or whoever is the planning agent, can make more provision for the future by first making a choice between the total amount of resources to be devoted to investment in relation to production for current consumption. Once this decision is made, the welfare of future generations can best be served by using discount rates that measure the marginal productivity of capital. For any given amount of real savings, the use of an artificially low discount rate will actually lead to a smaller future endowment.[27] Low interest rates increase the desirability of all forms of investment. Furthermore, they favor durable investment as opposed to short-lived capital. This effect upon the time structure of capital is often neglected. There is no reason for individuals or for society to use longer planning periods or lower rates of interest than those dictated by productivity considerations.

As an empirical matter, the concept of a social rate of time preference resulting from the working of the "general will" has not been established in the Western world. There is no evidence that shows a consistent pattern to shift explicitly the distribution of income in society toward the future by public means. This is not to deny that public investment is often approved by voters for many *other* reasons and that as a secondary effect there will be a redistribution of income toward the future. It is also clear that programs undertaken to redistribute income within the current time period may also have effects upon the distribution of income between present and future generations.

On a similar point, many writers fail to distinguish between social benefits and the concept of a social rate of interest for evaluating these benefits. There is no necessary reason why benefits, just because they are social, should also be discounted at a low rate of interest. I suggest that social benefits, somehow measured, should be subject to a rate of discount that reflects the marginal productivity of capital (with allowance for risk) as well as time preference.[28]

FUTURE GENERATIONS AND MORALITY

When all is said and done, it is clear that investment in natural resources has a moral flavor not deserved. All kinds of investment (public and private) may affect the welfare of future generations; [29] *all investment involves some redistribution of income and wealth toward the future.* Obviously, the more any society restricts its current consumption (increases real savings), the more resources can be devoted to investment in productive capacity, and the better off future generations will become. The inescapable moral question, then, is: What is the proper level of current consumption, i.e., what is the proper amount of total real investment? Can we rely upon the social consensus achieved in the market? Should we turn to the ballot box for an answer to this question? In fact, can we use individualistic preferences at all?

The search for a criterion that will point toward the "ideal" distribution of wealth over all future time periods is an impossible task. Interpersonal comparisons within a given time period are difficult enough. How can we go about making intergenerational comparisons? I see no way out but to count the preferences of those now living. Can we do otherwise? This, of course, can be done through either the ballot box or the market place. Personally, I see no reason why the question can be solved more readily by one process than by the other. There is need for the use of both processes here. Apparently, some writers in the field of welfare economics believe that these questions are ones to be decided solely in the political realm and not in the market place:

> We can safely conclude that no real solution to the problems we have been discussing in this chapter is to be found in concentrating on contemporary households and letting them decide how far to look ahead and how much to provide for posterity. These are not decisions which households, acting separately, are equipped to make. There is no satisfactory "competitive solution" to the problems of the horizon and terminal capital equipment or of investment generally. Households must act collectively—if they are to act at all. And, in the absence of unanimity, the decisions must be imposed on those who disagree with them. Politics—or paternalism—is involved.[30]

I do not accept this position. Can contemporary individuals make more nearly optimal decisions in regard to the welfare of future generations through political processes than in the market process? How does one derive a standard for intergenerational ethics? More importantly, it is clear that this position explicitly says that households acting in the market place should not and cannot be allowed to determine the general level of investment and consumption! Instead, these matters are deemed to be collective, political, and undoubtedly paternalistic. All this raises basic questions as to the assumed wisdom of the paternalistic decision-maker and the validity of denying individual choice.

Why is it that individuals are assumed or believed to act more rationally in the polling booth? Why are elected political representatives all-wise and free from fault? Why is it that so many writers fail to analyze in comparable fashion all the alternative means for making economic decisions for the future? Most welfare economists are extremely facile in demonstrating the "shortcomings" of individuals acting in the market, but very little of their keen analytical talents are applied to alternative choice mechanisms. Analysis of the defects in the market mechanism does not prove that political choice processes are any more free of error.

About the only thing we can be fairly sure of from a study of history, barring the possibility of nuclear wars, is that future generations will be wealthier than we are. Deliberate redistribution in favor of the future may well involve a transfer of wealth from a poorer to a richer group.

IMPERFECTIONS IN THE MARKET AND POLITICAL PROCESSES

Each process has a number of similarities to the other; each has unique features. Both have a role to play in natural-resource policy. Neither can be used to the exclusion of the other. For example, the market process always has to function within a system of property rights and general rules of the game. These considerations are basically political in nature. Furthermore, market-generated prices and costs are always conditioned by the existing distribution of means and wealth. When this distribution is altered by political decisions, market relationships may change. It is difficult to imagine, however, that any socially sanctioned redistribution of income would change the structure of market prices very much for natural resources. Actually, there is reason to believe that the present distribution of income has considerable social sanction.[31] Above all, it should be stressed that governmental intervention to deal with market imperfections may or may not improve matters—depending upon the imperfections in governmental processes. The choice processes may not function smoothly in terms of their own framework. Real-life operation may fall short of theoretical standards. Second, they may fail to produce "correct" decisions because their theoretical frameworks do not take into account all the variables required for ideal solutions. Certainly, this discussion is not more than suggestive of the general terrain.[32]

Turning to the first consideration, we must note that economists are prone to stress the operational imperfections in the market mechanism. Some of these faults are monopoly, problems of scale, indivisibility, capital-market imperfections, externalities, ignorance and imperfect knowledge, inertia and immobility of resources, desire for the quiet life, and so on. My feeling is not to belittle or underplay any of these imperfections. Some of them will be explored below. I do wish to emphasize two points:

1) All these imperfections are applicable to the operation of the price system in general and do not have, for the most part, special meaning for natural-resource use.
2) Most of the items on the list have their counterparts in the democratic political process.

In the political sphere we find such operational imperfections as voter ignorance and apathy, bureaucracy, log-rolling, the spoils system, party machines, corruption, failure to represent minority views, and the like. Lack of competition for votes may lead to the same sort of results that obtain from business monopoly. Economies of scale in the operation of political parties may make it difficult to have "workable competition" for votes.[33] Ignorance on the part of voters and elected officials can be deadly. Brand names, the "hard-sell," the "waste-makers," and the hucksters are not uncommon in the political arena.

Perhaps all this appears as heresy to "true" believers in each process. My feeling is that each process works imperfectly. This means that a choice between them should be determined by analysis of their relative desirability, and not by blind assertion of "faith." Some element of sheer belief is probably involved in all such judgments. I must confess to a preference for use of a system of market values in many cases. The conclusion still remains, however, that the selection of choice processes for natural-resource decisions should be made upon a case-by-case basis.

I shall comment in more detail upon three types of market imperfections often said to raise special problems for natural resources: ignorance on the part of resource owners, imperfections in capital markets for resources, and the presence of externalities. My view is to question the degree of relevance in the first two cases. I believe that these problems are applicable to almost all economic decisions. This position is not widely accepted. Most writers argue that many resources, particularly soil and forests, are exploited on a small scale. Small wood-lot owners and small farmers are said to lack adequate knowledge of the technical conditions of production and of prices and costs. Moreover, limited access to capital markets in rural areas by small resource entrepreneurs tends to cause diseconomies of small-scale operation and undesirable resource depletion.

All this, of course, is quite plausible and possible. The economics of ignorance has received insufficient attention. Even the ascertainment of market price is not an easy task.[34] Actually, at least two sorts of questions are involved here. One concerns the special ignorance of small resource owners in relation to ignorance displayed by other types of small business, by individual voters, and by small units of government. A second level of questioning might deal with the issue of whether size and knowledge are positively correlated. I am not aware of studies showing either that smallness generally leads to more ignorance than largeness or that small resource owners are necessarily more ignorant than decision-makers in other small business and political units. My guess is that problems of ignorance are pervasive and are not strongly correlated with scale or size or type of activity.[35]

Be that as it may, the cure for ignorance is knowledge. Knowledge can never be perfect, especially in regard to the future. Neither perfectly functioning markets nor wise governments can escape this fact. Although reduction of ignorance provides benefits, provision of education is costly. Do the returns more than offset the costs? To whom do the benefits accrue? Who pays the costs? There is widespread acceptance of the need for government to support education in general. In addition, a case can often be made for dealing with particular pockets of ignorance in natural resources and elsewhere by public means.[36]

Many of these same considerations also apply to resource capital markets. Are capital markets more imperfect for resource production than for other types of economic and political activity? What is meant by imperfection? Is this imperfection reduced by an increase in the scale of activity? Prevailing opinion seems to say yes to the last question, to be divided on the second, and to be silent on the first.

I do not know how imperfect capital markets are in general. In my opinion, they are much more competitive than is commonly granted. The wide spectrum of money rates that exists at any one time, or even over time, may indicate a failure of competition; it may also be due in large part to variations in length of loan, cost of administration, and riskiness. Interest rates are generally high to all small borrowers. Is this due to the lack of bargaining power on the part of the borrower or to higher risk for the lender? Probably both factors are present. In so far as natural-resource firms are small, they are subject to high interest costs. No one has shown that this is necessarily an imperfection or that owners of natural resources are victims of special discrimination.

Perhaps the best case for taking market imperfections into account may be found under the general label of externalities. This is sort of a catch-all category for all cases in which a decision-maker fails to take into account the impact of his actions upon other units. Externalities are also known as spill-overs, neighborhood effects, external economies and diseconomies, and divergencies between private and social costs (and benefits). Quite glaring examples of externalities exist in the field of natural resources, though they are not confined to this field by any means.

It is important to distinguish between technological and pecuniary externalities.[37] Pecuniary spill-overs are external consequences that affect the prices or incomes of other units in the economy but do not affect their physical or technical ability to produce. In the case of any interdependent economy, *every* action is bound to have *some* effects upon others. Pecuniary effects are manifested by changes in economic rents, incomes, and prices of competing and complementary inputs and outputs. This pecuniary effect may be illustrated by the development of a new oil field that reduces the value of old oil reserves. Technological spill-overs, on the other hand, are those actions which do change the physical productivity of other units; for example, the pumping of oil from a common pool by separate decision-makers or the pollution of water by upstream users. Such actions also have price and income effects upon other producers and products, but these stem from changes in the technical ability to produce.

Should these spill-over effects be taken into account, and, if so, how? Both types have implications for the distribution of wealth and income. When distributional matters are under consideration, it follows that both pecuniary and technological externalities should be counted. Only technological effects should be counted, however, when we are concerned with questions of economic efficiency.

In general, the solution to a technological spill-over problem is to expand the scale of decision-making to correspond with the effects of the action. This can very often be done by coordinating fragmented property rights, as in the case of unitization of oil pools and ground water basins. An incomplete definition of property rights is usually at the heart of the matter. Changes in these property rights, either to make them specific or to enlarge the scale of action, are frequently called for. Very often the pricing system itself may take into account many types of spill-over costs and gains.[38] In some cases direct governmental intervention is the only available solution. This is the case when the scale of action is too large to be encompassed by ordinary property rights, as in a river basin or an ocean, or when it is simply impossible to establish a mechanism to give private owners incentives to take into account spill-over social benefits and costs, as in the case of air pollution.

It should be clear that large river basins cannot be exploited efficiently in piecemeal fashion. Upstream and downstream uses are interdependent and must be co-ordinated somehow. Incomplete property rights limit the use of the price system as a guide to costs and benefits. Furthermore, production of multiple products—such as hydroelectric power, stream regulation, navigation, and water supply—requires co-ordination. Governmental intervention to centralize or to co-ordinate these interdependent decisions would seem to be mandatory to maximize economic returns. But this is where some sheer irony comes in: political processes, ostensibly required to promote economic efficiency, often produce partial or complete abandonment and disregard of economic principles. An outstanding example is found in the operation of the Texas Railway Commission. Under the guise of promoting efficiency in a classic commonality situation, the Commission actually functions as a price-raising cartel. Political imperfections are then substituted for market imperfections. This is another case in which we have failed to compare the total product yielded by alternative social choice mechanisms. We cannot assume that an ideal political alternative is available to deal with an imperfect market situation. Even if one is available, what assurance is there that it will be used? [39]

In my opinion, pressure for federal development of river basins may stem not from sound legal and economic reasons, but often from special-interest groups that hope to profit from the provision of subsidized benefits. Typically, navigation and flood-control facilities are provided almost entirely at federal expense; the costs of hydroelectric power and irrigation features are partially borne by federal taxpayers. Because of this, prospective beneficiaries have extremely strong incentives to push for more federal development. All projects benefit some groups, but the difficult questions are concerned with determining how great the costs will be and who is to bear them.

But it may be asserted that the goal of river-basin development or of other public-resource projects is not economic efficiency at all; instead, the goal may simply be a deliberate redistribution of income and wealth from the taxpayers to the project beneficiaries. Furthermore, it could be argued that the fact that the

projects are approved indicates political acceptance of this redistribution on the part of the majority. The point is well taken,
but I would question this line of reasoning. I doubt that the
electorate is really informed at the time the decision is made,
because accurate information as to what the costs and benefits
are and who is to bear and receive them is seldom provided.

Neglect of economic analysis and provision of subsidies for
special-interest groups have long been characteristic features of
political decision-making processes for natural-resource development. Is this an imperfection comparable in magnitude to market
externalities? Should we view many federal water and soil projects as the operation of the "pork-barrel system"? Or, instead,
do these projects represent the attainment of "distributive justice" for the underprivileged? Perhaps the answer is yes to all
three questions.

Apart from the perplexing and ever-present operational imperfections, it is important to acknowledge that each process has
some inherent and unique limitations. The market process cannot work in the provision of two types of want-satisfaction—the
provision of intangible services and the provision of collective
goods. It is also not a useful device for determining rules of the
game.

Intangibles are those wants or values that cannot be directly
measured by the common denominator of dollars and cents.
Major gains and costs to society cannot be ignored just because
they are incapable of dollar measurement, because they cannot be
bought and sold, or because organized markets for them do not
exist. Examples of alleged intangible values in the resources
field stem from national defense considerations, the theme of
balanced development, the family farm, the saving of human life,
and the preservation of historical or scenic sites. But the inadequacy of the market in providing intangibles does not mean
that they should be exempt from rational consideration or from
at least some economic analysis. No intangible has infinite value.
All intangibles have costs. The least that can be done is to
specify and to make very clear to all concerned the cost of
obtaining the intangible. As a *minimum* the intangible must be

worth as much as it costs in terms of alternatives sacrificed if it is to be approved. Second, it is often possible to place a *maximum* value on the intangible if it can be produced by alternative means. For example, the value of a particular facility for preserving human life can be worth no more than the cost of preserving human life in other ways. Such considerations may reduce the common tendency to consider intangibles as exceptions to economic calculation. Undoubtedly there are even alternative ways of saving human souls that vary in cost and productivity.

Collective goods may be defined as those that are consumed collectively by the entire community rather than by individuals as such. An important aspect of such goods is the inability of the market to provide them because of the absence of the power of "exclusion"; i.e., individual sellers must be able to deny access to the service if prices are to be charged. National defense is a classic example of a collective good. Flood-control protection is another example. The establishment of flood-control facilities upstream will inevitably protect all persons and lands located in the flood plain. Provision of flood control, national defense, or lighthouses for *one* person means that all of the group automatically receive benefit. Rational choice, just as with intangibles, will be furthered if a careful study is made of the costs and the benefits. The mere fact that consumption must be collective does not mean that economic principles should be scrapped. Allocation and identification of benefits accruing to individuals within a flood plain may be difficult, but it is clear that they can be calculated in rough fashion for the basin as a whole. Land values usually rise in dramatic fashion as testimony to the capitalization of these benefits. Why is it that the costs of federal flood-control protection are always borne by all taxpayers rather than by just those persons living in the flood plain? Perhaps we should consider the provision of collective goods apart from attempts to redistribute income and wealth.

The ballot-box process also has its inherent limitations. Short of unanimity or complete social consensus, it is necessary to rely upon some form of majority rule. This will always involve some coercion of the minority. Once individual preferences are polled,

the collective choice becomes binding on all. Other voting limitations are involved in the indivisibility of votes and of choices, the
infrequency of voting, and the necessity of predicting how other
voters will vote. To this latter uncertainty is added uncertainty
concerning the consequences of a particular decision.[40] Furthermore, how much incentive does an individual voter have to
study issues carefully? For one thing, an individual vote has only
an imperceptible effect on the outcome. The decision will be
reached whether a particular individual votes or not; so why
study the issues?

IV

AN OVERVIEW

In this paper I have attempted to explore some of the
economic considerations that should govern natural-resource
policy. For the most part, I have not tried to break new ground
either in the field of economics or in social-welfare theory.
Instead, I have argued that much of existing theory in both
areas, while often crude to the purist, can be directly carried over
to the field of natural resources. Over and over, I have stressed
that natural resources are not to be given any special consideration; they are only a part of our total social capital.

Evidence was reviewed suggesting that our natural-resource
picture is not critical. Special problems do exist. This is especially true in situations where property rights are incomplete or
nonexistent. The problem of externalities is perhaps best illustrated in the cases of air and water pollution. Here the major
hurdle to be overcome is the lack of an adequate structure and
organization of business and political leadership to tackle the
problem. Devices can be suggested for the establishment of
co-ordinated or centralized decision-making so that these spill-
over effects can be taken into account. The use of centralized
decision-making, however, makes it all the more important that
an accepted method of attaining efficiency be applied. I am sure

that a rational benefit-cost calculus can be developed for both public and private investment here. Such a calculus is particularly needed to deal with the investment and planning soon to be required within the urban resources setting. We need to base public policy for common resources on much more than an emotional reaction to the obvious failings of fragmented decision-making.

I have not implied that all is well with the world. It is evident that both the market and the political allocation processes have theoretical as well as operational imperfections. Little comfort is given to the extreme positions in the debate between proponents of the public sector and the private sector. Neither sector can function well without the other. The market system has a much greater role in natural-resource direction than is usually admitted. The public sector, on the other hand, should not be starved, although in some areas it is clear that a change of menu is required—more lean meat at the expense of surplus fat from the "pork barrel."

The cry of natural-resource scarcity should not be used to frighten the electorate into hasty, ill-considered action. There is nothing mystic about natural resources, the market system, or the political process. No earth-shaking action is called for. Indeed, what is needed is calm and deliberate appraisal. With all their imperfections these two allocation processes probably satisfy most of the goals and axioms of individual choice. It is perhaps "poetic," but true, that the heritage of unborn generations will be enriched only if freedom of individual choice is protected and preserved in both the public and the private sectors.

NOTES

1. I wish to acknowledge helpful comments received from Jack Hirshleifer, Joseph L. Fisher, Vernon W. Ruttan, Marshall R. Colberg, and from the participants in the Symposium.
2. I shall not dwell here on what constitutes a natural resource as opposed to so-called man-made resources. Obviously, in some contexts man himself is a natural resource. Distinctions can also be made between re-

newable versus exhaustible resources; stock versus flow resources; and migratory or fugitive resources versus fixed resources. It is also clear that resources become economic goods *only* in so far as they become scarce in relation to demands placed upon them. This latter point means that the world's resource base should not be viewed apart from an assumed structure of demand. For a definitive discussion of the concept of resources, the reader should consult: Erich W. Zimmermann, *World Resources and Industries* (New York: Harper & Bros., rev. ed., 1958), chap. I.

3. *Message from the President of the United States Relative to Our Natural Resources,* U.S. 87th Cong., 1st Sess., House Doc. 94 (February 23, 1961), p. 1.

4. Edward S. Mason, "The Political Economy of Resource Use," in Henry Jarrett, ed., *Perspectives on Conservation* (Baltimore: Johns Hopkins Press, 1958), p. 184.

5. James W. Knowles, *The Potential Economic Growth in the United States,* prepared for the Joint Economic Committee of the United States Congress, U. S. 86th Cong., 2nd Sess., Study Paper, No. 20 (January 20, 1960), chap. II. Edward F. Denison, *The Sources of Economic Growth in the United States and the Alternatives before Us,* Committee for Economic Development, Supplementary Paper, No. 13, 1962.

6. Edward F. Renshaw, *Toward Responsible Government* (Chicago: Idyia Press, 1957), pp. 22–24.

7. Nathaniel Wollman, *Water Resource Activities in the United States: Water Supply and Demand,* for Select Committee on National Water Resources, U. S. 86th Cong., 2nd Sess., S. Committee Print, No. 32 (Washington, D.C.: Government Printing Office, 1960). These limitations are explicitly recognized by Wollman, but not by most of the persons citing the study.

8. J. W. Milliman, "Water Law and Private Decision-Making—A Critique," *Journal of Law and Economics,* II (October, 1959), pp. 41–63.

9. For an incisive discussion of the meaning of resource scarcity, *see* Harold J. Barnett, *The Measurement of Change in Natural Resource Scarcity,* Reprint No. 26, Resources for the Future, Inc. (March, 1961).

10. For a more complete dicussion, *see* Anthony Scott, *Natural Resources: The Economics of Conservation* (Toronto: University of Toronto Press, 1955), chap. I. A less comforting view may be found in *Resources for Freedom,* President's Materials Policy Commission (Washington, D.C.: Government Printing Office, June, 1952), I, 17–18.

11. Here are some of these recent studies. The list is by no means complete
   1) *The Adequacy of Resources for Economic Growth in the United States,* by Joseph L. Fisher and Edward Boorstein, prepared for the Joint Economic Committee, U. S. 86th Cong., 1st Sess., Study Paper, No. 13 (December 16, 1959).
   2) Harold J. Barnett, *Measurement of Change in Natural Resource Scarcity and Its Economic Effects;* Neal Potter and Francis T. Christy, Jr., *Employment and Output in the Natural Resource Industries,*

1870–1955. Both of the studies appear in Reprint No. 26 (March, 1961), published by Resources for the Future, Inc.
3) Orris C. Herfindahl, *Three Studies in Minerals Economics,* Resources for the Future, Inc. (1961). See especially the essay entitled, "The Long-Run Cost of Minerals."
4) Orris C. Herfindahl, *Copper Costs and Prices: 1870–1957* (Baltimore: Johns Hopkins Press, 1961).
5) Sam H. Schurr and Bruce C. Netschert, *Energy in the American Economy, 1850–1975* (Baltimore: Johns Hopkins Press, 1961).
6) Bruce C. Netschert, *The Future Supply of Oil and Gas* (Baltimore: Johns Hokins Press, 1958).
7) *Timber Resources for America's Future,* U. S. Dept. of Agriculture (Washington, D.C.: Government Printing Office, 1958).
8) Marion Clawson, Burnell Held, and Charles H. Stoddard, *Land for the Future* (Baltimore: Johns Hopkins Press, 1960).
9) Harvey S. Perloff, Edgar S. Dunn, Eric E. Lampard, and Richard F. Muth, *Regions, Resources and Economic Growth* (Baltimore: Johns Hopkins Press, 1960).
10) Neal Potter and Francis T. Christy, Jr., *Trends in Natural Resource Commodities* (Baltimore: Johns Hopkins Press, 1962).
11) V. W. Ruttan and J. C. Callahan, "Resource Inputs and Output Growth: The Contest Between Agriculture and Forestry," Journal Paper No. 1698, Purdue University Agricultural Experiment Station, Lafayette, Indiana (November 28, 1960).
12. See the work of the following authors for extreme pessimistic views: Harrison Brown, Robert C. Cook, Charles Galton Darwin, Samuel H. Ordway, Fairfield Osborn, Palmer Putnam, Hyman Rickover, and William Vogt. Earlier studies that are fairly optimistic are: *America's Needs and Resources, A New Survey,* J. Frederic Dowhurst and Associates (New York: Twentieth Century Fund, 1955), and *Resources for Freedom,* President's Materials Policy Commission, Faley Report (Washington, D.C.: U. S. Government Printing Office, June, 1952).
13. It is interesting to see that an examination of United States political and economic history shows that the birth and continuation of the "conservation movement" in this country can be explained largely on grounds *other than* a general economic scarcity of natural resources. Much of the impetus for conservation has come from:
    1) Forces of nationalism and national self-sufficiency.
    2) Identification of big business and financial power with "waste" of natural resources.
    3) A desire to stop the fraud and violence that accompanied the use and disposal of public lands, forests, oil reserves, and minerals. Many of the problems here arose from the interests of special groups in the division of the "spoils." It is clear that the *problem was not so much a failure of the system of private property as a lack of it.*
    4) Desire to "develop the West" and to foster certain interest groups, particularly agrarian interests.

5) With the coming of the "New Deal," public-resource projects were used as tools to attack unemployment and to achieve social redistribution of wealth. Multipurpose projects in river basins were also designed to achieve co-ordination of interdependent activities.

For penetrating discussions of the United States conservation movement, *see* Scott, *op. cit.*, chap. III, and Ross M. Robertson, *History of the American Economy* (New York: Harcourt Brace and Co., 1955), chaps. XI and XVIII.

14. Herfindahl, *Three Studies in Minerals Economics*, p. 34. Emphasis added.

15. Fisher and Boorstein, *op. cit.* The page numbers in the summary refer to the study.

16. Barnett, *op. cit.*, p. 91. Agriculture, mining, forestry, and fishing are classified as extractive. All other economic activity is nonextractive.

17. Potter and Christy, *op. cit.*

18. Barnett, *op. cit.*, p. 99.

19. Marion Clawson, "Land Use and Demand for Land in the United States," *Modern Land Policy*, sponsored by Land Economics Institute (Urbana: University of Illinois Press, 1960), p. 12.

20. It should be pointed out that these projections and estimates were taken "from work in progress" at Resources for the Future, Inc. *See* Fisher and Boorstein, *op. cit.*, pp. 47–48. As a result, very few of the crucial assumptions behind the figures are at all evident. I would hazard a guess that the "estimated demands" may be extrapolations of current consumption patterns rather than true economic demands.

21. *Ibid.*, p. 50.

22. *See* E. Ayres and C. A. Scarlott, *Energy Sources—Wealth of the World* (New York: McGraw-Hill Pubishing Co., Inc., 1952), and Palmer C. Putnam, *Energy in the Future* (New York: D. Van Nostrand Co., Inc., 1953).

23. Mason, *op. cit.*, p. 179.

24. J. J. Rousseau, *Social Contract*, Bk. I, chaps. i, vi.

25. James M. Buchanan, "Social Choice, Democracy, and Free Markets," *Journal of Political Economy*, Vol. LXII, No. 2 (April, 1954), p. 119.

26. Raleigh Barlowe, *Land Resource Economics* (Englewood Cliffs: Prentice-Hall, 1958), pp. 310–311. The statement in the text is paraphrased from Barlowe's discussion, which generally supports the statement. For other examples of this general point of view, *see* Robert Dorfman, "Water and Welfare," paper delivered at Econometric Society meeting, St. Louis, Dec. 27, 1960, and Edward S. Mason, *op. cit.*, p. 185. Mason says: "In estimating, for purposes of projection, the relationship between present costs and future benefits in this area [land resources], the appropriate rate of interest may well be close to zero." Dorfman argues that public water projects should be appraised with the use of a discount rate based upon social time preference.

27. Jack Hirshleifer, James C. de Haven, and Jerome W. Milliman, *Water Supply: Economics, Technology and Folicy* (Chicago: University of Chicago Press, 1960), pp. 116–121.

28. I have argued this point previously: J. W. Milliman, *Decision-Making for Public Investment: Discussion* (Santa Monica: RAND Corporation, January 15, 1961), P-2252, p. 11.

29. Perhaps it should be stressed again that the market system usually gives private entrepreneurs incentives to plan for the future.

30. J. de V. Graaff, *Theoretical Welfare Economics* (London: Cambridge University Press, 1957), p. 105.

31. These last two statements apply primarily to the United States. In some countries of the world there might be a question about consensus in support of the existing distribution of wealth. Also, radical changes in this distribution could well exert a large change in the structure of prices.

32. For more complete discussions of market imperfections, *see:*
    1) Francis M. Bator, "The Anatomy of Market Failure," *Quarterly Journal of Economics,* Vol. LXXII, No. 3 (August, 1958), pp. 351–379.
    2) R. A. Dahl and C. E. Lindblom, *Politics, Economics and Welfare* (New York: Harper & Bros., 1953).
    3) De Graaff, *op. cit.*
    4) Hirshleifer, De Haven, and Milliman, *op. cit.,* chap. IV.
    Some excellent insights concerning the political process are to be found in:
    1) Gary S. Becker, "Competition and Democracy," *Journal of Law and Economics,* I (October, 1958), 105–109.
    2) James M. Buchanan, "Individual Choice in Voting and in the Market," *Journal of Political Economy,* Vol. LXII, No. 2 (August, 1954), pp. 334–343.
    3) Anthony Downs, "An Economic Theory of Political Action in a Democracy," *Journal of Political Economy,* Vol. LXV, No. 2 (April, 1957), pp. 135–150.
    4) Richard A. Musgrave, *The Theory of Public Finance* (New York: McGraw-Hill Publishing Co., Inc., 1959), especially chap. 6, "Budget Determination Through Voting."
    5) Hirshleifer, De Haven, and Milliman, *op. cit.,* chap. IV.

33. For a discussion of the role of competition in the democratic process, *see* Becker, *op. cit.*

34. George J. Stigler, "The Economics of Information," *Journal of Political Economy,* Vol. LXIX, No. 3 (June, 1961), pp. 213–225.

35. It may be true that a large firm might be able to spend more money in pursuit of knowledge than a small firm, but it is not clear that this action will make the large firm more knowledgeable in relation to the larger size of its market. It is quite conceivable that a small firm may know more about its market than a large firm. All this does not deny that there may be economies of size in the development of knowledge or even that there may be optimum levels of ignorance.

36. Compare with F. A. Hayek, *The Constitution of Liberty* (Chicago: University of Chicago Press, 1960), p. 371: "It cannot be denied that there are some facts concerning probably future developments which government is more likely to know than most of the individual owners of

natural resources. Many of the recent achievements in science illustrate this. There will always exist, however, an even greater store of knowledge of special circumstances that ought to be taken into account in decisions about specific resources which only individual owners will possess and which can never be concentrated in a single authority. Thus, if it is true that government is likely to know some facts known to few others, it is equally true that the government will necessarily be ignorant of an even greater number of relevant facts known to some others. We can bring together all the knowledge that is relevant to particular problems only by dispersing downward the generic knowledge available to government, not by centralizing all the special knowledge possessed by individuals."

37. A most helpful discussion of this point is found in Roland N. McKean, *Efficiency in Government through Systems Analysis* (New York: John Wiley and Sons, 1958), chap. 8.

38. Ronald A. Coase makes this point in convincing fashion in a critique of the current economic literature relating to the problem of externalities. *See* "The Problem of Social Cost," *Journal of Law and Economics,* Vol. III (October, 1960), pp. 1–44.

39. Vernon W. Ruttan has suggested to me that governmental control may not necessarily provide centralized operation for dealing with interdependencies. Instead, the management may be parceled out among different agencies with varying objectives and constituencies, thus eroding the potential for an efficient system of operation even under government development, as in the Columbia River Basin System.

40. Buchanan, "Individual Choice in Voting and the Market," *op. cit.,* p. 335.

6

Public Policy and the Foreign Sector

WILSON E. SCHMIDT

The Federal Government, in fulfilling its constitutional prerogative to regulate the foreign commerce of the United States, has persistently pursued uneconomic policies. When it has striven for excellence in international economic affairs, it has too often done so for the wrong reason or has attempted a worthy objective with senseless methods. The government has wasted public funds through inept policies, and it has caused the private sector to waste its scarce resources as well.

There is a fundamental principle that the government has violated: economic progress and national well-being are best served by giving purchasers the maximum freedom of choice and by buying in the cheapest market, foreign or domestic. The ideas behind this principle are elementary and well known. When the number of items among which a consumer may choose is increased, the consumer's well-being is obviously increased. If a man can select among eight-, six-, and four-cylinder cars, his chances are greater for obtaining what best suits his needs and his pocketbook than if he is forced to choose only between an eight and a six. An economy that produced nothing but one-family houses would provide less satisfaction to many consumers than one that provided apartment buildings as well.

The public sector should maximize its own freedom of choice

in order to increase, not its own well-being, but that of the private sector, for which the government in effect has a proxy. It chooses among goods and services to provide the people with things which they are believed to want, but which they are unable to supply at all or as efficiently themselves, e.g., national security. In public construction, if private contractors and government architects were free, as they are not, to choose between foreign and domestic marble or glass mosaics, the opportunity to look abroad as well as at home would offer greater possibilities for pleasing government structures.

By destroying artificial obstacles to international trade, government can give a new efficiency to a nation, and its people will enjoy, as a whole, higher incomes, measured in terms of the physical goods and services available to them. Suppose, for example, that a particular item can be bought abroad for $1 and that, because of a tariff of $.50, the item sells for $1.50 in the United States. Because competition among American enterprises forces equality between prices and costs of production, United States producers will manufacture it, if the item can be produced at all in the United States, at a cost of $1.50, including the normal profits of the producers. That is, it will take $1.50 of United States resources—land, labor, capital, and management—to produce the item. In contrast, if the item is bought abroad, it requires only $1 of United States resources; this is the value of the land, labor, capital, and management that must be put into some other product to be exported from the United States to obtain a dollar's worth of foreign currency with which to pay for the imported item. If, by breaking down the barrier to international trade, we were to substitute one imported unit for a domestically produced unit of the tariff-protected product, the nation would save $.50 worth of resources. Instead of devoting $1.50 of resources in order to produce the item at home, we would need only a dollar's worth of resources to obtain it indirectly by first producing an export commodity and using the proceeds of its sale to buy the imported commodity.

As domestic resources are displaced by increased imports, they would shift to more productive employments, moving to new activities in different geographical locations or finding new opportunities as new enterprises move to them. In this way, the total output of the nation would be enhanced, its base for economic growth would be increased, and the people as a whole would enjoy greater supplies of goods and services, which are the stuff from which real income is made.

There are instances in which obstacles to international trade may increase real income, and there are situations in which economic objectives should bow to other national goals, e.g., security. Cadres of American businessmen and labor-union leaders have draped themselves and their industries in the flag in order to justify protection from imports for themselves before Congressional committees and the executive branch, but their arguments have been so often rejected by competent authority —the Office of Emergency Planning has accepted only one plea for protection on defense grounds, and even that decision is widely disputed—that it is hard to justify any widespread trade restriction on the basis of national security.

There are two situations in which trade restrictions can increase the real income of a nation: where the price we pay to foreigners for their products can be forced down by artificially reducing our demand for them through trade restrictions, and where external economies, broadly defined, prevail. The latter situation is too abstruse to detain us here and, in any event, is nonoperational to such an extent as to be, for the most part, irrelevant to policy. A tariff policy designed to reduce the price paid to foreigners on the things we import suffers in that there is little private demand for trade restrictions that will in fact reduce these prices, because the price decline limits the protective effect afforded to the domestic industry through trade restrictions. The United States Government has shown little disposition to pursue a policy oriented toward reducing the price paid for imports except in some strategic materials purchases during the Korean War; in the one instance where the policy could easily succeed because of the dominance of the United

States in the market, namely, coffee, the government is, at this writing, supporting financially the efforts of foreign suppliers to raise their prices.

A. *The Public Sector*

The Federal Government, purposely, consciously, and to the disadvantage of the taxpayer, has thrown away the advantages of international trade in its own transactions.

1. FEDERAL PROCUREMENT

The Post Office Department, a few years ago, prohibited the purchase of foreign-made office machinery at the same time that it was demanding increased postal rates of the Congress.

The Department of Defense is required by law to buy all its food, fiber, and fabrics within the United States, no matter what the additional cost over foreign sources may be, and even if they are to be used abroad by the Department of Defense. The restrictive effect of the law is enhanced by the fact that all the components and subcomponents of the products must be entirely of United States origin. Estimates of the additional cost of this law to the taxpayer may be wide of the mark, because the prohibition on foreign procurement has meant that procurement officers have not been in touch with foreign prices. But the Department of Defense estimates that the difference between foreign and domestic prices in 1958 was big enough to allow a saving of $70 million through foreign procurement, a sum equal to the cost of seventy missiles for the Polaris submarine. This estimate does not include the savings that would be gained on goods purchased for use overseas through reduced transportation costs, decreased lead-times, and reduced stocks in the pipeline.

Since 1933, all federal procurement has been subject to the Buy American Act, which forbids foreign procurement for use in the United States, with certain exceptions, specifically, unless the cost of the domestic item is unreasonable. Of course, on our earlier reasoning, the domestic cost is unreasonable if it is higher than the cost of a comparable imported item. But the Executive Branch has chosen to define "unreasonable" in other dimensions. Up to 1954, the domestic price could exceed the import price by 25 per cent plus the tariff on the imported item and still not be regarded as unreasonably high. Inasmuch as this differential was measured against the price of the imported item including tariff, domestic handling, and the cost of domestic components, the differential on the foreign component of the product was often substantially greater than 25 per cent—easily 60 per cent, according to one estimate.[1] In 1954, the Executive Branch redefined "unreasonable," putting the differential at a minimum of 6 per cent; it could be greater if national defense industries were involved or if the domestic procurement was from an area with heavy unemployment. But the reduction in the differential was ordered in sufficiently loose terms to permit the Tennessee Valley Authority to apply a 20 per cent preference to domestic procurement.

It is exceedingly difficult to arrive at a firm estimate of what the Buy American Act has cost the taxpayer. One estimate, admittedly subject to an extremely wide range of error, put the figure at $200 million annually, composed half in higher procurement costs and half in tariff revenue on imports which otherwise would have been received.[2] The effectiveness of the United States Government procurement policy in restricting imports is suggested by the fact that in 1958 the ten most important government agencies spent only 1/20 of one per cent of their procurement funds on foreign goods, and in 1959 only 1/5 of one per cent;[3] in contrast, for the nation as a whole, imports were equal to three per cent of total purchases of goods and services.

If aggregate estimates of the cost are difficult, we are on firmer ground in specific cases. In 1953, in the first of the Chief Joseph dam cases, a British supplier underbid domestic producers by $1 million on certain generators and transformers, and, in addition, the Treasury stood to gain $600,000 in additional tariff revenues, all this on a purchase involving $6.2 million; but the

British supplier lost all but the less profitable transformer contract. In a subsequent Chief Joseph case, the same British supplier offered the Treasury a saving of $1.5 million on a transaction of about $6 million, but he lost the contract because of the unemployment exception. Had the selection of bids been delayed only a few months, the unemployment exception could not have been invoked to reject the British bid, because the level of unemployment in the affected domestic area soon fell below the percentage that permitted invoking the unemployment exception.

Indeed, the government works at cross purposes with itself in its procurement policy. This was shown early in 1961, when the General Services Administration, which was established by Congress to cut costs of procurement for the Federal Government, had to plead before a special panel of the Department of the Interior for permission to buy oil in the cheapest market. The United States Government limits, through quotas, the amount of oil that may be imported, and, inasmuch as foreign oil is considerably cheaper than domestic oil, there is a substantial advantage in having a license to import. The General Services Administration was not granted such a license. Consequently, according to testimony of GSA officials, the procurement cost of oil for use in the Washington, D. C., area was increased by $660,000 in 1961.[4] The Department of Defense has testified that the oil import program at minimum has cost it $20 million since April, 1959.

The recent gold and balance-of-payments problems of the United States have led to shifts in government procurement policy that have added unnecessarily to the costs of government. For example, late in 1960 the Department of Defense ordered that commodities and services that normally would be purchased abroad for use abroad be procured in the United States if the cost differential does not exceed 25 per cent. This was subsequently raised to 50 per cent on a wide range of products. Some insight can be gained into the significance of these measures if we assume that the differential is collected in the form of money. In that event, they wipe out more than one-quarter of the possible reduction in the ratio of customs receipts to imports which might be achieved under the widely heralded 1962 Trade Expansion Act, using 1960 imports as a base.

The leading case under the new policy concerned the purchase of coal for United States facilities in Germany. The White House, motivated chiefly by the balance-of-payments problem but admittedly concerned with the welfare of West Virginia, required the purchase of some 440,000 tons of anthracite coal in the United States at an additional cost of $2.8 million over what it would have cost if bought in Germany. The only voices heard to object publicly to this transaction were those of the American maritime industry—and its Congressional representatives—who complained that the Kennedy Administration failed to require that the coal be carried in American ships.

While the pressing problem of the United States balance-of-payments deficit would seem to support such measures, it is often overlooked that there are economic and uneconomic methods of solving the balance-of-payments problem. To the extent that we meet a balance-of-payments problem through measures designed to expand our exports, we need to restrict our imports less in order to achieve balance in our international payments and receipts; therefore, we can enjoy more of the gains from international trade. Hence, the best solution is a measure or a set of measures that will increase receipts from abroad as well as reduce payments abroad.

Furthermore, the optimum solution is one that gives equivalent stimuli to change all kinds of receipts and payments. For example, if, in the face of a balance-of-payments deficit, we were to restrict the imports of product A greatly while doing nothing about imports of product B, we would be worse off than if we restricted both A and B to achieve the same total reduction in imports. Suppose that A and B both cost $1 abroad and that we impose a $.50 tax on imports of A to reduce the balance-of-payments deficit. In response to the protection afforded by the tax, United States producers will expand the production of A within the United States until the cost of production rises to $1.50. In these circumstances, if we subsequently reduced the tariff on *A* slightly so that imports of *A* rose by $1, and if we simultaneously imposed a small tariff on *B* so that imports of *B* fell by $1, the balance-of-payments position of the United States would be unaffected, but the country would be better off. By buying one more unit of *A* abroad to substitute for United States production of *A*, we would set free $1.50 of United States resources currently producing *A* in the United States; by restricting imports of *B* by one unit, we would have to employ, depending upon the size of the slight tariff on *B*, slightly more than $1 of United States resources to produce *B* within the United States. Hence, there would be a net freeing of United States resources for other uses.

As this illustration suggests, selective restriction of imports is an uneconomic method of cutting total imports. A 25 per cent tax on government imports, which is what the new policy amounts to, without a 25 per cent tax on private sector imports, violates the rule of nonselectivity. The optimum measures are those that have effects across the board, giving equal stimulus to the expansion of all exports and the reduction of all imports. The leading examples of these are exchange-rate and/or internal general price-level changes.

2. GOVERNMENT SURPLUS PROPERTY

Another area of public waste in international transactions concerns United States Government excess property abroad. Under law, no one purchasing this property can import it into the United States without specific approval by the Department of Commerce, and, from time to time there are disapprovals: over 40 per cent of the applications were rejected in 1960. Since the United States is the largest single area in the world in terms of purchasing power, this law automatically reduces the demand for, and thus the price of, the overseas excess property that the United States Government offers for sale.

The philosophy underlying this law, as displayed by the relevant administrative rulings, is notable for its forthright rejection of the gains from international trade. Foreign Excess

Property Order No. 1 (Revised) states the fundamental criterion for approval of imports, namely, that ". . . . the importation of such property would relieve domestic shortages or otherwise be beneficial to the economy of this country."

It further states: "The importation of foreign excess property must have special benefits over and beyond any benefits to be derived in the market place by an added supply of goods and materials through imports." Specifically, "The price at which foreign excess property is acquired, or the price at which it can be sold in the domestic market, will not be considered as an adequate benefit to the economy to justify importation. . . . ." [5]

3. BARTER

In some of its international transactions the United States Government has forgotten the advantages of using money, well known even by the most primitive of peoples for centuries. For example, the United States Government barters surplus agricultural products for strategic materials. A private contractor provides the government with imported strategic materials and receives in return surplus agricultural products that must be sold abroad. Inasmuch as the private contractor is usually a specialist only with respect to commodities on one side of the barter transaction, the barter technique forces him to deal in unfamiliar commodities or obliges him to make arrangements, for a fee, with some specialist in the commodities on the other side of the transaction in order to dispose of them. The result is that the cost to the private contractor of undertaking the barter transaction is increased. As a consequence, the United States Government has been obliged, on a few occasions, to pay more in surplus commodities for strategic imports than if it had bought them for cash. As a rule, however, the government does not like to exchange strategic and surplus commodities at exchange values different from their current market values under cash transactions. But the contractors are loath to bear the extra costs and reduced trading margins imposed by barter. Therefore, the contractors, when commercial business in a particular commodity is active, do not undertake barter transactions for the United States Government. This, however, slows the achievement of the stockpile objectives and retards the disposal of the surplus agricultural products.

Another example of barter is found in the foreign aid program, in which the United States Government transfers surplus agricultural products to workers in underdeveloped countries in part payment for their labor on economic development projects. Penalties are assessed if the worker finds any of the food in excess of his needs, relative to other products, and therefore sells it. Besides suffering the disadvantages of barter, this procedure is exactly the opposite of one means of stimulating economic development: the expansion of the money economy, which facilitates specialization and increases productivity.

Against these criticisms it may be contended (1) that the United States surpluses should be utilized by starving people rather than accumulate as shameful abundance, (2) that it is better to store strategic products, which do not deteriorate as easily as the agricultural products, (3) that the surplus disposal program saves us the heavy storage costs imposed on the taxpayer, or (4) that we achieve political objectives abroad at no cost because we would not use the surpluses ourselves. However, these points, right or wrong, are irrelevant to the issue at hand, namely, the inefficiency of barter, because all these purposes could be better achieved through cash sales and purchases.

4. FOREIGN AID PROCUREMENT

The foreign aid program has provided a number of opportunities for the waste of public funds through uneconomic procurement policies. Until recently, the United States foreign aid agencies, with the exception of the Export-Import Bank, generally pursued a policy of world-wide procurement, buying products wherever they saw fit. But late in 1959 the Development Loan Fund, the major agency of the United States Government at that time for making loans for economic development abroad, shifted to a policy of placing primary emphasis on United States procurement. Subsequently the International Co-operation Administration, another foreign aid agency, initiated a policy designed to shift purchases to the United States.

While very little is known about the effects of the shift in policies since 1959, we do know that the government had serious problems in forcing procurement to the United States before the announcement of the general policy in 1959. For example, in 1955 the Foreign Operations Administration, a predecessor of ICA, sought to direct a substantial volume of its orders for coal into areas in the United States suffering from labor surpluses. According to the Department of State:

. . . . innumerable controversies arose as to specifications, allocations, terms, and conditions. Certain areas were picked out as a source of supply. This antagonized every State where coal is produced but which was not on the list for procurement. This attitude was uniform, even though the coal could not possibly be competitive in price. . . .

There were complaints that awards were going to mines employing nonunion labor; that the coal specifications were either too restrictive or not restrictive enough; some States complained that they did not obtain a coal order, while those that were successful complained that it was not large enough.[6]

Some of the consequences of domestic procurement were revealed when the Foreign Operations Administration decided to finance the purchase of locomotives and railway cars for India's railroads.

Interest was expressed by the Netherlands, the United Kingdom, France, Belgium, Switzerland, Germany, Italy, Yugoslavia and Japan, and bids were solicited and received. However, because of the strong urging from United States concerns to limit procurement to the United States, agreement was obtained from the government of India that it would procure approximately half in the United States and half in other countries. Additional costs would be borne by FOA. The government of India agreed, in full knowledge of the fact that it would receive only 5,000 cars instead of the 5,000 plus which they could ex-

pect for $30 million from world-wide sources. Pursuant to this agree-
ment, an additional $8.5 million was made available by FOA for the
extra cost of limiting half the procurement to the United States.

After considerable difficulties, such as additional allowances in price
to insure that United States firms used all United-States-made components rather than importing certain parts for assembly, the government of India received 100 steam locomotives and 5,430 rail cars.
. . . . Had the commodities been bought on the bids as originally
received, the government of India would have obtained for the $30
million, 100 locomotives and 11,220 cars, and FOA would have saved
$8.5 million . . . . for other important aid to India or elsewhere.7

As indicated by the Indian railway case, to the extent that
United States prices are higher than those prevailing abroad
for specific commodities needed in the aid program, domestic
procurement either forces the foreign aid agencies to give less
assistance in terms of real goods and services or obliges the
Congress to increase aid appropriations in order to maintain
the level of real assistance to be provided. Either there is a
reduction in real assistance to foreign countries at the same
cost to the United States, or there is an increase in the cost of
providing a given amount of real aid. No matter where one
stands on the question of foreign aid, this policy does not make
sense. Those who favor foreign aid should lament the reduction
in real assistance if appropriations are not increased to offset the
higher costs imposed by United States procurement, while those
opposed to foreign aid can surely argue that, if we are going
to reduce the real amounts of assistance provided, we should
obtain a tax reduction for it.

The domestic procurement policy reduces the effectiveness of
the aid program by limiting the range of projects that can be
financed and forcing the donor agencies to select less favorable
opportunities for assisting foreign economic development. In
particular, projects requiring expenditures of large amounts of
the currency of the aid-recipient country to buy resources in
the recipient country must be de-emphasized. If we buy the
currency of the aid recipient with dollars, it is difficult to assure

that the dollars that the aid recipient gains will be spent directly in the United States; and when the aid recipient's normal trade patterns are not with the United States, it is difficult to arrange for the import of United States products into the recipient country for sale for the recipient's currency.

The chief justification for shifting procurement to the United States has been our difficult balance-of-payments position. The Secretary of the Treasury testified in 1961 that "the preponderant part of foreign-aid expenditures will be spent in the United States. Such expenditures, which are accompanied by American exports, have no adverse impact on our balance of payments." [8]

This argument for domestic procurement is seriously misleading. It is true that domestic procurement will expand our noncommercial exports and thereby help the balance of payments. However, the expenditure of foreign aid funds in the United States will add to demands upon our economy. It will press prices upward or prevent them from falling further. This will reduce our commercial exports or stimulate imports and indeed worsen the balance of payments. Hence, it is far from correct to argue that foreign aid expenditures, accompanied by United States exports, have no adverse effect on our balance of payments. At any given moment of time, the excess of our exports over our imports equals the difference between our total output and total spending; equilibrium will be restored to our balance of payments only when we raise the ratio between total output and spending in the United States economy. Policies such as domestic procurement, which impose higher costs and reduce our real output and real income, make the necessary steps to obtain the appropriate ratio more difficult.

5. AID AND TRADE INCONSISTENCY

Finally, the United States Government policies on foreign aid and on trade are at loggerheads. Between 1949 and 1959, United States imports from underdeveloped countries totaled $57.4 billion, while United States aid to them, exclusive of military assistance, was less than $12 billion. Trade is far more important than aid to the underdeveloped countries in providing foreign exchange. Yet in 1956 the United States Government levied duties on imports from Africa equal to seven per cent of the dutiable imports from Africa, duties equal to ten per cent in the case of imports from Latin America, and duties in excess of ten per cent for imports from Asia, excluding Japan, Australia, and New Zealand.[9] In 1960, the United States Government collected revenues of over $9 million on imports of tropical agricultural and forestry products, chiefly from underdeveloped countries, which were not produced in appreciable quantities in the United States.

Furthermore, because our tariffs on processed goods tend to be higher than those on unfinished products, our tariff structure hinders the development of exports of light manufactures in the less developed nations. In addition, we impose import quotas on a number of products produced by the poor countries, including such items as petroleum, lead, and zinc, which further depress our imports from them; the quotas specifically mentioned are not simply hangovers from long-past decisions but were actually imposed when the government had fully established its policy of large-scale assistance to the underdeveloped countries.

A complete catalogue of United States Government restrictions on imports from the underdeveloped countries is impossible, but they are numerous and varied. For example, a recent reduction in the tolerance for foreign matter in cacao shipments established by the Food and Drug Administration, after the tolerance had been considered satisfactory for almost three decades, will probably affect adversely the exports of some underdeveloped countries. The government-granted right of collective bargaining may on net balance have harmed the developing nations. For example, the maritime strike of 1961 cost the banana-exporting countries untold millions in income on stems that could not be sold for shipment to the United States because they would deteriorate.

The significance of United States trade restrictions for our aid levels is readily apparent from the estimate that the complete removal of United States import restrictions would increase our annual imports from Latin America alone by between $850 million and $1.7 billion; [10] in contrast, the Kennedy Administration proposed public assistance of $1 billion to Latin America under *Alianza para el Progresso.*

B. *The Private Sector*

The Federal Government not only has wasted public funds through inept procurement policies, but it also has succeeded in inducing the private sector to waste its scarce resources by restricting its dealings with foreigners. In particular, over 60 per cent of all United States imports in 1960 were subject to extra taxes beyond those that would have been paid if the imported items had been produced in the United States; in addition, there are a number of quotas on imports.

The government has sought since 1934 to reduce our tariff barriers through the reciprocal exchange of tariff reductions with other countries, and these have paid dividends. For example, a recent estimate holds that the 2½ percentage point reduction in duties obtained in 1956 on about $1.7 billion of imports added up to $31.5 million to the real income of the United States.[11] However, the government has been exceedingly slow to reduce taxes on trade. After twenty-seven years, it has reduced the ratio of tariff revenue collected to total imports by 12.8 percentage points, or by .5 percentage points per annum, and part of this reduction is attributable, not to the efforts of the government, but to inflation in the prices of imported products subject to duties that are fixed in monetary terms.

While the authority to reduce tariffs has been extended numerous times by the Congress, the President, to whom this authority is granted, has increasingly been hemmed in by "fringe protection." For example, after the war, the law was amended to require the United States Tariff Commission to establish so-called "peril points." These are dramatic labels for those levels below which the President may not reduce a tariff without injuring some American industry. Since these points are determined in secret tribunal, and the Commission has never informed the public of the methods of determining them, there is little that can be said about them. We do know, however, that peril points have been established for imports that had no direct competitive effect in the United States, and we know that single peril points have been set for so-called basket categories of many items, even though items in the category appeared to differ significantly. Furthermore, the notion that no industry should be injured by tariff reductions is foreign to the elementary logic of the case for expanded trade set forth earlier. One of the advantages of a competitive enterprise system is that the price of progress *must* be paid by those resources and persons who stand in its way; the forces of the market push them out of their pockets of low productivity. If those who will be hurt by progress can defeat the forces of economic development by artificial means, then progress is slowed or stopped.

1. ESCAPE CLAUSE

Another element in fringe protection is the escape clause, which was introduced into the legislation early in the last decade. Responsibility was placed on the Tariff Commission to determine if a tariff reduction has caused serious injury to an American industry, and, if injury is found, the Commission recommends to the President that he reinstate stiffer trade restrictions. The clause requires the Tariff Commission, on its own volition or after the complaint of any party:

. . . . to determine whether any product on which a [tariff] concession has been granted under a trade agreement is, as a result, in whole or in part, of the duty or other customs treatment reflecting such concession, being imported into the United States in such increased quantities, either actual or relative, as to cause or threaten serious injury to the domestic industry producing like or directly competitive products.

. . . . the Tariff Commission, without excluding other factors, shall take into consideration a downward trend in production, employment, prices, profits or wages in the domestic industry concerned, or a decline in sales, an increase in imports, either actual or relative to domestic production, a higher or growing inventory, or a decline in the proportion of the domestic market supplied by domestic producers. Increased imports, either actual or relative, shall be considered as the cause or threat of serious injury to the domestic industry producing like or directly competitive products when the Commission finds that such increased imports have contributed substantially towards causing or threatening serious injury to such industry.

. . . . the terms "domestic industry producing like or directly competitive products" and "domestic industry producing like or directly competitive articles" mean that portion or subdivision of the producing organizations manufacturing, assembling, processing, extracting, growing, or otherwise producing like or directly competitive products or articles in commercial quantities. In applying the preceding sentence, the Commission shall (so far as practicable) distinguish or separate the operations of the producing organizations involving the like or directly competitive products or articles referred to in such sentence from the operations of such organizations involving other products or articles.

As Learned Hand said with respect to another law, "The words he must construe are empty vessels into which he can pour nearly anything he will." The problem was underlined by the Chairman of the House Ways and Means Committee, which is responsible for this clause, when he stated that "as I read some of the provisions, I am at a loss to understand what they mean." [12] And then there is the lament of the Chairman of the Tariff Commission, who explained that in a decision the Commission does not cite previous cases that it has decided ". . . . because each individual case is so different in this field that there just isn't any precedent." [13]

How serious must injury be in order to be "serious injury"? Surely the nation has imposed an immensely difficult task upon the members of the Tariff Commission, for they have four different degrees of injury to interpret: injury, serious injury, material injury, and substantial injury. As the Chairman of the Commission once testified, ". . . . we weigh the difference as to what Congress intended between serious injury, which I think is at one extreme and the bare word 'injury,' which is at the other extreme, with 'substantial' and 'material' in between That is not an easy task to interpret that." [14]

And then there is the problem of defining the domestic industry whose circumstances will determine whether injury has been done. The Commission once voted to recommend a tariff increase on garlic even though, for the most part, garlic farmers grew it as an incidental part of a vegetable and sugar-beet business and had ample opportunity to increase the production of other crops if they were dissatisfied with the return on garlic. But on another occasion the Commission combined two separate complaints, tartaric acid and cream of tartar, to report its decision, because they were produced by one company in a single plant. And the Commission chose to define the United States meat-packing industry and not sheep raising as the competitive domestic industry in the case of lamb and mutton imports in the form of carcass meat. As the Chairman of the Tariff Commission once testified, "The concept of industry is one of our troubles and one of our difficulties. . . . . Commissioners will have different opinions on what constitutes the industry." [15]

There is also the problem of deciding whether imports have been a sufficiently significant cause of injury when purely domestic forces are also contributing to an industry's difficulties. In some cases, imports appear to have been made the scapegoat when in fact the principal cause of difficulty in a domestic industry lay elsewhere. For example, the Commission recommended relief from import competition for the briar pipe industry when the major cause of the industry's troubles was a shift in consumer preferences away from pipes. It also recommended relief for the domestic spring clothespin industry when the trouble was caused by the development of a new product, namely, the automatic dryer.

The Commission is instructed to employ, as evidence of injury, either an absolute increase in the level of imports or an increase in imports relative to domestic production. If domestic production were rising but imports were rising faster, so that domestic producers failed to capture their proportionate share of the expanding market, the Commission could find injury. Injury may be found even if an industry loses something it never had. This involves just about as much injury as that suffered by the man who complains that he lost money on a stock that he failed to buy because it went down in price after he did not buy it. Though it is a sticky point to prove, because so much depends upon the base period selected, these circumstances have prevailed in several cases sent to the President with recommendations for relief. In the acid grade fluorspar and wood clothespin complaints, domestic production was substantially higher in the last full year before the Commission's decision was rendered than in several, though not all, of the immediately preceding years. In the stainless steel case, there had been a steady increase in the value of the domestic industry's sales, almost doubling in five years.

2. NATIONAL DEFENSE AMENDMENT

Another postwar amendment to the trade agreement program requires the Office of Emergency Planning to hear complaints that imports are injuring national defense industries.

By far the most important of the national security cases to be decided was the oil import complaint. It displays the problems of the United States Government in restricting imports through quotas; the program of oil import restriction has been in almost constant turmoil since it started in 1959. Some of the chief difficulties have concerned the allocations of the right to import. Inasmuch as foreign oil is considerably cheaper than United-States-produced oil, an import license is a valuable right. It is reported that, in a process known as "quota-peddling," companies have been willing to pay premiums equivalent to $1 or more a barrel to those who had rights to import. After the first allocations of import licenses, no less than one-third of the importers complained about the size of the allocations that they received. And there have been almost continuous protests from those who did not receive import rights. For example, only those firms that were importing in 1957 were granted licenses to import residual fuel oil. A number of oil marketers handled imported oil in 1957 but did not receive import licenses because they were not the importers of record, i.e., they purchased the foreign oil from other firms. Hence, they were obliged to buy domestic oil or imported oil at premium prices and to compete with marketers who, by virtue of their import licenses, could buy cheap foreign oil. As the representative of one company testified, ". . . . elimination of our company from the import program has caused us untold hardship, has cost us nearly a million dollars, and has done us irreparable damage." [16] Later he added, "Suppose that some government administrator told you that, because you lived in a certain house on one side of the street in 1957, you must live there for the rest of your natural life. Would you stand for such a dictate in these free United States? And yet in substance that is exactly what the Oil Import Administration has been dictating to certain oil men during the past two years." [17]

At a Department of the Interior hearing early in 1961, concerned chiefly with the proper level of oil imports and the allocation of import licenses, the last witness, appearing close to midnight in a session that started at 10:00 A.M., was sufficiently discouraged by the day's proceedings to say, "If the American way is to take something that we fought like hell for and split it up, somebody says five per cent, somebody says fifteen per cent, and hand this out as a dole, I think it is time we nationalize the oil industry and let the government run everything. How small can we creep? How filthy can we permit ourselves to walk through this?" [18] In a somewhat calmer assessment, the Secretary of the Interior, Stewart Udall, stated, "I think this is a problem that might very well baffle King Solomon himself." [19]

Most, if not all, of the problems involved in allocating import rights could have been avoided if the United States Government had chosen to restrict imports through a higher tariff rather than a quota. The higher tariff would restrict the total volume of imports, but, unlike the quota, would not have restricted the imports of particular firms. Those firms which were willing to pay the higher tariff could freely obtain the oil they desired. Furthermore, a tariff would permit the Federal Government to absorb the difference prevailing between the cost to the importer of foreign oil that he is allowed to bring in and the scarcity price at which he can sell it domestically.

A tariff is undoubtedly superior to a quota as a means of restricting imports. But there is an even better method of achieving the professed objective of the oil import restriction program, namely, the maintenance of an adequate domestic oil industry for purposes of national security. As it stands now, if we accept the argument that oil import restrictions are necessary for national security reasons, New England, which relies heavily on residual fuel imports, bears a disproportionate share of our national security costs. One estimate suggests that the price increases caused by the import restriction cost consumers on the East Coast $1.2 billion in 1961 alone.[20] Would it not be fairer to allocate among all Americans the cost of maintaining the domestic oil industry through general taxation rather than on the basis of accidents of geographical location, both of people and of fuel? If so, the United States Government would achieve its objective more equitably through a direct subsidy to the domestic oil industry from the United States Treasury.

3. VOLUNTARY QUOTAS

The newest form of fringe protection, initiated by the Eisenhower Administration and expanded by the Kennedy Administration, is the voluntary quota. It arose when the United States textile industry complained vigorously about harm by Japanese textiles. The government, casting aside the established procedures, induced the Japanese government to require its businessmen to restrict textile exports to the United States under the threat that if this were not done "voluntarily," restrictive measures would be imposed by the United States Government.

The Kennedy Administration multilateralized the voluntary quota system by bringing together the major textile exporting and importing countries for an international agreement on voluntary quotas. The agreement established the principle that a country could restrict its textile imports from another country if the exporting country, upon request of the importing country, did not voluntarily restrict its exports of textiles.

This was a big-stick policy. It by-passed the normal procedures established under law for handling injury problems. No compensatory reductions in other trade barriers were offered to the textile-exporting nations, as is the usual procedure under the General Agreement on Tariffs and Trade, which provides rules of international commercial policy. This major innovation was not even deterred by the prospect that high officers of the Departments of State and Commerce, in all dignity and seriousness of purpose, would have to discuss with equally high officials of a sovereign and allied power the proper levels of imports of certain ladies' unmentionables.

The results of the United States–Japanese voluntary quota system were exceedingly inequitable. With Japan's entry into the United States market limited, new suppliers sprang up, particularly in Hong Kong, and, inasmuch as these new supplying areas were unwilling to agree to voluntary restrictions, Japan's share of our textile market fell precipitously. Had a tariff been imposed across the board, this discrimination would not have occurred.

The quota on Japanese textiles did not simply limit Japan's over-all textile exports, but divided them into some twenty-five categories, placing a limitation on each kind, with only restricted possibilities for shifting goods among categories. The recent multilateral agreement negotiated by the Kennedy Administration raises the number of categories to more than sixty. Through categorization, the restrictive effect of the quota was increased, for it tended to thwart the desires of consumers to satisfy their preferences as they shifted. For example, several years ago there was a shift from slacks to Bermuda shorts among American males. But when importers tried to respond to this shift, the quota relevant for Bermuda shorts stopped them. Another effect of the categorization has been partly to cause Japan to fail to fulfill its total textile quota. As demand patterns and cost conditions shifted among various textile products, Japan lost markets in particular items but was unable to compensate for these losses by increased exports of other textiles because the specific quotas prevented it.

Still one other effect of the voluntary quota system should be noted. The imposition of a quota, by restricting supply within the importing country, raises the price of the imported product within that country without raising it abroad. In the case of the oil imports, we noted the payment of premiums on foreign oil in the United States market, which indicates that Americans are paying less to overseas suppliers for the oil they import than the price at which they are selling it in the United States market. But in the case of sugar quotas, United States importers on average pay a price to foreign suppliers which is very close to that prevailing in the United States market and several pennies per pound more than the world price of sugar. Foreign sugar suppliers, by restricting their offers, have managed to absorb the gap in prices created by the quota. America pays more to foreigners for each unit of imported sugar because of the quota. The same thing has apparently happened in respect to some of the products subject to voluntary quotas, in particular, velveteen; the price paid to Japanese exporters for it has risen over fifteen per cent since the quotas were imposed. Such effects are facilitated by the fact that the voluntary quota system works through associations of Japanese exporters, and it may be added that the large Japanese enterprises are not wholly displeased with the quota system because of the market control that it affords. In sum, the voluntary quota system has increased the cost to the United States of our imports by more than a tariff, because foreign suppliers have been able to raise their export prices; and it has done this without providing any more protection to the domestic industry, because a tariff could have been established to provide the same degree of import restriction.

Conclusion

The record of the United States Government in international economic intercourse is far from satisfactory. The economic waste that its inept policies cause should give pause to those who would grant more power to the government.

NOTES

1. *Staff Papers Presented to the Commission on Foreign Economic Policy* (February, 1954), p. 316.
2. *Ibid.*, p. 318.
3. Laurence A. Knapp, "The Buy American Act," *Columbia Law Review* (March, 1961), p. 450.
4. *Official Report of the Proceedings Before the Department of Interior in the Matter of Aspects of and Problems Pertaining to the Residual Oil Import Program*, Vol. I (February 20, 1961), p. 161.
5. This regulation is fascinating for its high ratio of bad economics to the total length of the regulation. For example, it states, "In general, a shortage in the market for any particular type or class of goods or materials exists when the demand is greater than supply." In clarifying this statement, there is no reference to price.
6. Department of State, *The United States Economy and the Mutual Security Program* (April, 1959), p. 23.
7. *Ibid.*, pp. 27 f.
8. *International Development and Security*, Hearings, Committee on Foreign Relations, U. S. Senate, Pt. I, 87th Cong., 1st Sess., p. 94.
9. *The United States and World Trade*, Report to Committee on Interstate and Foreign Commerce, U. S. Senate (March 14, 1961).
10. L. O. Delwart, *The Future of Latin American Exports to the United States* (Washington: National Planning Association, 1960), p. 99.
11. M. E. Krenin, "Effects of Tariff Changes on the Prices and Volumes of Imports," *American Economic Review*, June, 1961, p. 321.
12. *Renewal of the Trade Agreements Act*, Hearings before Committee on Ways and Means, House of Representatives, 85th Cong., 2nd Sess., p. 187.
13. *Ibid.*, p. 212.
14. *Ibid.*, p. 189.
15. *Ibid.*, p. 178.
16. "Official Report . . . . ," *op. cit.*, p. 507.
17. *Ibid.*, p. 514.
18. *Ibid.*, p. 527A.
19. *Ibid.*, p. 467.
20. Federal Reserve Bank of Boston, *New England Business Review*, November, 1961, p. 2.

7

The Expansion of the Public Sector through Foreign Policy

J. FRED RIPPY

With the complete imposition of totalitarian Socialism (Communism) or the adoption of full-scale democratic Socialism, the private sector of any economy is absorbed by the public sector. So far, only the first type of Socialism has succeeded in virtually eliminating the private sector. Democratic (parliamentary) Socialism is more gradualist. It expands the public sector by selective take-over and by generally hampering the operation and growth of the private sector. Most of the non-Communist economies of today are described as "mixed" economies. They are neither completely private nor entirely public, the "mix" differing from nation to nation.

Both Socialism and Communism require an all-encompassing centralized government machinery. As its result we see the expansion of state functions to regulate, control, tax, and spend. Governments may seize a few or many of the means of production, but in the process they cannot avoid restricting free enterprise in general by intervention or domination and by increasing taxation and the size of the regulatory bureaucracy. Moreover, in this climate there appears to be an inevitable tendency to berate and abuse the private sector, often accusing—sometimes falsely—those who run it of all sorts of economic crimes (see the essay by Commissioner Mason).

The survival of the private sector in contemporary economies may in part depend upon a better understanding of the causes, agencies, functions, and intended or unintended consequences of interventionist government in the United States.[1]

The Proximate Causes of Expanding Government in the United States

1. Large-scale businesses, inviting regulations
2. Labor-union monopolies
3. Business cycles
4. Unresisted demands by pressure groups for special benefits
5. Political and bureaucratic ambitions
6. Global enthusiasms for the salvation of mankind
7. Involvement, eager or reluctant, in world politics and economies
8. The disposition of people to believe that the government can solve most of the problems perceived in the modern "complex" world.

Of course, there is some overlapping among the above categories. They are merely intended as a general checklist.

The existence of large corporations and labor unions and the need to control monopolistic tendencies are obvious. There are also several "natural monopolies" that require regulation in respect to rates and services because of the impracticality of competition. However, it would be difficult to maintain that economic monopoly per se is a genuine cause of big government. If this were true, we should expect less government today than in 1900. And we remember, of course, the Great Depression and the numerous "alphabetical agencies" established in the vain effort to achieve "full employment and economic prosperity." The fourth cause, the demands by pressure groups for government favors, has been in operation since the beginning of our nation. The significance of such words as tariffs, bounties, "pork barrel," quotas, and subsidies should be well known. A multiplicity of government favors not only requires a multitude of public employees but also tends to give rise to bloc voting and electoral corruption through "platform bribes."

The personal ambitions of politicians, demagogues, and bureaucrats to make history or at least widen their jurisdiction also cause growth and extravagance in government. This trend, curiously enough, is no longer fully noticed by the general public of our time. The warnings of the founders of the limited governments of the Old World and the New have been forgotten. For the promotion of their welfare, people now seem to expect more and more from the state and less and less from their own efforts and ingenuity.

The sixth and seventh causes are closely related and will form the crux of my analysis. But first a few observations about the context. Big government operates in ever larger measure through agencies of various types which have restricted the free enterprise of the people but which also have tended to wring from the Congress more and more autonomy and thus have removed themselves ever farther from the inspection and control by the representatives of the people. Many of these agencies are attached to the various federal departments headed by the President's Cabinet officials. These posts have increased considerably during the past century. The most recent addition was a Secretary of Health, Education, and Welfare. And the most likely addition in the near future will be a Secretary of Urban Affairs and Housing. Some agencies, such as the Bureau of Federal Revenue, have themselves become so autonomously fragmented that contradictory decisions arise within them. A more numerous group of agencies stand apart from both the federal executive and the federal legislative body. Nobody seems to know the exact total of both types. Estimates run as high as 2,500.

Classified in respect to function, perhaps the majority of these agencies can be reduced to the following categories: [2]

1. Monetary and fiscal agencies, including collectors of revenue
2. Quasi-judicial agencies
3. Procurement agencies

4. Regulatory agencies
5. Agencies concerned with domestic security and order
6. Conservation agencies
7. Subsidizing and welfare agencies
8. Agencies engaged in production and distribution
9. Agencies, both military and civil, engaged in the preservation of national security, the conduct of foreign relations, and the promotion and protection of foreign trade and foreign investments.

For present purposes I am mainly concerned with the agencies that conduct foreign relations, including the promotion and protection of foreign trade and investments and the expenditure of public funds for these purposes. But a few more general remarks about the broad setting may be in order.

The more or less unintended consequences of big government are numerous and often oppressive or even fatal for personal liberty and national prosperity. The following list is probably incomplete.

1. Enormous and often wasteful expenditures of public funds
2. A federal debt approaching $300 billion
3. Federal taxes which take an average of more than 20 per cent of the national annual income
4. Draining of the sources of state and local revenues, as well as a growing tendency toward double taxation
5. A propensity to transform national elections into grand auctions in which rival candidates bid against one another for the votes of the electorate with promises to spend the people's money
6. An inflation that has reduced the purchasing power of our dollar to less than 47 cents in comparison with its purchasing power in 1939
7. The linking of wages and salaries of federal employees and officeholders to the inflationary kite, thus removing a major bureaucratic motive for preventing the continuous rise in the cost of living

8. Curtailment of personal freedom, particularly freedom to spend, invest, and conduct private business enterprises
9. Gradual substitution of government economic activity and government doles for private self-reliance, initiative, ingenuity, and industry.

In its attempts to promote global justice, prosperity, and peace, our Federal Government has granted and loaned a total of more than $90 billion, without counting the administrative costs of the numerous international organizations established largely at its behest since 1945. The United States has forced its taxpayers to provide from one-third to more than one-half of the compensation of these international income-tax-exempt employees. Compulsory spending for foreign aid has been utilized repeatedly as an argument for extravagant federal appropriations for domestic purposes. In line with governmental attitudes and practices acquired and cultivated in the foreign-aid field, our Federal Government now employs funds taken from the taxpayer to induce or force state and local governments to intervene in various private sectors or else to accept federal intervention.

Federal Intervention in Foreign Trade and Foreign Investment

I now invite attention to trade and investment intervention in the international sphere. Probably necessary in some instances, if foreign governments cannot be dissuaded from taking similar action, it is the sort of activity that tends to break through all restraints. Already it involves more agencies, bureaus, and commissions than I can enumerate here, and no doubt it likewise involves considerable overlapping and overstaffing. Important in this category are the Export-Import Bank, the Tariff Commission, the Bureau of Foreign Commerce, an office of Tourism, the Commodity Credit Corporation, the General Services Administration, commercial and agricultural attachés scattered around the world, an agency in charge of trade fairs, a host of bureaucrats in the State and Agricultural Departments busy with the negotiation of sales and barter agreements required by

Public Law 480 of 1954 and subsequent amendments, legislation designed to dispose of farm surpluses by means of grants, sales, and barter—all these and many other agencies and employees are involved.

Subsidies are provided for our Merchant Marine and our International Airlines. Attempts are made by federal bureaucrats, chiefly for political reasons, to manipulate import quotas for petroleum, sugar, and other commodities. And our woolgrowers are given bounties for the same purpose. Capitalists who invest their funds, equipment, and skills abroad are guaranteed by our government against almost every hazard except bad judgment and defective management. A billion dollars in such guaranties is already authorized. Ironically, these guaranties apply only to new investments. The Cuban and Bolivian expropriations and confiscations revealed that no such guaranties are provided for older investments. Such guaranties, however, undermine any determination to exact prompt and adequate compensation for losses of capital in sugar, petroleum, tin, and other enterprises. Finally, the large grants and loans made to foreign countries in connection with our so-called "mutual-assistance" programs are motivated in part by the desire to promote exports of capital goods as well as consumers' goods. And if, in the process of stimulating exports, a number of industries turning out consumers' goods or producing primarily for the domestic market are injured by the manipulation of tariffs and import quotas, these industries must be compensated by federal subsidies to both their owners and their workers. Free enterprise and individual liberty would be far better served by international agreements to desist from the utilization of these complex and costly efforts to promote trade and investment.

Foreign-Aid Programs and the Public Sector

The total cost of our foreign-aid programs for the fiscal years 1946–1961 has been estimated, as already noted, at some $90 billion in government grants and loans. But this does not include the many millions contributed by our Federal Government to the administrative expenses of a multitude of international organizations, global and regional, established during the postwar period, many of them at the urgent suggestion of our own high officials.

Whatever the doubts we may have about the talents of our politicians and bureaucrats in the conduct of foreign relations, their talent for the multiplication of public agencies must be admitted. The total that they have sponsored for the management of international relations and the promotion of universal prosperity and peace during the years since the end of World War II is certainly not less than seventy-five. And in addition to expensive participation in all these organizations of an international or regional type, our Federal Government has set up numerous special organizations of its own for the purpose of engaging partly or exclusively in foreign-aid programs. Among the latter are the Export-Import Bank, the International Cooperation Administration, the Development Loan Fund, the United States Information Agency, the Office of Cultural Relations, the Peace Corps, and several agencies charged with administering the provisions of Public Law 480 and with the task of bartering farm commodities for stockpiles of minerals and metals. Because of overlapping between these and the many international organizations, co-ordinating agencies are beginning to be created —and surely we shall soon have co-ordinators to co-ordinate the co-ordinators.[3]

I have my doubts regarding the inevitability of the course of world politics (supposedly) forcing our top-level politicians to attempt too much too soon in setting out to redeem the inhabitants of our planet. More pertinent for this occasion is an attempt to assess the weight and quality of our performance since World War II. Does the postwar participation of our country in world politics show or promise more satisfactory results than were achieved by the efforts of Woodrow Wilson, F. D. Roosevelt, and their collaborators? I have not been able to put aside my misgivings about the possibility of attaining within any short time the announced goals of freedom, justice, prosperity, and peace for all mankind, particularly through the economic means employed by our government.

Except for the threat of Soviet aggression, most of Western Europe, owing in part to the economic assistance received from the United States, probably is in a much better condition than at any time in the past. But a very large part of the rest of the world is far from showing a reasonable result of the billions poured into it. In the Orient, in Africa, and in much of Latin America, turbulence and violence and extreme economic and social tensions, partly caused by the glowing expectations aroused and fostered by the United States, the United Nations and its special agencies, and the utopian promises of the Soviet bloc, are hampering political, economic, and social progress. Growth in population is outrunning growth in production, and production is impeded by statism.

Thorough inspection of our assistance programs has revealed mismanagement, waste, and corruption wherever such inspection has been made: in Laos, Cambodia, Korea, Formosa, South Vietnam, and Iran; in Haiti, Bolivia, and Peru. Although most of those guilty of corruption are natives of the various countries, much of the waste and inefficiency must be charged against the agents and agencies of the United States. If despots are now fewer in Latin America than before the programs were initiated, despots have become more numerous in the rest of the under-developed world (e.g., Ghana, Egypt, Indonesia, to name a few). The immediate benefits of our aid, such as they have been so far, have rarely reached the masses of the people. The major part of our so-called "free world" is neither free nor prosperous, and we are gravely dissipating our resources in attempts to bring freedom and prosperity to them.

Our noble intentions and our benevolence have rarely developed gratitude or confidence, good will or respect. Governments that formerly asked for help as a favor are now demanding it as a right and threatening to join the Sino-Soviet bloc if our help is denied. Thinly veiled blackmail is becoming a habit in many instances. Neutralism with reference to the global conflict between totalitarian tyranny and political, personal, and economic freedom is spreading in the Orient and Africa, and even in the Western Hemisphere. Dependence upon government rather than private initiative and enterprise, fostered—probably for the most part unintentionally—by our aid programs, is being increasingly emphasized almost everywhere. Our government has not even been able to negotiate a consensus in respect to the Communist regime set up by Fidel Castro in the Caribbean danger zone.

Hardly anywhere in this vast and populous underdeveloped world, I repeat, can the impartial observer discover a strong determination to promote the private sectors of national economies and contrive protective equilibriums against the encroachment of the public sectors. If any exceptions are to be found, they might be in Latin America—maybe in Argentina, Peru, or Colombia, or in some of the small countries of Central America —although the evidence is not yet convincing to me. Nor do I believe that our cheap public loans and grants will serve to promote the private sectors in these countries; on the contrary, there are already indications that free funds are likely to be used to buy out foreign holdings of private enterprise and expand the public sectors.

It is difficult to discover facts showing that any of these Latin neighbors are more favorably disposed toward private enterprise—particularly foreign private enterprise—than before they began to receive economic and technical assistance from our government. Public ownership and operation of the means of production seems to be spreading in most of the nations south of the Rio Grande. The public sector, which has long included telegraph systems and a few railways, most of the locally owned steamship firms, a few telephone systems, and several electric utilities and water and sewer installations, has now taken over many more of these, and has begun to add to them, beginning with the petroleum industry (after the earlier Mexican and Argentine examples) and extending to banking, finance, and insurance, the new steel plants, the mining industry, broadcasting and television, and several others.

Price stabilization and production controls are expanding in agriculture—and our government, at the recent conference in Punta del Este, and on other occasions, has agreed to speed this movement into the public sector. The state bureaucracies are growing like mushrooms during the rainy season. Many of the state enterprises incur deficits year after year, so that inflated currencies continue to purchase less and less. But, as I have said, I have not succeeded in ferreting out any convincing evidence of a strong disposition to reverse or even interrupt the general trend. Nothing that our government can do, or seems willing to do, appears likely to redress the balance and create the equilibriums required for the efficient functioning of stable national "mixed economies." [4]

Meantime, our foreign policies, political and economic, have fostered the advance of our own country's public sector until it threatens to crush the private sector by heavy taxes and a maze of regulations and controls. Although our foreign policies have not initiated this expansion, they have accelerated the advance, and accelerated it more than has been necessary in order to deal with the crises of our century.

Suggestions Regarding Policy

In spite of all my pessimistic utterances and apparent defeatism, I am still an optimist with respect to my own country and a few others in the Western world, provided our people and theirs can be aroused from their apathy.

I propose an appealing statement of freedom's basic creed. My personal belief is that the creative spirit and the energies of the individual are the major impulses of all progress, and that every restraint imposed upon them not only retards progress but hampers the pursuit of happiness as well. Every expansion of government—i.e., of unappealable power by men over men—except expansion for the purpose of preserving order, safeguarding national security, promoting justice, and preventing monopoly, constitutes a reduction of the liberty of those governed.

Regarding every proposal to multiply the functions of government, this fundamental question should be asked: Does this proposed new function restrict the creative spirit and energies that freedom provides? This ought to be the crucial test; and whatever the language employed to clothe this basic creed, it should be constantly reiterated by all our public officials and by all who take part in the formation of public opinion. Any political, economic, or social order established upon a widely different foundation is bound to weaken and eventually destroy the principle of the sacredness of the individual human being and his inherent rights.

To the extent that we feel our nation must assume global responsibilities in the national interest, I propose that our foreign policies should be designed to extend this creed to other nations and peoples, and that every operation in the realm of foreign affairs should harmonize to the maximum extent possible with this creed; that departure from it in the name of expediency should be reduced to an absolute minimum; that representatives of our government charged with the management of our external relationships and interests be selected in as strict accord with this principle as possible; and that vigorous and tactful efforts be made to persuade nations and peoples receiving our support and assistance to act in harmony with it. This will mean, of course, that our aid may have to be cut off from some of the ninety-seven countries to which it has been granted, but perhaps most of these are beyond our redemptive powers in any event if they cannot be induced to accept our philosophy of the individual. This may likewise mean that not a few of our incumbent statist bureaucrats, both at home and overseas, should be removed.

I must confess that all those who are engaged in this global effort to accelerate the economic and social progress of this vast aggregation of retarded nations and peoples arouse my deepest sympathy. They arouse my sympathy because, like the leading actors in a classical Greek tragedy, they are likely to be doomed to frustration and failure. According to my view, there is only one way to develop the underdeveloped inhabitants of this earth without doing violence to human dignity and human rights, and that one way is freedom's way: free enterprise, hard work, honesty, efficiency, a long preliminary period of low wages and fairly high profits regularly and prudently invested, and a government that confines itself mainly to improving transportation, education, and health and to providing conditions that will foster private investment, both domestic and foreign. Unless the many millions now said to be involved in this "revolution of rising expectations" can be convinced that austerity must precede affluence and that an expansion of the capacity to produce must be achieved before launching a multiplicity of welfare programs, their anticipations will never be realized. Unless they move along this highway in their pursuit of higher levels of living and happiness, all the economic aid that the more affluent nations can provide them, all the personnel that may be sent overseas to assist them, will do them little good.

Perhaps we can find some reassurance in the address by Robert L. Garner, President of the International Finance Corporation, delivered on September 21, 1961, at the annual meeting of the Board of Governors of the World Bank in Vienna. I conclude with a few quotations from it:

Obviously there is need for governments to provide the basic facilities and services. To do this in adequate measure will strain their human and financial resources. It seems sensible, therefore, to give the greatest scope to private initiative and capital in all fields which are not necessarily in the public sector.

There is convincing proof that this is the most assured method of getting development. The most productive economies which have brought the highest standards of living to the most people have been those which have permitted private initiative to control the widest range of activities. This system has worked in Europe and Japan with the long-established societies.

Over the past fourteen years I have visited some fifty countries, most of them in earlier stages of development. The most substantial progress I have observed has come from the private sector, where it has been provided with basic facilities and a political and administrative climate in which it could exercise its talents.

NOTES

1. Professor Calvin B. Hoover's *The Economy, Liberty, and the State* (Garden City, New York: Doubleday, 1961) is a cautious treatise on this subject, dealing, however, only with Europe and the United States.
2. *The World Almanac* contains a long list of these agencies and commissions. Consult the *United States Government Manual* for fuller information. Among the functions listed, there is considerable overlapping. Among the ones that have expanded most are those involving regulation, conservation, subsidization and welfare, and those related to national security and foreign trade and investment. Production and distribution of commodities include water for irrigation, electric power, the repair of ships, and world-wide operation of housing and hotel facilities and post exchanges, to mention only a few of the most important.
3. This and the preceding paragraph are based on the *Hearings* of the House Subcommittees on Appropriations for the State Department, the United States Information Agency, and the International Co-operation Administration. I refrain from a mass of detailed citations.
4. The following works contain impressive data on Latin-American propensities to expand the public sector: Harry Stark, *Social and Economic Frontiers in Latin America* (Dubuque, Iowa: Wm. C. Brown, 1961); J. Fred Rippy, *Latin America and the Industrial Age* (New York: Putnam's, 1947); and *British Investments in Latin America* (Minneapolis, Minnesota: University of Minnesota Press, 1959). Consult especially the chapters on industry and public services, including railways.

   The *Congressional Record* (Sept. 23, 1961), pp. 19799–801, contains an account of an electric-power seminar held in Mexico City during the previous August. Written by Alex Radin, a public-power advocate from the United States who attended the conference, it points out that the governments of Latin America own and operate 60 per cent of the region's installed electric-power capacity and that most of these governments are advocates of the further expansion of the public sector into this phase of their economies. The conference was attended by representatives from the United Nations and its special agencies as well as from the Latin American countries and the United States.

   The *Congressional Record* (Sept. 25, 1961), pp. 19846–854, offers an illuminating discussion of the shortcomings of "mutual assistance" by Senator Prescott Bush of Connecticut, who had just returned from a conference of representatives of various multilateral financial agencies engaged in efforts to speed the development of the retarded countries.

Senator Bush quotes at length from the high officials of the global banking organizations: World Bank, International Finance Corporation, International Development Association, and International Monetary Fund. I emphasize this quotation from the head of the IFC:

Over the past fourteen years I have visited some fifty countries, most of them in earlier stages of development. The most substantial progress I have observed has come from the private sector. . . . .

8

The *Contraproducente* Consequences of the Foreign-Aid Program in Bolivia

WILLIAM S. STOKES

Introduction

In a letter to President Víctor Paz Estenssoro of Bolivia (released May 14, 1961, in the United States and May 17 in La Paz, Bolivia), President Kennedy declared that the United States was now ready to assist Bolivia in a long-range economic program to achieve higher standards of living, economic progress, and social justice. President Kennedy promised loans and grants for the state tin and oil enterprises, roads, surplus agricultural products, an airport and a sugar mill (totaling $50,000,-000, including the West German credits), with other projects, such as low-cost worker and farmer housing to be undertaken as soon as the planning and programing could be completed.

In the last paragraph, President Kennedy said: "This great revolution has blazed a path for others to follow." [1] In the official translation of the letter in Bolivia, the sentence reads: "This great revolution has opened the road for other countries to follow." In the headlines to the letter as it was published in the official newspaper of Bolivia is the phrase: "Kennedy Eulogizes the National Revolution." [2]

145

Is this a "great revolution"? Has it "blazed a path for others to follow"? Should the President "eulogize" it? Is it worthy of long-range foreign aid?

Bolivia has already been the recipient of aid from the United States (from July 1, 1945 through June 30, 1960, a total of $191,-200,000 in Mutual Security and Economic Program aid; $191,-700,000 if military aid is included).[3] President Kennedy has determined that the country should receive more, and apparently he and his distinguished advisers are convinced that the *Revolución Nacional* is a model for other Latin American countries to follow. It therefore seems legitimate for the scholar and citizen to examine the nature of the *Revolución Nacional* and the aid it has received from the United States preliminary to a determination of the consequences of the President's "strong leadership" and "bold, imaginative program."

The Ideology and Politics of the "Great Revolution"

I have described elsewhere the origin of the *Movimiento Nacionalista Revolucionario* or MNR.[4] In association with a military lodge, the MNR seized power by force on December 20, 1943. The civilian-military oligarchy proceeded to govern by terror. At least eleven outstanding Bolivians were murdered in the period November 20–25, 1944, alone. The assassinations, tortures, and official thievery became so universally known that Sumner Welles said that the Government had ". . . . turned Bolivia into an immense concentration camp" and, "torture and assassination were daily occurrences." [5]

Led by professors and university students, urban masses exploded into a direct, frontal assault on the centers of dictatorial power in La Paz in July, 1946. When they burst into the governmental palace and finally found President Gualberto Villarroel hiding in a closet *(armario)*, they shot him in the chest, and pushed his body out on one of the balconies that front on Ayacucho Street. From there they threw him to the mob below, which finished him off and hung his remains to a lamppost.[6]

Those leaders of the MNR who escaped began immediately to plan their return to power. In August, 1949, they initiated such mass violence that it probably could be said that a state of civil war prevailed in the country. The army suppressed the uprising in three weeks of fighting. The next attempt, which was successful, was a two-day attack on La Paz, the center of political power. The fighting from April 9–11, 1952, was fierce. A two-column analysis of the violence, published in *El Mercurio* of Santiago, Chile, on April 11, 1958, asserted that at least 5,000 lives were lost.

The original ideology of the MNR was basically Marxist-Leninist, although it was revisionist in not contemplating immediate affiliation with international Communism. Theorists such as Walter Guevara Arze and José Fellman Velarde accepted historical materialism and the class struggle as central parts of their thinking. Ideally, the exploited masses should destroy the bourgeoisie and establish an economic system of socialism and a political system of dictatorship of the proletariat ("people's democracy"). The theorists argued, however, that Bolivia was obliged to import a third of its food and obtain foreign exchange by marketing minerals in other countries. Whether Bolivia could have socialism, therefore, depended upon whether socialism first succeeded in the large countries. A further difficulty was that class consciousness was not sufficiently developed among the Indians and mestizos to permit dictatorship of the proletariat at once. If Bolivia could not have socialism and dictatorship of the proletariat immediately, what could and should it have? The MNR theorists answered: *Revolución Nacional*. "The *Revolución Nacional*," Dr. Guevara Arze asserted, "does not deny the class struggle but is not based upon it." He added that later, depending upon the world development of socialism, Bolivia could base a revolution on the class struggle.[7]

The original program of the MNR included: Opposition to "Judaism" and liberal democracy; prohibition of foreign capital in the media of communication; prohibition of the use of foreigners in command posts in the army; registration and control of all foreign employees in the country; absolute prohibition of the immigration of Jews; abolition of the "great private monopolies"; state control of commercial activities; nationalization of public services; class warfare through a union *(alianza de clases)* of the proletariat, peasants, and the middle classes against the "anti-national superstate" (usually called the *rosca*) and its servants; and public education and social welfare directed by the state along political and nationalistic lines.[8]

Fellman Velarde, who was Minister of Education in 1961, described the programmatic objectives of the MNR in this way: ". . . . it is necessary to eliminate imperialism and the great bourgeoisie that serves as its agent, returning to Bolivia the exploitation of its mines, redistributing the land, and diversifying the economy by means of the creation of new sources of wealth." [9]

The men who affixed their signatures to the act establishing the MNR were: Augusto Céspedes, Carlos Montenegro, Víctor Paz Estenssoro, Hernán Siles Zuazo, Walter Guevara Arze, and José Cuadros Quiroga. In addition, there were eight other leaders who aided significantly in the campaign for power that followed.[10] Most of the original founders and their principal supporters have published works that expose their views. Although Marxist-Leninist conceptions are important in almost all cases, it must be emphasized that the MNR sought nationalistic applications of Communist formulae. Both Montenegro and Céspedes, for example, assert again and again that the MNR managed the data of historical materialism better than the scientific Marxists. By this they meant that the "reality" of Bolivia negated the possibilities of a successful class revolution. They therefore opposed the native Marxist activists and the trained members of the international apparatus who wished to impose the "revealed" truth of Marxism-Leninism on Bolivia in orthodox Communist fashion.[11]

A major work of Hernán Siles Zuazo published in 1954 revealed intellectual affiliation with Marxism,[12] but in his address to Congress in 1958, President Siles Zuazo repudiated class dictatorship, criticized the Communists, and associated himself with "Christian democracy." [13] Even Siles Salinas (who insists that President Paz Estenssoro clearly is a Marxist) asserts that Siles Zuazo is not a "dogmatic Marxist." [14] A Congressman concerned with Latin American affairs told me in Washington in July, 1961, that Secretary of State Dean Rusk had assured him that President Víctor Paz Estenssoro is not a Marxist. On the basis of the books, documents, and interviews available to me, I must conclude that President Paz Estenssoro is a revisionist Marxist-Leninist, whose policies have encouraged Communism in Bolivia.

There is less disagreement as to the Marxist orientation of the leaders of the great labor unions, such as Juan Lechín, Vice President of Bolivia and head of both the Central de Trabajadores de Bolivia and the Confederación Minera de Bolivia, and Mario Torres Calleja, Secretary General of the Federación Sindical de Trabajadores Mineros de Bolivia or FSTMB. Stalinists and Trotskyites drew up the famous *Tesis de Pulacayo* (approved on May 18, 1946), which was adopted as the *Programa de Principios* of the FSTMB. The essence of the *Tesis de Pulacayo* was a commitment of the miners to subordinate temporary possibilities of economic gain to the greater task of achieving the proletarian revolution. The specific provisions of the *Tésis* and the *Programa* paralleled almost exactly the "reforms" of the MNR after the seizure of power in 1952. When Lechín arrived at Huanuni on May 7, 1961, after a trip to the United States to discuss foreign aid, he made a twenty-minute speech to union members to the effect that his visit to the heartland of "imperialism" did not mean a give-away *(entreguismo)* or betrayal of the working class. He told his audience that they must be prepared to "zig-zag" if they expected to achieve their objectives, and on this point he reminded them that even Stalin made a temporary alliance with Hitler as a part of his long-term strategy.[15]

Perhaps the most important single source of information as to the ideological orientation of the MNR at the present time is the Program of Government for 1960–1964. The program was drafted for the purpose, among other things, of persuading the United States to part with even larger amounts of foreign aid.

Nevertheless, the program defends the politically unliberal and economically unsuccessful "reforms" achieved since 1952, some of which were contained in or alluded to in the first program, already discussed. In addition, the part that deals with the nature of the state and the role of law and certain institutions, such as the armed forces and the police, is clearly Marxist-Leninist. According to the MNR, the state is an instrumentality at the service of the classes that control the means of production. "Legal norms—which are not mere abstractions removed from reality but part of the social phenomenon—reflect the interests of the economically dominant classes and are obligatory upon the members of society. . . . The armed forces constitute the apparatus of force of the state and of the social classes that have public power and are designed to fulfill two principal functions. The first consists of defending the state from its internal enemies. This means defending the groups or social classes that have in their hands the management of the state, as opposed to those social groups with contradictory interests. This constitutes the function of conserving public order . . . . and necessarily implies a political identification between the armed forces and the dominant classes.

"In the modern state the police are one of the instruments of coercion of the social classes that possess public power." [16]

The government established by President Víctor Paz Estenssoro in 1952 could not by any stretch of the imagination be described as democratic. The President and his advisers evidenced from the very beginning a passionate intolerance of the opposition. They arrested a former foreign minister, former minister of economic affairs, former chief justice of the Supreme Court, leaders of the major political parties, and many other prominent, even distinguished figures. Secret police organized under a bureau known as Political Control ferreted out the opposition, using unconstitutional methods that rivaled in ferocity those employed by the Nazi and Communist tyrannies. The jails were literally filled with thousands of political prisoners, and President Paz Estenssoro created concentration or "work" camps to accommodate the overflow. Among such camps were Curahuara de Carangas, near Laz Paz, and those at Corocoro, Catavi, and Uncía.[17] The media of communication were intimidated. President Paz Estenssoro ordered the closing of *La Razón* in La Paz, a newspaper owned by Carlos Aramayo. In Cochabamba, MNR mobs burned and destroyed the daily *Los Tiempos*.[18] The leaders *(dirigentes)* of the MNR arrogated to themselves "super-legal immunities" and acted above constitution, law, or court. It has been alleged that they looted the public treasury and engaged in fiscal irregularities probably without parallel in Bolivia's history. As late as July, 1961, it was revealed that about $1,000,000, which was supposed to be used to purchase 4,000 tons of lard, had disappeared.[19]

When elections were scheduled for June, 1956, with power to be transferred in August, it was obvious to Bolivian and foreign observers that the official candidate, Dr. Hernán Siles Zuazo, Vice President under Paz Estenssoro, would win. All effective political opposition had been suppressed. In addition, the MNR instituted universal suffrage, which meant, in effect, giving the vote to illiterates. Whereas only about 160,000 citizens were eligible to vote in the 1951 elections, approximately 1,200,000 were eligible to cast ballots in 1956.[20] To be certain that no embarrassing slips would occur, the government created an *ad hoc* committee to draft an electoral statute that would guarantee the effectiveness of the *imposición* (rigged election). They gave the illiterate Indians their colored ballots *(papeletas de colores)*, and Dr. Siles Zuazo became president.[21] Paz Estenssoro departed for England to perform ambassadorial duties but returned to win the 1960 "elections" and assume the presidency once more (with former President Siles Zuazo departing for Uruguay to perform ambassadorial chores).

President Siles Zuazo closed the concentration camps, succeeded (early in July, 1957) in removing some extreme left-wing influence from the cabinet and party leadership, and permitted freer expression of opinion in the press. In addition, the President stated that the thousands of political exiles could return to Bolivia. In fact, however, most requests for the special transit visas *(permisos de retorno)* were reported to have been denied. Although administrative corruption "reached unknown limits," and Siles had to denounce certain members of the previous administration for having enriched themselves at public expense, it is contended that not one person was punished for the *operaciones fraudulentas.*[22]

The MNR endeavored to eliminate the traditional army and to create proletarian armed militias dedicated to the defense of the *Revolución Nacional.* Juan Lechín, who is credited with having formed the militias, has claimed that the rural people *(campesinos)* made up fifteen regiments, the miners, 10,000 men, the railroad workers, 2,000, and the factory workers, 3,000. When a union was organized, its leaders immediately asked the government for arms for each man.[23] It was reported late in 1958 that at the last mining congress at Colquiri, the following resolution was adopted: "The militias should be strengthened, their command centralized, and their discipline ought to be based on the most profound class convictions. The Federation of Miners will arm the workers and at the same time provide them with an ideological conception of class. The armament of the proletariat and the peasants is one of the great conquests of our class and especially of the miners. The revolution has no more defense than that of the workers' militias." [24] However, the use of violence for political purposes, instead of protecting person and property, has sometimes failed to serve the MNR. Sometimes the militias have refused to follow orders or have acted contrary to government policy. Therefore, in recent years the MNR has begun to rebuild the professional army. The army is reputed to total about 80,000 soldiers at the present time,[25] and in the 1961 budget the Ministry of Defense received 52,700,000,000 bolivianos (with only debt service and education receiving more).[26]

Although the MNR has always officially repudiated the class revolution and professes to represent an alliance of workers, peasants, and members of the middle class, it is a fact that the MNR's policies have desperately injured the middle class, perhaps even more than the upper class. The government's policy of inflation, for example, meant that many members of the middle class were compelled to debase their standards. Many intellectuals and trained people left the country. Others abandoned their professions for black-marketing. Those with capital exported it in order to prevent government seizure. The Zondag report declared that inflation ". . . . is about to wipe out the small middle class of Bolivia, which . . . . is practically the only one that has the necessary education and management ability to give direction to the country." [27] Some writers argue that the MNR should have boldly eliminated the *latifundistas* (large landholders) as a social class in the first place.[28] There is little evidence that the MNR has curbed Communist infiltration from 1952 to the present. Indeed, there is demonstration of Communist presence and influence in the cabinet, legislature, court system, police, unions, and education.[29] There was enough support in the Chamber of Deputies in 1960 to approve a resolution introduced by Deputy Roncal calling for aid for the Cuban Revolution ("to defend the Cuban Revolution is to defend the Bolivian Revolution").[30]

Since returning to power in 1960, President Paz Estenssoro has "reorganized" the court system, permitted the Minister of Economy to "intervene" in the management of the newspaper *El Diario* of La Paz, decreed an *estado de sitio* (suspension of constitutional guarantees for ninety days beginning June 7), and forced Walter Guevara Arze, Chief of the Movimiento Revolucionario Nacional Auténtico, and thirty-one followers, to flee to Peru. The Congress converted itself into a Constituent Assembly, in a manner that seems clearly unconstitutional, in order to add more than a hundred amendments to the organic statute. Some of the amendments purported to give constitutional sanction to previous "elections," while others gave the executive authority to effect economic change without approval from the legislature. Finally, the Communist assault on the Catholic Church has intensified class conflict and resulted in the closing of a Catholic radio station.[31]

The "Great Revolution" and the Agrarian Reform

The Zondag mission described traditional agriculture in Bolivia as economically and socially backward and concluded that reform was "absolutely necessary." [32] The problems were many. Some men owned too much property *(latifundismo)*, and some too little *(minifundismo)*. The 1950 census revealed that 4.5 per cent of the rural landowners possessed 70 per cent of all private landed property. On the other hand, the small and medium farmers, who made up 90 per cent of the rural population, held only 30 per cent of the land.[33] The evils of the *colonato* system, characteristic of the central valley and *altiplano* (highlands) of Bolivia, have been described by many writers.[34]

So inefficient was the system of agriculture that large percentages of the foodstuffs domestically consumed had to be imported each year: for 1925–1929, 22.3%; 1940, 23.9%; 1952, 30%; 1953, 37.84%.[35] This situation was unnecessary. Bolivia has literally millions of acres of undeveloped land that studies have proved to be suitable for agricultural, pastoral, and extractive enterprises. For example, the possibilities for cacao and Brazil nuts are great. Bolivia's rubber is high grade and not likely to be replaced by synthetics. The climate and labor conditions in Yungas are favorable to tea-growing (of which 155 tons worth $200,000 were imported in 1953). Pyrethrum, bananas, corn, rice, sugar, yucca, vegetable oils, tobacco, hard fibers, cusi palms for palm oil, honey, tumeric, cotton, caranday palm wax, quebracho—all could be produced. Although low, governmentally controlled prices for coffee discourage its production, without such artificial barriers the possibilities were virtually unlimited. Quinna, grown in the Bolivian highlands, is a cereal extremely rich in vitamins and protein content. New varieties of wheat could be grown on the high plains, freeing the valleys for other crops. With an estimated 128,000,000 acres of forest, Bolivia is one of the most richly endowed countries in the world in this resource.[36]

Instead of concentrating agrarian reform on national lands,

the MNR enacted a decree-law on August 2, 1953, which provided for expropriation and distribution of lands that were already in use. The official program of the MNR for 1960–1964 describes the agrarian reform as the "most transcendental" of all its *conquistas* because it liberated more than 2,000,000 *campesinos* from serflike conditions.[37] The boast evokes sympathetic response, but the facts must be explored to determine what the effects of the agrarian reform have been.

There is evidence that the main ideological influence in the drafting of the expropriation decree was Marxist-Trotskyite.[38] According to Article 156, *hacendados* or *latifundistas* (large landholders) whose lands are expropriated in whole or in part are to be offered compensation in the form of two per cent, twenty-five-year "agrarian bonds." The value of the land was based on the formula of current tax assessment, which must have been calculated to take private property virtually without compensation. The vicious inflation that the MNR initiated further eroded the worth of the bonds. Article 160 provides that the beneficiaries of the land program can pay for the land on the same terms—price according to tax assessment, twenty-five years for amortization, two per cent interest. Article 162 sets up a National Service of Agrarian Reform headed by the President. Article 164 gives the President "supreme authority" over the entire administrative system including (in section *d*) the final decision, without judicial appeal, on all concessions of titles to land. The Agrarian Law, therefore, provides for a centralized system of administration without checks or controls on the executive. The President is authorized to appoint whomever he chooses to administer the program, and he himself has the final vote. As I wrote in 1959, "This kind of unlimited, unchecked authority invites arbitrary action and abuse." [39] Let us see how the scheme has worked.

As soon as the decree was signed on August 2, 1953, many Indians seized land "militarily." They took and used whatever they found, including about $15,000,000 worth of cattle, many of which were prize breeding-stock. Although the *haciendas* (large farms) had been supplying the cities with food, the people

who seized or received land proceeded to grow food for themselves alone. The reason for this was that the prices the Bolivian
Government offered the farmers for their produce were too
low. When there were surpluses, the farmers smuggled their
livestock, corn, rice, and other products into neighboring countries where they could sell at a profit. Bolivia, the home of the
potato, was compelled to import this food from Argentina. Thus,
the initial result of the agrarian reform was famine in the
cities, which the United States was called upon to alleviate.
However, about one-third of the food supplied by the United
States was smuggled out of the country, and much of the rest
went into black markets. Little reached the consumers who
needed it most, although they waited hours in lines *(colas)* to
get it. In December, 1956, prices of United States food were
raised from their formerly artificially low points of ten to
twenty per cent of cost to market levels. Price controls were
abolished. These actions encouraged local production to some
extent.[40]

The National Service of Agrarian Reform was characterized
by "dishonesty, ignorance, and negligence." The local administration—called *juntas rurales*—produced "anarchy" and "insecur-
ity" in the countryside. Trips to acquire data to implement the
reform became expeditions of "pillage." Aside from "gifts" in
kind, the members of the *juntas* collected "fees" from the
Indians they were supposed to benefit. A law of December 22,
1956, replaced the *juntas* by a new administrative system, but
the results were no better. The new appointees, like the old,
demanded food, drink, gifts, and fees for their "labor." In many
instances, the owner was not present at the time his property
was investigated, but the officials proceeded to sign the form
declaring that the proprietor had ceded his property to the
Indians "freely and voluntarily." It usually took several months
to conclude the preliminary part of the paper work. When the
documents were transferred to higher authority, they entered
a "long winter sleep," although awakened promptly by "gifts."

From the National Service of Agrarian Reform, the documents passed to the Minister of *Campesino* Affairs, and from

there to the Legal Department of the Presidency, and finally to the *Primer Mandatario* (the President) himself. In the long meantime, the *campesinos,* "orphans without direction," became adventurers. They sacked houses, occupied properties, and subjected the owners to terror and extortion. Many of the agitators who encouraged such activity were members of the MNR.

The lawyers prolonged land cases to increase their fees. The administrative and legal work was done so poorly that a second examination was often required (called a *replanteo*) to correct the mistakes made. The surveyors demanded "gross sums" for their services (such as 50,000 bolivianos each from 320 ex-*colonos* of the property "Cocamarca" in the province of Arque in Cochabamba). The *campesinos* were thus compelled to pay for lawyers, surveyors, judges, secretaries, and other officials, as well as for sealed paper, stamps, etc., in order to obtain titles to land. The total amount invested often was more than the market value of the land. For this reason, ". . . . a great number of ex-*colonos* prefer to buy their parcels." [41]

In his address to the national congress in 1958, President Siles Zuazo estimated that it would take thirty to forty years to complete the agrarian reform.[42] However, Beltrán and Fernández (1960) have calculated that if the "rhythm" of the first period of the reform—1953–1956—were followed, it would take 485 years to redistribute the land. If the increased pace of the 1956–1959 period were to continue, it would take 108 years.[43] As of May, 1960, the government had granted 63,414 titles to 44,100 heads of family, involving 1,510,832.57 hectares, of which only 820,707.82 hectares went into individually held plots. In addition, 23,431 titles were almost ready for distribution to 12,670 heads of family.[44]

The average size of holding extended to *campesinos* has been 3.61 hectares.[45] Production has increased in some crops, especially sugar. It has fallen in others, such as wheat. However, it seems plain that the agrarian reform, even in instances in which a farmer has been able to secure title to land, has created fractionalized plots too small to encourage hopes of prosperity among the masses of rural peoples. Benjamín Maluenda, a Chilean

agronomist, reported in November, 1958, that the agrarian reform had had only one result: the subdividing of property.[46]
Martínez Márquez, writing in June, 1961, concluded that after
eight years, the agrarian reform had not resulted in increased
production, lower prices of products, improvement in the living
conditions of the peasants, or lessened political tensions in the
country.[47] State interventionism in agriculture may have produced political consequences, however. Two Bolivian deputies
have charged that an "immense tonnage" of coca leaves are
being processed into cocaine in a factory in Santa Cruz, which
is managed by Senator Luis Sandoval Morón, the "right arm
of the government." The cocaine is allegedly exported to pay
for arms flown in from Cuba, stored in Santa Cruz and Cochabamba, and from there distributed in Bolivia, Peru, Chile, and
Argentina in preparation for other *fidelazos* (Castro-like coups).[48]
Finally, even Augusto Céspedes, one of the founders of the MNR
and editor of the official newspaper, *La Nación,* admitted that
the agrarian reform had produced *contraproducente* consequences (the reverse of expectations), at least in the rich
Cochabamba valley. He uses such words and phrases as the
following to describe what has happened: "Unproductive," "anarchy," "new tyranny," "disorder," "lower agricultural production," and "negative results." [49]

The "Great Revolution" and the Nationalization of the Tin Mines

In response to their enchantment with nationalization of the
means of production and the planned economy, the MNR seized
the three great tin interests—Patiño, Aramayo, and Hochschild
—on October 31, 1952.[50] Both evidence and logic argued strongly
against nationalization. The Bohan report (1942) concluded
without qualification that the three large companies ". . . . are
without a doubt superior to any staff which the Government of
Bolivia, alone or with official American assistance, could put into
the field." [51] However, the leaders of the MNR and their left-
wing supporters had the terms of an ideology to fulfill, and in

addition they could see that the companies were prosperous. They thought that by seizing the tin mines they would make a great killing. For example, Anaya—a Marxist-Leninist—declared that the nationalized mines would make enough money to pay for the agrarian reform; the electrification of the country; the colonization program; the construction of light and heavy industry; petroleum development; the building of schools, hospitals and the like on a "great scale"; and the development of water, air, and land transportation and communication.[52] Dr. Hernán Siles Zuazo, one of the founders of the MNR and President from 1956–1960, read a paper at the Universidad Mayor de San Simón in Cochabamba on October 11, 1954, in which he declared: "For many years, Bolivia will depend on the production of its extractive industry." [53] The best proof of the grandiose expectations of the MNR nationalizers and planners is found in the statement of the President of the Corporación Minera de Bolivia (COMIBOL), the state mining enterprise, made in 1959. Guillermo Bedregal asserted that from the very moment of the decree of nationalization it was their expectation to finance "all our ideals of social justice" through operation of the mines.[54]

The leaders of the MNR and their supporters had long depicted the tin companies as exploitative, imperialistic enterprises that contributed little to the welfare of the country. The decree of nationalization itself asserts that the tin companies paid to the government only a "tiny part" (*mínima parte*) of the value of tin exports. The companies, the decree states, "were practically exempt" from the payment of taxes. What they paid to the government would scarcely cover the most essential needs of the country, while the owners were "accumulating enormous fortunes" for themselves. The fact is that the mines before nationalization paid a large part of the taxes collected by the government. René Ballivián shows what the revenues were for the period 1921–44,[55] and even Anaya admits that the taxes the mines paid in 1948 amounted to 47.45 per cent of the total revenues of the government.[56] The Bohan report demonstrated that Bolivia, almost alone among tin-producing nations, taxed its exports of tin very highly. There were thirty separate tax laws dealing with export duties. The result was that twenty per cent of the CIF value of tin exported was returned to the government.[57]

Although the MNR did not formally nationalize the medium and small mines, almost the same effect was achieved by government policy. The Ford, Bacon, and Davis survey of 1956 said: "As a result of this extreme taxation of private mines, the government has maneuvered the significant private mines into a position where they are, in effect, nationalized without the government having the headaches of their operations." The government's take was often 100 per cent of the profits, and the survey found that 25 per cent of the mines were operating on a nonprofit basis as of June, 1956. The MNR took 41–56 per cent of net sales income without regard to the profit or loss of the mine or its replacement needs. In addition, the MNR established a complete monopoly of purchase and sales of all minerals, control over all imports of necessary equipment, and complete control of the Central Bank in regard to foreign exchange for the private mines. The number of small private mines declined by over 1,600 in the period 1953 through 1954. More would have ceased operations if it had been possible to do so without confiscation by the government. "The major reasons for these conditions are attributable almost entirely to the unfavorable political climate and adverse economic environment for private initiative and private investment." The Ford, Bacon, and Davis survey concluded: "No other country in the Western Hemisphere takes so much from industry profits, and no other mining country in the Western Hemisphere has created such a condition of exhausted working capital and lack of self-sustaining mine operations as has Bolivia."[58]

The management of the nationalized tin mines by the government of the MNR was an immediate and disastrous failure. As Víctor Andrade, long-time member of the MNR and Ambassador to the United States at the time, admitted in 1957, "Most of the tin mined since 1952 has been at a loss. . . . . Almost every pound of tin taken from the Bolivian mines since 1952 has been at a loss."[59] Utilizing figures supplied by Guillermo Bedregal,

President of COMIBOL,[60] I have prepared a chart that demonstrates what has happened through 1958:

RECORD OF MANAGEMENT OF NATIONALIZED BOLIVIAN TIN MINES

	TIN PRODUCED, KILOS, FINE	TIN EXPORTED COMIBOL	VALUE, TIN, COMIBOL
1952	27,346,902	25,245,369	$65,090,390
1953	26,034,007	29,974,273	61,360,919
1954	25,850,417	25,141,095	49,684,404
1955	23,484,543	23,793,512	48,035,681
1956	22,996,621	22,843,206	49,632,838
1957	21,648,353	22,389,816	45,488,068
1958	17,384,476	14,074,511	28,482,446

Although the above official figures do not go beyond 1958, studies of more recent COMIBOL statistical data indicate that the MNR has not been able to correct its mistakes. Production continues to decline. Costs continue to increase. One analysis (COMIBOL figures) shows a 59 per cent decline in production of the nationalized mines from 1952 to 1960.[61] Pacheco Arana, with the aid of official sources, concludes that the losses of the state enterprises from November, 1952, to December, 1959, amounted to 307,517,365,657 bolivianos.[62] Losing money on eighteen out of twenty nationalized mines in 1960, the government sustained a total loss for that year of 149,243,733,581.45 bolivianos.[63] According to Guillermo Bedregal Gutiérrez, President of COMIBOL, the loss was approximately $10,000,000 in 1960 and $60,000,000 for the entire period of state operation.[64] The cost of production for the years immediately preceding April 9, 1952, was estimated to be $.70 per pound. According to COMIBOL, the cost rose to $1.17 by 1959 and $1.29 by 1960.[65]

Why could private enterprise operate the tin mines profitably? Why have the state enterprises failed to do so? The question evokes agreement on some points and basic disagreement on others. Let us examine first the areas in which there is substantial agreement.

It cannot be denied that the MNR and its leftist supporters encouraged the belief for years that, when the state nationalized the tin mines, the workers would achieve "gains" such as higher wages, shorter hours, less discipline, less work, and more fringe benefits. Aside from the fact that the unions were led by Marxists-Leninists-Trotskyites and anarchosyndicalists for the most part, the masses of the workers wanted their gains, and at once. They got them.

A decree of December, 1953, created the so-called "worker control" *(control obrero)* under which the unions would elect representatives for one year to participate in the management of the mines. The consent of the *control obrero* was required for all personnel changes—hiring, firing, promotion, demotion, transfer; the *control obrero* must approve action on absenteeism, theft, sabotage; supervise allocation of housing, commissary supplies, distribution of mining materials and explosives; sign all purchase orders; check on health and safety conditions; report to union officials and workers; and he had the right of veto over management's actions. If the management should object, the issue is referred to COMIBOL and the miners' federation. If no agreement is reached, the case then goes to the Ministry of Mining. As the Minister of Mines is "always a leading member of the union" (for example, in 1961 the Minister of Mines was the Marxist Nuflo Chávez Ortiz), the records of the cases show that most of the decisions have favored the *control obrero*. I am indebted to the Ford, Bacon, and Davis report for the above data.

The report also asserts that ". . . . the mines are very much lacking in competent supervision, and the working conditions have greatly deteriorated." There was a decrease in underground labor efficiency averaging 15 per cent in the first five years of state operation of the mines. The working force of the nationalized mines continually increased, rising from 28,998 in 1952 to 34,500 in 1955. Safe practices and conditions were "much below minimum standards." The report declares that there was a lack of materials, lack of discipline, disrespect for safety rules, lack of enforcement authority, pilfering of critical materials, lack of safety training, and interference from political groups. There was an increase of 61 per cent in the frequency of fatal accidents per 1,000,000 shifts worked in 1955 as compared to 1953. The commissary *(pulpería* is the word used in Bolivia) subsidy in some mines amounted to more than the total direct mining and milling costs at the mine. The workers enjoyed eighty paid holidays in 1955.[66]

The findings of the Zondag and Freeman reports were essentially the same. Zondag found that contrary instructions poured in on the mine managers from many and different sources—the Minister of Mines, the Board of Directors of the Mining Corporation, the General Manager of the Mining Corporation, the union, and the *control obrero.* Labor had six channels of recourse to higher authority over their own management. The union exercised actual control over the commissary in many of the mines. The stealing of minerals and supplies was prevalent. There were daily interruptions of work for union meetings. The foremen and supervisors could not exercise their authority, as the unions refused to approve any dismissals. Many workers used up their sick leave at the urging of the unions. The mine doctors were afraid to reject workers with "subjective complaints" for fear of losing their jobs. Zondag found much "featherbedding" in COMIBOL's mines. The Freeman report indicated that the average mine worker earned almost as much as a cabinet officer, although the Bolivian miner produced only one-tenth that of a United States miner in a comparable type of work.[67]

When Siles Zuazo was president, he boasted about the social security "gains" Bolivian workers enjoyed. "I should like you to show me," he challenged, "any other underdeveloped country which has so high a percentage of its workers covered." [68] I would argue that it is hard work, low wages, saving, few fringe benefits, and productivity—all leading to capital accumulation—which is what underdeveloped countries need if they desire to improve themselves economically. President Siles Zuazo's own figures indicated that the Social Security system added greatly to the costs of production and contributed to the state's vast deficits. Zondag found that Social Security costs were 67.5 per cent of the employee's wage: Family subsidy, 13 per cent of wage; rent allowance, 14 per cent; social security, 5.5 per cent; professional risks, 5 per cent; two extra months' pay and other benefits, 10 per cent; Sundays and bonus holidays, 20 per cent. Ever since 1954, wages must be paid for seven days per week even if no work is performed by anyone on Sunday. Two months' extra salary are paid at the end of the year; medical and pharmaceutical supplies are furnished free if there are over 80 employees in the enterprise; regular wages are paid for 90 days to sick workers; 90 days' notice or three months' wages are required for dismissal; with proper notice a fired employee is entitled to one month's pay for each year with the company; if the employee has worked in one place for eight or more years, he gets this amount even if he resigns; finally, the employer is prohibited by decree from reducing the number of his employees.[69]

The psychology *(mentalidad)*, encouraged by the MNR, that to work less means to gain more, has resulted in a large number of strikes and work stoppages. Martínez Márquez estimates that the average number of strikes per year was 300 for the period 1952 to 1957. In 1958, the total was about 600.[70] The president of COMIBOL reports, somewhat sadly, that the union and its representative in the Ministry of Mines succeeded in getting $7,600,000 for "fictitious labor." [71] COMIBOL even resorted to an incentive system as a means of persuading the miners to work a little more. On October 31, 1958, the government announced that those workers who stayed on the job for a year would be granted a substantial increment. Some districts took advantage of the offer. Now, however, the union—the FSTMB—insisted that the offer represented a labor gain *(conquista laboral)* and demanded that all districts should receive the bonus, including those that had struck so much and done so little that the state enterprise suffered a $4,000,000 loss as a result of their activity.[72] Very recently the MNR has appealed to the unions to replace the *Tesis de Pulacayo,* which had a Marxist-Leninist proletarian revolution as its purpose, with the *Tesis de Telamayu,* which has as its purpose subordinating temporary workers' "gains" for the "vital necessities" of the *Revolución National.*[73]

Siles Zuazo argues that the reasons for the failure of the state to operate the mines economically are: low prices, insufficient capital, worn-out machinery, inadequate electrical power, and an excessive number of workers who are kept on because of "elementary social justice." [74] Beltrán and Fernández assert that what Bolivia imports costs about 300 per cent more than in 1945. Tin was selling for $.65 per pound in 1945; therefore, Bolivia should get three times that price of tin or $1.95 per pound just to "break even." [75] If this kind of argument is accepted, then it would follow that an international commodity or cartel agreement with the United States buying tin at high fixed prices would be logical. The United States has already purchased much tin from Bolivia for political purposes, and our stockpiles exceed strategic requirements (as of July, 1961) by about 150,000 tons.[76]

In any event, the contention that low prices explain state failure is erroneous. According to the *Statistical Bulletin* of the International Tin Council in London, except for the higher prices produced by the Korean "police action" in 1951 and 1952, the price per pound, fine, prior to expropriation was: 1948, $.98; 1949, $.98, and 1950, $.93. Since nationalization, "low prices" and the Soviet dumping of tin in 1957 and 1958 cannot explain the deficits of the Corporación Minera. Using the above source, we find that the price in 1953 was $.91; 1954, $.89; 1955, $.92; 1956, $.98; 1957, $.94; 1958, $.91; 1959, $.98; and 1960, $.99. Other explanations are put forth, but they are hardly credible. López Rivas, for example, blames the "democratic," "capitalistic," "monopolies" of foreign countries for the state's failures.[77]

Basic disagreement exists as to whether socialism or capitalism can best operate the means of production. All the independent studies, surveys, and reports that I have been able to read take the position that the inherent difficulties of socialism negate the possibilities of successful operation of the mines. The Keenleyside report, written before the MNR seized the mines, states: "Even if nationalization of the mining industry were theoretically desirable, it would be wholly impracticable in Bolivia under present conditions. The government has neither the financial resources nor the technical and administrative competence to undertake any such task." [78] The United States has supplied the MNR with more than $191,000,000 in financial assistance and promises more, but the management of the state mines still lacks technical and administrative competence. A lawyer's group within the MNR (La Célula de Abogados del MNR) issued a public statement in August, 1961, which accused the management of COMIBOL of such administrative ineptitude and dishonesty that state operation of the mines could only be termed "disastrous." The group called for the immediate resignation of the top officials, including Guillermo Bedregal, President of COMIBOL.[79]

All the recent reports assume that socialism will not prove economically viable and that therefore the MNR must return to a free economy. The Zondag report insists that a free economy is required ". . . . because only a free economy can stop the present drain caused by the activities of speculation and runners of contraband. Only a free economy can force people to work again instead of making a few pennies by standing in line. Only a free economy will create confidence in the foreign investor which, once established, will result in the Bolivian investor bringing back vast amounts of capital now hoarded abroad." [80] The Ford, Bacon, and Davis survey, the most complete and thorough of all the studies, asserts: "Both the technical and economic problems are surmountable, and the industry should be able to overcome its present difficulties provided the government takes the necessary steps in the available time to give Bolivia the economic and investment climate it needs." The same survey makes absolutely clear that it is not price or lack of subsidization that is causing the trouble: "It must be noted that during the past four years the nationalized mining of Bolivia has enjoyed the highest metal prices in the history of the industry, and, furthermore, the country has been subsidized by United States government tungsten contracts to the sum of about six and one-quarter million dollars annually. The Bolivian tin industry has been subsidized through all the Longhorn smelter contracts to an amount estimated at about three-quarters of a million annually." The survey concludes finally that Bolivia's only hope ". . . . is through revival of private mining activity." [81]

It is not only the nationalized tin mines that are mismanaged and deficit-ridden, but all the other socialized industries as well.

The president of COMIBOL stated in 1959 that 70 per cent of the economic activities of Bolivia were state-owned and operated. This figure included not only the mines but factories, railroads, the state oil enterprise and other activities.[82] Even in the face of the most overwhelming evidence that socialism is a failure in Bolivia, the United States has almost literally leaped to support the system. For example, the MNR called in Salzgitter A.G., a West German Government holding company with mining activities, to survey COMIBOL. There were some reports that Salzgitter might assume managerial responsibility under a production contract. At this time the Soviet Union allegedly announced that it was prepared to give Bolivia a $10,000,000 tin smelter. The United States almost instantly changed its policy position of refusing credits to COMIBOL as a state enterprise born of expropriation. The United States agreed to put up $10,000,000 for re-equipment and concentration plants as well as exploration work to find new tin deposits.[83]

The United States should have told the Bolivian planners and the unions—one of which threatened to march on the capital if the Soviet offer was not accepted—[84] that a tin smelter does not make economic sense for them. The Bohan report made this point clear as long ago as 1942. The Ford, Bacon, and Davis survey established that the direct operating costs of a tin smelter in Bolivia would involve an estimated $491 per fine ton, about 90 per cent higher than in foreign smelters, mainly because of the costs of imported materials and supplies. Also, there should be proved ore reserves for twenty-five years of operations in order to justify a smelter, something that is lacking in Bolivia.[85] Despite the evidence that the Soviet offer should have been described as spurious, the United States responded to the Communist "challenge" by establishing the important policy that this country is now prepared to subsidize nationalized industries whether just compensation is provided or not. Although the United States accepted Mexican expropriation of private oil properties with a token compensation, it had been a policy of this country, until President Kennedy's edict, not to reward confiscators.

What about payment for the expropriated mines? The government promised to pay in the decree of expropriation. The decree in Article 3 listed certain values that it said would be taken into account when a final settlement was reached. The government promised in Article 10 to reach a final settlement before December 31, 1953. In reaching the figure of real worth of the properties, the decree threatened in the preamble to subtract sums for alleged nonpayment of taxes or alleged noncompliance with fiscal provisions of the law in the past. Prior to settlement with the companies, the government promised in Article 11 to pay three per cent interest on the values described above, and in Article 12 to deposit in the Banco Central de Bolivia two per cent of the gross value of all minerals exported by the nationalized mines to be used as a fund to begin paying the owners of the mines for their property. Under the "retentions" system, the Patiño, Aramayo and Hochschild groups received through September, 1959, a total of $16,825,581.34, according to the President of COMIBOL.[86] Even these sums were apparently given grudgingly. The President of COMIBOL says they were paid as a "necessity" and an "imperative" in the face of "sabotage" and "judicial embargoes" initiated by the former owners.[87] As the New Frontier increases Bolivia's stipends under the foreign-aid program, there might be enough money to make up the deficits and even to pay the former owners for the mines.

There were other consequences of the *grandes conquistas* and *transformaciones profundas* of the MNR. When the state enterprises failed and incurred great deficits, the planners printed paper money. This had the effect of producing a fantastic inflation. By December 31, 1958, the *Revolución Nacional* had printed and put into circulation ninety times as many bolivianos as existed in 1952, when they seized power by force. The exchange rate in 1952 was reported to be about Bs 110—$1 up to Bs 160—$1 on the free exchange. By 1955, the exchange rate was up to about Bs 14,000—$1. On December 16, 1956, the government was persuaded to accept and put into effect a stabilization program devised by United States experts. The boliviano was to be stabilized at Bs 7,750—$1, but by January, 1959, the exchange rate was Bs 12,500—$1. The plan failed, even though the United States provided $25,000,000 to back up the boliviano. The Banco Central, as of March 31, 1952, had in its vaults 344,961 gold pounds sterling and 17,765 kilos in gold bars. By December 31, 1957, only 2,921 kilos of gold remained. An editorial in *Ultima Hora* dated January 3, 1959, asserted that not even an *adarme* (the sixteenth part of an ounce) of the gold remained.[88] According to official data, the general index of the cost of living in Bolivia (1953–100) had risen by August, 1960, exactly 3,031 per cent or 30.3 times.[89]

The "Great Revolution" and United States Foreign Aid

In the following quotations, I hope to provide some of the flavor of the United States foreign-aid program in Bolivia ($191,200,000 as of June 30, 1960) through a sampling of comments from a 1960 document of the United States Operations Mission to Bolivia [90] (emphasis mine).

In a letter from Rey M. Hill, Director, to Juan Haus Solís, Minister of Economic Affairs (1960), there is a reference to *"an inadequate control system."*

As of August 6, 1960, the Government of Bolivia/Distributors owed Bs. 16.5 billion. This amount has been outstanding two to four years.

As of August 6, 1960, Government of Bolivia/Distributors owed Bs. 4.1 billion. This amount has been outstanding three to four years.

A portion of the funds that was used to purchase new commodities has been *poorly handled.*

Also sight should not be lost that *the Government of Bolivia/Importers did not abide by the terms of payments* as outlined in these agreements.

. . . . *large sums were still outstanding. As of August 6, 1960, the Government of Bolivia/Importers owed Bs. 6.3 billion. This amount should have been paid two years ago to the stabilization account.*

The end results are that *poor records* were maintained, some of the *equipment was sold without accountability,* and the *sales proceeds used for other purposes.*

The Mission on a monthly basis since August, 1957, has requested the Government of Bolivia to provide information on the funds accruing to it. *To date no reports have been submitted.*

The largest single amount as of August 6, 1960, due the special account counterpart is *Bs. 9 billion owed by the Government of Bolivia/Y.P.F.B. for Avgas. This amount has been owed since 1958.*

In re United States dollar aid:

Co-operating governments usually assume the leading role to control the aid commodities/equipment and submit to the United States Mission reports regarding the arrival, distribution, usage, and storage of the commodities equipment. . . . *In Bolivia the information required for these purposes has not been furnished by the Government of Bolivia.*

Costly errors are in abundance

The real difficulty regarding the monitoring and auditing of local currency projects has been the failure of the project sponsor to establish a separate bank account for the project funds and to submit quarterly progress and financial statements. Here again the key to the solution lies with the Ministry of Economy. *One solution that is considered rather drastic is to cut off funds to the project until the project sponsor abides by the terms of the project agreement.* Less drastic would be an educational program of utilizing the press and word of mouth that any project agreement entered into must be abided by. *Since for six years most of the project sponsors have not abided by the reporting requirement of the agreements,* it is considered advisable to begin the educational program immediately, and if this measure is not effective, commence to take drastic steps to cut off funds beginning January 1, 1961.

As of August 6, 1960, the Mission had issued 210 reports containing 506 recommendations to the Bolivian Government. *"Unfortunately seldom have any of these recommendations been acted upon."*

ICA equipment valued at $20,500 *"remained in the ports for two years."*

No replies have been received to any of the above correspondence.

Many other recommendations pointing out misuse of funds, nonuse of equipment, etc., that have not been acted upon.
Since no reports have been forthcoming from the Bolivian Government on the amount of funds accruing for deposit. . . .

In re some Bs 3 billion:

This amount was not deposited to the special account counterpart in accordance with the economic assistance agreement between our two governments but was transferred directly to the Ministry of Finance.
Since the present handling of import duty funds *is not in conformity* with the Mutual Security Act of 1954. . . .
. . . . *the failure of the Government of Bolivia to provide reports of any nature or have the project sponsors abide by the terms of the project agreement.*

End-Use/Audit Reports:

It was necessary for this staff to work two and one-half years to account for the amounts owed by distributors who, as agents for the Government of Bolivia, sold the ICA food and cotton arriving during the 1954–1958 period. These reports are available to the Government of Bolivia. *They point out that Bs. 20.6 billion is still owed. . . . .* For the past year a part of the End-Use/Audit staff has field-checked the use of the ICA hardware items. These field checks have included two detailed surveys of the ICA commodities/equipment *that has remained for long periods of time in the Chilean and Peruvian ports.* . . . . . These reports point out *ICA financed equipment remaining in the ports from one to three years and deteriorating, equipment purchased for certain projects and remaining in its original crates for long periods of time after arriving in Bolivia, misuse of local currency funds, and failure to file insurance claims within the statutory period.*

A letter (n.d.) from Rey M. Hill, Director, to Juan Haus Solís, Minister of National Economy, refers to *manipulations of Counterpart Funds.*
In a letter from Jorge Tamayo Ramos, Minister of Economic

Affairs, to the Superintendent of Banks, dated June 6, 1960, in re Point IV funds: *"This action could be considered embezzlement with the aggravating circumstance of swindle."*

". . . . many irregularities have taken place."

Exhibit A—Montellano & Company: "Crédito Hipotecario *has illegally retained the amount of Bs. 52,262,420 for its own use."*

Exhibit C—American Export Company: "The report submitted by the Controller's Office End-Use Inspector states that two Willys Jeep Station Wagons were handed over to the Minister of Economy without sale slip.

"The Cochabamba Mayor's Office received two jeeps under the same condition."

Other recent United States government documents merit at least brief examination. Some of the words and phrases from the Selden-Fascell Report for the House Foreign Affairs Committee (1961) are: ". . . . great excess of miners. . . . inability to fire featherbedded laborers. . . . . decreased agricultural and mineral production, voluminous contraband traffic, inflationary monetary policies. . . . ." In regard to the Ford, Bacon, and Davis survey: "Due to political pressure . . . . the Bolivian Government took no action on the recommendations. The government's ability to implement its decisions is further handicapped by the existence of an armed militia of workers and peasants, infiltrated by Communists." On the United States aid program to Bolivia: "It should be tapered off as soon as possible, and assistance directed to specific projects." [91]

Some data relevant to the MNR in Bolivia may be found in the 1961 Hearings of the Subcommittee of the Committee on Appropriations of the House of Representatives. Although Dr. Gordon was an administration witness and favored the President's proposals for more aid for Bolivia, this exchange took place:

> Mr. Passman: "Did not some of your witnesses testify that Bolivia last year was near bankruptcy?"
> Mr. Gordon: "It was and is near bankruptcy."

Further on in the hearings:

Mr. Montoya: "And I notice where they were not suffering any paucity of funds because of such small revenues because last year Bolivia, under the mutual security program, received $23 million in special assistance. That is $2 million more than their total revenues. They received $8,870,000 in technical assistance, or a total of $31,870,000. But let us go further with respect to Bolivia.

"They received a loan from the DLF of $4 million. That far exceeds their total revenues.

"But let us go further than that. This is what adds to the shock—the Export-Import Bank loaned them, during 1958 and 1959, $47.3 million, or approximately, in total United States funds, a ratio of about 3 to 1."

Mr. Gordon, ". . . . It is true . . . . we have made, relative to the Bolivian Government revenues, enormous financial assistance in loans and grants together. The Bolivian case is, as I think I mentioned the other day, a particularly tragic case. None of us are happy with what happened there, either with respect to their own financial situation, or with respect to the failure so far of our aid program really to get the Bolivian economy even approaching getting on its feet. . . . . I am sure that the future policy should differ very substantially from the past policy in the Bolivian case." [92]

On the other hand, in neither public nor private Bolivian sources can one find anything even remotely approaching enthusiasm for the United States foreign-aid program. The kindest words are found in President Siles Zuazo's message to Congress in 1958. He made several very brief noncommittal references to United States aid and then finally used the phrase, "the generous co-operation of the people and North American Government," in respect to the program.[93] All the official Program of Government of the MNR for 1960–1964 says is, "The results obtained up to now are, in general, satisfactory." This is scant praise, and the next sentence says that the results can be improved by application of better methods.[94] Guillermo Bedregal, President of COMIBOL, says only (1959) that United States assistance is necessary to pay "public expenses." [95]

Mario Torres Calleja, Secretary General of the miners' union (the FSTMB) and a Trotskyite, has provided a detailed criticism of United States foreign aid to Bolivia. The truth, he argues, is that in large part the "aid" the United States sent to Bolivia was food and fiber products that the United States overproduced and channeled into Bolivia as a dumping ground. To administer the "aid," the United States has created a gigantic bureaucracy in Bolivia made up of "inept" and "ignorant" men who have contrived to waste the dollar aid so that all Bolivia sees of it are ciphers on paper. The "aid" never involved bringing machines or instruments of production. The United States' objective was simply to dispose of surplus farm commodities in order to solve the farm crisis and to "destroy the agriculture and national industries and frustrate the diversification program and self-sufficiency plans begun in 1952." The North American "experts" are characterized by "incredible ineptitude," the Eder plan for monetary stabilization was antinational and antiworker, and "imperialist control of the minerals market" has injured Bolivia. The union leader is against "Yankee plutocracy," "monopolists," and "multimillionaire Yankees." Torres concluded by saying that his union would continue the "anti-imperialist struggle, expressing its solidarity with the Cuban Revolution." [96]

Similar ideas are developed by Beltrán A. and Fernández B. in a serious study published in 1960. The principal reason for United States foreign aid in Latin America is to protect the 30, 40, and 50 per cent earnings "on capital invested" of "North American monopolies." As Latin America is of "enormous" importance to the "monopolies," the United States has put into play "a new form of slavery through the deceiving etiquette of American aid." The food program (of Public Law 480) is not disinterested. The purpose is twofold: (1) to permit the maintenance of high prices in the United States by "dumping" the surpluses in Latin America; and (2) to prohibit the development of a healthy agriculture in Latin America that might compete with the United States. In this way, it is possible to subjugate the Latin American countries and keep them in a perpetual state of dependency. The United States can use foreign aid to protect both its sources of raw materials in Latin America and also the markets for the manufactured goods of its "monopolistic enterprises." The United States uses "surplus food" *(excedentes agrícolas)* for the purpose of financing military dictatorship and furthering political corruption in order to guarantee a favorable climate for the investments of "North American monopolies." The United States also provides "technical assistance" to Bolivia, but the means employed are "absolutely fragmentary and superficial." The authors conclude that United States foreign aid has caused all the failures of the MNR. On the other hand, "the cause of the countries that fight for their liberation can count on the definite help of the socialist world, aid that is a guarantee of the success of an enterprise." [97]

Concluding Remarks

If it can be assumed that the foregoing analysis is supported by sufficient evidence to merit the judgment of substantial accuracy, then it becomes crystal clear that President Kennedy's "eulogy" of the *Revolución Nacional* as a "great revolution," which has "blazed a path for others to follow," is a profound blunder the consequences of which may prove disastrous for the United States. Undoubtedly the President was advised by trained, traveled, and talented specialists in Latin American affairs to write the letter, promise the aid, and praise the MNR. The names of such men and the reasons for their advice have not been revealed, however.

The *Revolución Nacional* is not a "great revolution." It has not "blazed a path for others to follow." It has lessened political liberty and retarded representative government. What is the direction of the present government? A scholar working in Bolivia writes (early 1961): ". . . . Paz Estenssoro, willingly or un-

wittingly, placed himself in the hands of the far left of the MNR";
and ". . . . the drift is toward the left." The same scholar's words
and phrases support the thesis of this paper that the MNR's system of socialism and the planned economy is an ignominious
fracaso or failure: "stagnating agrarian reform"; "plummeting
tin production"; "hyperinflation"; "rising cost of living"; "mass
exodus of professionals." [98]

The United States must have selected all its officials in Bolivia
from the ranks of "imbeciles" and the "deaf," "blind," and
"dumb" not to know what has happened in that country in the
past eight years, one Latin American writes.[99] Ramírez R. tells
us, "We view with surprise the measures adopted by the United
States, handing over enormous quantities of dollars to their own
enemies." [100] In the view of Siles Salinas, United States aid to
Bolivia is designed to provide an example to other Latin American countries of what not to do—seize land, nationalize, and
"plan." [101] One increasingly notes the use of the word *antie-
jemplo* (literally, "counterexample") in Latin American publications to describe the *Revolución Nacional* in Bolivia. The feeling
has assuredly developed, among some Latin Americans at least,
that the quickest way to debase a country's economy is to nationalize it. This may well be the only positive consequence of
the United States foreign-aid program in Bolivia.

I submit that the evidence does not and cannot support the
view that the MNR is a defender of the ideals and values of
American culture. Massive United States aid has nullified the
American policy of nonintervention in the internal affairs of
other countries in the Western Hemisphere. The aid program
has resulted in rendering the leaders of the MNR subject to
extended tutelage by selected United States officials. Even so,
no basic principles of the MNR have changed, and only a minute
impact on policy can be claimed.

I am aware of the fact that it can be argued that the political
authoritarianism of the 1952–1956 period has been moderated in
certain particulars. Some have insisted, erroneously in my judgment, that the presidential elections of 1956 and 1960 were
"democratic." The *reforma agraria* has so far permitted indi-

viduals to possess, if not to acquire legal title to, land, but there are influential elements in the MNR who agitate constantly for co-operatives or collectives. The public monopoly in oil has been mitigated to permit private exploration under prescribed circumstances. Some recognition of the value of private initiative is to be found in the Program of Government for 1960–1964. Furthermore, Dr. Rowland Egger, Special Representative of President Kennedy, addressed high officials in the Government of the *Revolución Nacional* in November, 1961, and said: "Bolivia is destined to a social and economic future of incomparable brilliance," (*La Nación,* La Paz, November 12, 1961). However, the basic principles and policies of the MNR, it must be reiterated, have resisted assault. Is there anything in the expanded program of aid to the public sector, to which President Kennedy has committed this nation, that will persuade the MNR to revise its principles and policies in a more fundamental and substantial way? In candor, one must recognize that, as of July, 1961, President Paz Estenssoro was reported to be intent upon soliciting $150,000,000 in aid from Premier Khrushchev and whatever else he might "cadge" from Red China.[102]

Foreign aid, overtly or unconsciously, has become an instrumentality of American foreign policy. If this is true, then it follows that the foreign-aid program should be used to defend and advance the interests of the United States. One of the few interests on which the executive and Congress and the great majority of American citizens seem to be agreed is that Communism should not inherit the earth. Modern-day Communism is principally Leninism, and much can be learned about its nature and tactics by examination of Lenin's *The State and Revolution* and *Imperialism: The Last Stage of Capitalism.* Communism operates as an international conspiracy with highly developed techniques of internal subversion and sophisticated employment of force and threats of force in international relations. Any country that demonstrates a desire to eradicate internal Communist subversion and external Communist pressure and coercion should be aided by the United States by specific measures designed to accomplish specific results.

However, some in the United States assume that the only way to prevent the Latin American countries from becoming Communist satellites is to extend massive support to left-wing, collectivistic movements. When the question is raised why such an assumption should be accepted, the reply usually given is that people are in a hurry to achieve the benefits of technology, and that rapid progress can be won only by permitting the government to control the means of production. In my opinion, this assumption can and should be challenged. Is not Japan developing more rapidly than India? From what I could see of East Germany with socialism and West Germany with capitalism (summer, 1960), the latter had "turned the clock back" to a superior economic system. Better still, visit the heartland of socialism, the Soviet Union. In so far as the great masses of human beings are concerned, the Soviet Union is a primitive, backward country. This was, at least, my own observational conviction. However, the best illustration of the falsity of the line of reasoning that the United States can oppose Communism only by supporting left-wing "revolutions" is seen in Bolivia. Massive aid has been given. The "public sector" has planned and expanded, but the results have been *contraproducente*.

The President of the United States has provided a considered solution to this dilemma: Extend even greater aid to left-wing political authoritarianism and economic socialism. To do this, to refer to the *Revolución Nacional* as a model, is to produce confusion and consternation among those public figures of virtue and integrity in Latin America who support principles of individualism, voluntarism, representative government, and private initiative and enterprise. Only the Marxists-Leninists and left-wing nativist collectivists, who seek to do in other Latin American countries what the MNR has done in Bolivia, can possibly derive aid and comfort from the policy of the United States. Bills have already been introduced in Chile to expropriate United-States-owned copper mines at a fraction of their real value, with payment to be provided indirectly through funds from the *Alianza para el Progreso* program.[103]

To those who argue that there are no alternatives, that there is only one course possible, I must insist that there is always another way, and not infrequently a better way. Such matters are appropriate considerations for another paper and should not unduly encumber the purposes and findings of this investigation. However, if the United States desires to inhibit the growth of Communism in Latin America through the expenditure of public funds, then it must make such funds available to those men who by conviction and policy oppose Communism. If the United States desires to spend public funds to aid other peoples to achieve higher material standards of living, it must make such funds available for governments and policies that make private initiative and enterprise possible. Books, documents, reports, interviews, and observation all lead me to conclude that Bolivia possesses the human and material resources appropriate for individual and collective life immensely superior to anything so far enjoyed in that country. The evidence suggests, in my opinion, that the *Revolución Nacional* cannot advance the good life, even with massive United States aid. At this point in the argument, the supporters of the MNR usually insist that withdrawal of foreign aid to the *Revolución Nacional* would instantly mean that Bolivia would become a Communist satellite. It is my judgment that United States support of the MNR has already led Bolivia closer to Communism than at any time in the history of the country, and that continued support of the men and policies of the *Revolución Nacional* will continue to advance the cause of Communism. If United States aid to Bolivia were withdrawn, the MNR would fall from power, and probably very quickly. Other Bolivians—talented, educated, competent, patriotic—and dedicated more to the ideals, values and objectives of the United States and the Western World than the MNR'ers, are ready to assume power. Those familiar with Latin America know who these men are. It is possible that they and not the Communists would emerge with control of the state.

NOTES

1. Office of the White House Press Secretary, for release to A.M. papers, Sunday, May 14, 1961, Monday, May 15, 1961.
2. *La Nación* (La Paz, 7 de mayo de 1961).
3. International Co-operation Administration, Office of Statistics and Reports, *United States Foreign Assistance and Assistance from International Organizations* (March 31, 1961), p. 60.
4. William S. Stokes, "The *Revolución Nacional* and the MNR in Bolivia," *Inter-American Economic Affairs* (Spring, 1959), pp. 28–30.
5. *New York Herald Tribune* (July 31, 1946).
6. For details and documentation of this episode, *see* Stokes, *op. cit.,* pp. 30–32.
7. Alberto Cornejo S., *Programas políticos de Bolivia* (Cochabamba, Bolivia: Imprenta Universitaria, 1949), p. 164. See also pp. 159–164, 170–175. Other relevant sources include: Nestor Taboada Terán, *Antología de cuentos de la revolución* (La Paz: Talleres Gráficos Bolivianos, Publicaciones SPIC, 1954), *passim;* República de Bolivia, *El libro blanco de la independencia económica de Bolivia* (La Paz: Subsecretaría Prensa, Informaciones y Cultura, 1952), p. 188; Secretaría Ejecutiva del Comité Político Nacional del MNR, *El pensamiento revolucionario de Paz Estenssoro* (La Paz: E. Burillo y Cía, 1954), p. 303; Saturnino Rodrigo, *Diario de la revolución nacional* (La Paz: Librería Editorial "Juventud," 1955), p. 389; Andrés Townsend Ezcurra, "La revolución nacionalista de Bolivia," *Humanismo* (México, D.F.: No. 1, jul., 1952), pp. 49–50; Alberto Ostría Gutiérrez, *The Tragedy of Bolivia* (New York: Devin-Adair Company, Inc., 1958), pp. 103–118.
8. Cornejo S., *op. cit.,* pp. 147–151. *See also* Walter Guevara Arze, *Plan de política económica de la revolución nacional* (La Paz: Ministerio de Exteriores y Culto, 1955), p. 200.
9. José Fellman Velarde, *Víctor Paz Estenssoro: El hombre y la revolución* (La Paz: Alfonso Tejerina, 1954), p. 95.
10. Augusto Céspedes, *El dictador suicida* (Santiago: Editorial Universitaria, S.A., 1956), p. 245.
11. *See* Carlos Montenegro, *Documentos* (La Paz: Imprenta "Nacional," 1954), pp. 50, 52–55, 62–71; Céspedes, *op. cit.,* pp. 246–249.
12. Hernán Siles Zuazo, "Hacia la planificación de la economía boliviana," *Revista de la Facultad de Economía y Finanzas* (Oruro, julio-diciembre de 1954), *passim.*
13. Hernán Siles Zuazo, *Mensaje al honorable Congreso Nacional, 6 Agosto 1958* (La Paz: Talleres de la Editorial del Estado, 1958), pp. 8, 34, 60, 85, 95, 101.
14. Jorge Siles Salinas, *Lecciones de una revolución. Bolivia: 1952–1959* (Santiago: Editorial Universidad Católica, 1959), pp. 59, 62.
15. *El Diario* (La Paz, 8 de mayo de 1961). See also *El Mercurio* (Santiago, 13 de marzo de 1961); Mario Padilla A., "El Movimiento Nacionalista

Revolucionario," *Semana* (21 de noviembre de 1960); *Tesis de Telamayu* (La Paz: n.p., 1960), pp. 1, 6; *Presencia* (La Paz, 30 de mayo de 1961); *La Prensa* (Buenos Aires, 22 de junio de 1961); Samuel Mendoza, "La situación en Bolivia," *El Mercurio* (Santiago, 9 de marzo de 1961); *El Diario* (La Paz, 17 de abril de 1961).

16. *Programa de Gobierno. Movimiento Nacionalista Revolucionario. Tercer Gobierno de la Revolución Nacional, 1960–1964* (La Paz: E. Burillo, 1960), pp. 113, 115–116, 121.

17. *El Diario* (La Paz, 12 de febrero de 1958; 14 de mayo de 1958; 16 de noviembre 1958); *El Mercurio* (Santiago, 25 de octubre de 1958; 2 de agosto de 1961); *La Prensa* (Buenos Aires, 13 de julio de 1961); *Crónica* (Cochabamba, 31 de julio de 1961); Ostría Gutiérrez, *op. cit.*, pp. 205–219.

18. *Ultima Hora* (La Paz, 11 de abril de 1958); Ostría Gutiérrez, *op. cit.*, pp. 137–140; *La Nación* (Buenos Aires, 11 de marzo de 1958).

19. *Ultima Hora* (28 de julio de 1961); *El Diario* (La Paz, 18 de diciembre de 1958); *Presencia* (La Paz, 13 de febrero de 1958).

20. *New York Times* (June 15, 1956); Ostría Gutiérrez, *op. cit.*, pp. 128–129.

21. *Ultima Hora* (La Paz, 21 de febrero de 1958). For a defense of the Siles Zuazo administration, *see* Siles Zuazo, *Mensaje al honorable Congreso Nacional, op. cit.*, pp. 116 and appendices.

22. *Ultima Hora* (La Paz, 2 de abril de 1958); *El Mercurio* (Santiago, 25 de octubre de 1958; 11 de abril de 1958); *Ultima Hora* (La Paz, 10 de abril de 1958); *La Prensa* (Lima, 23 de noviembre de 1958); *see* also *El Diario* (La Paz, 16 de noviembre de 1958); Pedro Zilveti Arce, *La hora de la verdad* (n.p., 1958), pp. 13–16; Ostría Gutiérrez, *op. cit.*, pp. 219–220.

23. *Ercilla* (Santiago, 8 de septiembre de 1955); *see also* Mario Padilla A., "El Movimiento Nacionalista Revolucionario," *Semana* (Noviembre 21, 1960).

24. *Ultima Hora* (La Paz, 20 de octubre de 1958).

25. *La Prensa* (Buenos Aires, 18 de junio de 1961).

26. *El Diario* (La Paz, 3 de enero de 1961).

27. Cornelius H. Zondag, *Problems in the Economic Development of Bolivia* (La Paz: 1956), pp. 24, 42, 156–157.

28. Fausto Beltrán A. and José Fernández B., *¿Donde va la reforma agraria boliviana?* (La Paz: Talleres Gráficos Bolivianos, 1960), pp. 24, 185–186, 215.

29. Guillermo Bedregal, *La nacionalización minera y la responsabilidad del sindicalismo* (La Paz: n.p., 1959), p. 23; Guillermo Martínez Márquez, "El dilema boliviano," *La Prensa* (Buenos Aires, 4 de junio de 1961); *Crónica* (Cochabamba, 19 de junio de 1961); *La Prensa* (Buenos Aires, 18 de junio de 1961; 22 de junio de 1961; 13 de julio de 1961); *La Prensa* (Lima, 12 de agosto de 1961); *El Mercurio* (Santiago, 6 de julio de 1961).

30. *El Diario* (La Paz, 18 de agosto de 1960).

31. *La Prensa* (Buenos Aires, 16 de diciembre de 1960); Guillermo Martínez Márquez, "Bolivia en 'estado de sitio' otra vez," *La Prensa* (Buenos

Aires, 3 de marzo de 1961); *Crónica* (Cochabamba, 19 de junio de 1961); *La Prensa* (Buenos Aires, 18 de junio de 1961; 22 de junio de 1961; 13 de julio de 1961; 13 de agosto de 1961); *El Mercurio* (Santiago, 12 de agosto de 1961); *La Prensa* (Lima, 3 de agosto de 1961); *El Diario* (La Paz, 3 de agosto de 1961).

32. Zondag, *op. cit.,* pp. 78–79.
33. Beltrán A. and Fernández B., *op. cit.,* p. 18.
34. *See* Stokes, *op. cit.,* footnote, p. 38.
35. Zondag, *op. cit.,* p. 59.
36. Zondag, *op. cit.,* annex to chap. V, pp. 1–14, 150.
37. *Programa de Gobierno, op. cit.,* p. 41.
38. Stokes, *op. cit,* pp. 39–40.
39. Stokes, *op. cit.,* p. 41.
40. Roger A. Freeman, *The Revenue Problem of Bolivia* (ms. report by the Tax and Revenue Adviser, U.S. Fiscal Mission to Bolivia, La Paz, April 12, 1957. Supplement to Final Report on Assignment in La Paz, November 17, 1956, to April 24, 1957, dated April 29, 1957), *passim.*
41. Beltrán A. and Fernández B., *op. cit.,* pp. 58–71.
42. Siles Zuazo, *Mensaje al honorable Congreso Nacional, op. cit.,* p. 35.
43. Beltrán A. and Fernández B., *op. cit.,* pp. 75–76.
44. *Programa de Gobierno, op. cit.,* p. 44.
45. Beltrán A. and Fernández B., *op. cit.,* p. 83.
46. *El Mercurio* (Santiago, 24 de noviembre de 1958).
47. Guillermo Martínez Márquez, "El dilema boliviano," *La Prensa* (Buenos Aires, 4 de junio de 1961).
48. *La Prensa* (Lima, 12 de agosto de 1961). See also: *La Razón* (Buenos Aires, 2 de agosto de 1961).
49. *La Nación* (30 de octubre de 1960).
50. For the names of the companies that were seized and other details, *see* Stokes, *op. cit,* pp. 43–44.
51. Merwin L. Bohan, *Report of United States Economic Mission to Bolivia* (August, 1942), Pt. IV, p. 4.
52. Ricardo Anaya, *Nacionalización de las minas de Bolivia* (Cochabamba: Imprenta Universitaria, 1952), p. 338.
53. *See* Siles Zuazo, "Hacia la planificación de la economía boliviana," *op. cit.,* pp. 23–63.
54. Guillermo Bedregal, *La nacionalización minera y la responsabilidad del sindicalismo* (La Paz: n.p., 1959), p. 9.
55. René Ballivián C., *Tasas e impuestos sobre la industria minera en Bolivia* (La Paz: Otero y Otero y Calderón, 1946), p. 239. On the other hand, *see* the MNR position in Fernando Díez de Medina, *Pachukiti y otras páginas polémicas, con la denuncia por defraudación de impuestos contra los multimillonarios Patiño y Aramayo* (La Paz: n.p., 1948), p. 189.
56. Anaya, *Nacionalización de las minas de Bolivia, op. cit.,* p. 30.
57. Bohan, *op. cit.,* Pt. VI, pp. 31–32.
58. Ford, Bacon, and Davis, Inc., *Report on Mining Industry of Bolivia, Ministry of Mines and Petroleum* (La Paz: not published, 1956, 9

volumes), Vol. II, *Significant Aspects of the Bolivian Mining Industry*, pp. 25–35; Vol. I, *Summary*, pp. 14–15.

59. Víctor Andrade, "Bolivia and the Future," Address, Cosmopolitan Club of Pennsylvania State College, February 23, 1957, *Congressional Record* (March 14, 1957), p. A2095; Address, Morgan State College, Baltimore, April 17, 1957, *Congressional Record* (May 22, 1957), p. A3923.

60. Bedregal, *La nacionalización minera y la responsabilidad del sindicalismo, op. cit.*, Appendix.

61. *Ultima Hora* (La Paz, 11 de marzo de 1961).

62. René Pacheco Arana, "La nacionalización de las minas," *Presencia* (La Paz, 11 de abril de 1961).

63. *La Nación* (La Paz, 19 de agosto de 1961).

64. *Presencia* (La Paz, 28 de julio de 1961).

65. Pacheco Arana, *op. cit.*

66. Ford, Bacon, and Davis, Inc., *Report on Mining Industry of Bolivia, op. cit.*, Vol. III, *Significant Aspects of Bolivian Mining Industry*, pp. 27–28, 43–44, 73–77, 83–85.

67. Zondag, *Problems in the Economic Development of Bolivia, op. cit.*, pp. 97–100; Freeman, *The Revenue Problem of Bolivia, op. cit.*

68. Siles Zuazo, *Mensaje al honorable Congreso Nacional, op. cit.*, pp. 78–79.

69. Zondag, *Problems in the Economic Development of Bolivia, op. cit.*, p. 169.

70. Guillermo Martínez Márquez, "Bolivia en 'estado de sitio' otra vez," *La Prensa* (Buenos Aires, 3 de marzo de 1961).

71. Bedregal, *La nacionalización minera y la responsabilidad del sindicalismo, op. cit.*, pp. 26–29.

72. *Ibid.*, pp. 44–46.

73. *Tesis de Telamayu* (La Paz: n.p., 1960), pp. 1–7.

74. Siles Zuazo, "Hacia la planificación de la economía boliviana," *op. cit.*, p. 41; Siles Zuazo, *Mensaje al honorable Congreso Nacional, op. cit.*, p. 17.

75. Beltrán A. and Fernández B., *op. cit.*, p. 169.

76. *Hanson's Latin American Letter* (Washington, D.C.: July 22, 1961, Number 853).

77. Eduardo López Rivas, *Esquema de la historia económica de Bolivia* (Oruro: n.p., 1955), pp. 191, 202.

78. H. L. Keenleyside, Head of Mission, *Report of the United Nations Mission of Technical Assistance to Bolivia* (New York: UN, 1951), pp. 48–49.

79. *El Diario* (La Paz, 3 de agosto de 1961).

80. Zondag, *Problems in the Economic Development of Bolivia, op. cit.*, p. vii.

81. Ford, Bacon, and Davis, *Report on Mining Industry of Bolivia, op. cit.*, Vol. II, *Significant Aspects of the Bolivian Mining Industry*, pp. 2–4; Vol. I, *Summary*, p. 15.

82. Bedregal, *La nacionalización minera y la responsabilidad del sindicalismo, op. cit.*, pp. 53–54.

83. *New York Times* (January 11, 1961).

84. *Presencia* (La Paz, 5 de noviembre de 1960).
85. Ford, Bacon, and Davis, Inc., *Report on Mining Industry of Bolivia, op. cit.,* Vol. I, *Summary,* p. 48.
86. Bedregal, *La nacionalización minera y la responsabilidad del sindicalismo, op. cit.,* Appendix.
87. *Ibid.,* p. 38.
88. For documentation of the details of the Bolivian inflation, *see* Stokes, *op. cit.,* pp. 46–47.
89. Beltrán A. and Fernández B., *op. cit.,* p. 128.
90. *Memorandum for Information and Action of the United States Aid Program* (United States Operations Mission to Bolivia, September 1, 1960), in Spanish and English, pages not numbered consecutively throughout.
91. *Special Study Mission to Latin America: Venezuela, Brazil, Argentina, Chile, Bolivia, Panama,* Report by Hon. Armistead I. Selden, Jr., Alabama; Hon. Dante B. Fascell, Florida (Washington, D.C.: United States Government Printing Office, 1961), pp. 24–31, *passim.*
92. *Inter-American Programs for 1961; Denial of 1962 Budget Information, Hearings before the Subcommittee of the Committee on Appropriations, House of Representatives, 87th Congress, First Session* (Washington, D.C.: United States Government Printing Office, 1961), pp. 116, 266.
93. Siles Zuazo, *Mensaje al honorable Congreso Nacional, op. cit.,* pp. 43–44, 90, 92, 106.
94. *Programa de Gobierno, op. cit.,* p. 141.
95. Bedregal, *La nacionalización minera y la responsabilidad del sindicalismo, op. cit.,* p. 42.
96. *El Diario* (La Paz, 17 de abril de 1961).
97. Beltrán A. and Fernández B., *op. cit.,* pp. 9, 124–125, 174–184, 210–211, 217, 219.
98. Richard W. Patch, "Bolivia Today—An Assessment Nine Years After the Revolution," *American Universities Field Staff,* Vol. VIII, No. 4 (1961), pp. 4, 7, 10–11.
99. *Crónica* (Cochabamba, 5 de junio de 1961).
100. *La Mañana* (Asunción, 14 de abril de 1961).
101. Siles Salinas, *Lecciones de una revolución, op. cit.,* p. 43.
102. *El Mercurio* (Santiago, 4 de julio de 1961).
103. *Hanson's Latin American Letter* (Washington, D.C.: August 19, 1961, No. 857).

9

Trade-Unionism and the "Public Sector"

Sylvester Petro

For the United States, as for the world as a whole, the great issue of the twentieth century involves the role of the state in society. The fundamental alternatives are two: on the one hand, the totally empowered state, with socialism as the pure example; on the other, the strictly limited state, with laissez faire as the pure example. In the United States, this issue is more clearly drawn than in other countries of the Western world, for this country has a definite and increasingly articulate body of coherent laissez-faire opinion. But here too the issue is usually drawn in terms involving something less than the polar extremes. Most commonly it is drawn between the *ad hoc* interventions of the uncertain welfare state and those who resist each new proposal for intervention on particular grounds rather than on the basis of general principle.

The fundamental issue has taken a new form in the current debate in the United States between those who contend that the "public sector" is being "starved" and those who resist proposals for increased government expenditure because they feel that the "private sector" is being aborted by excessive taxation and other forms of government intervention. Of all participants in this dispute, the leaders of the large trade-unions are perhaps in the most interesting and the most uncomfortable position. They are fundamentally a part of the "private sector," with the long-run prospects for trade-unions essentially dependent upon the well-being of that sector. Yet they are politically and ideologically allied with the proponents of expansion of the "public sector"; moreover, they gain many short-run benefits from an active public sector.

Long-run considerations tend to influence the conduct of only a relatively few persons—those with a high degree of courage and statesmanship, men of intelligence and imagination. Such men are not to be found among the leadership of the large trade-unions in the United States. Many of those leaders adhere consciously to the Keynesian dictum that "in the long run we shall all be dead." The less literate trade-union leaders, unacquainted with Keynes, nevertheless act in accordance with the dictum because it is natural to them to prize short-run gains. All trade-union leaders are conscious that they, as individual persons, owe their present power and position largely to the kind of governmental favoritism that they can expect only from those who favor expansion of the public sector.

Although such expansion will diminish the position of all private associations in the long run, including trade-unions, the present leadership of the large trade-unions without exception is allied with the statists. Occasionally one hears of a high trade-union official who has praised the free-enterprise system. But this is only talk. No matter what form the ultimate issue may take in current events—federal intervention in education, in housing, in agriculture, in medicine, or in the regulatory areas—the leaders of the large trade-unions are always among the most vocal proponents of government expansion. As the most active lobbyists in the country today, their efforts are not confined to the merely vocal. Their political power and their political efforts are valued highly by the politicians they help, and dreaded profoundly by those they oppose.

If statism ultimately destroys the free society, the present leaders of the large trade-unions will have played a part in the destruction. Their part will not, however, have been either fundamental or critical. While they sometimes set destructive measures in motion, they are more a product than a cause of the measures that tend to destroy personal freedom and to advance socialism. The basic challenge for the opponents of statism and socialism is posed, not by the present leadership of the large trade-unions, but by the ideas and the measures which have brought the public sector to its pre-eminent position in society, and which have, along the way to this end, also given to trade-unions temporary powers and privileges that they cannot have at all in a coherently operated free society and that they cannot long retain in a system of totally empowered government.

A. *Reflections on the Concepts Involved*

The dispute over public versus private spending presupposes that there is something that can be usefully defined as the "public sector" and something else that can be defined as a "private sector," distinct from the former. As a matter of fact, a sharp distinction between the two does exist—but only in the theory of laissez faire. Laissez-faire theory holds that the state's authority and responsibility extend only to keeping the peace—safeguarding domestic tranquillity, providing for the common defense, and administering justice in private disputes among citizens. Here one finds a sharp distinction between the "public sector" and the "private," for all the rest belongs to the realm of free personal choice.

The same is, of course, not true of socialism, or of the incipient socialism known as the welfare state. Under socialism the direction of society is determined by the government, which has exclusive ownership and control of the means of production. Some socialists insist that their system will promote civil liberties even more effectively than the theory of limited government does. But printing presses are means of production, and if the state owns and controls all means of production, including printing presses, how can one seriously contend that civil liberties will endure? No, there can be no "private sector"—as tradition defines the term—under socialism. There can only be a public sector, with all expenditure and all activity determined by or under the tutelage of the central bureaucracy.

Current protagonists of the public sector in the United States commonly dissociate themselves from socialism. Professor Arthur Schlesinger, for example, has recently said that expansion of the public sector is today in fact the best method of avoiding full socialism. But this position, too, cannot be taken seriously. The welfare state is built around the assumption that it is the duty of government to take care of all serious matters that cannot be left to the "unreliable" and "unpredictable" operation of the free market. Sometimes advocates of the welfare state declare that under their philosophy it is the duty of government to do for people all those things which they cannot do for themselves, or which they cannot do as well as government can.

Fundamentally, there is only one function possible to government that private persons cannot perform. That is the basic function that laissez faire allots to government: the function of keeping the peace by discouraging lawbreakers at home and invasion from abroad. Individual persons cannot do this; only the agency representing the full power of society can do it; and that agency is called government. Since proponents of the welfare state and other advocates of expansion of the public sector obviously reject this method of delimiting the function of government, they must have something else in mind.

In exploring their position, one discovers that however much they may dissociate themselves from full socialism, that system is the inevitable outcome of their program. This conclusion is rigorously compelled by the inner workings of the system known as the welfare state. If the government takes from A to increase the well-being or security of B, A's ability to provide for himself is diminished. If the state could somehow draw to a sharp halt after aiding only B with A's resources, A might still be able to provide for himself. He would not necessarily be forced to go to the state in his own turn for help. But both logic and experience establish that the state cannot come to a halt after aiding B. C and D and E and F and so on all feel that their claims are as exigent and as meritorious as B's. The farmers who insist on subsidies today contend that they are injured by the tariffs that protect manufacturers and the special privileges that the government has given trade-unions. On the local level, those who play golf insist that the county government should provide public golf courses, since it provides so many other public facilities. Soon the bowlers and the ping-pong players will see the injustice of a system that taxes them to help the golfers.

When the United States government assumed responsibility for the economic security of superannuated workers, it established a premise and a precedent with implications that only full socialism can exhaust. Medical care for the aged cannot be neglected by a government that has assumed general responsibility for old-age security. If for the aged, why not for the young? For after all, "a nation's future lies in its young people." With each advance along the frontiers of the welfare state, the private citizen's ability to take care of his own problems diminishes, and his incentive to go to the government increases.

The chief popularizer of "public sector" arguments, Professor J. K. Galbraith, has admitted that socialism and the welfare state provide no method of distinguishing between the "private" and the "public" sectors. In *The Affluent Society,* he said:

There will be a question as to what is the test of balance—at what point may we conclude that balance has been achieved in the satisfaction of private and public needs. The answer is that no test can be applied, for none exists.[1]

Professor Galbraith goes on, however, to insist that "The present imbalance is clear," notwithstanding his admission that there is no test for detecting whether an imbalance exists. And then he proceeds to assert, despite the inherent contradiction of his position: "The direction in which we move to correct matters is utterly plain." [2]

Many have observed that in the last fifty years or so the percentage of national product spent by government has increased from less than ten to more than thirty. In view of this fact, disinterested persons might well take the position that, while

Professor Galbraith is correct in detecting an imbalance, the imbalance is precisely the opposite of the one he identifies: that is, government is spending too great a portion of the national product, rather than too little, as Professor Galbraith suggests.

Be that as it may, Professor Galbraith's position amounts to a concession that the size and scope of the "public sector" are to be left to the exigencies of politics and to the judgment of those who advise the politically powerful. The long-term result of such a policy is clear. If the distinction between the private sector and the public sector is not defined in the sharp terms provided by laissez-faire theory, it must disappear entirely, until there is only the public sector of full socialism. Human needs and desires constitute a continuum. Once the state sets itself the task of serving those needs, there is no logical or practical place to stop. Furthermore, each new activity of the welfare state, benefiting some at the expense of others, creates an ineluctable force for more of the same kind of thing. The protagonists of the public sector, whether consciously or not, are moving toward a system that can tolerate no other sector. There will be a public sector, and that is all.

B. *Trade-Unions in the Advanced Welfare State*

There is no place for free, autonomous, independent trade-unions in the society that contains only a public sector. On this, experience in the United States and other countries leaves little room for doubt. In joining forces with those who seek expansion of the public sector, the trade-union leaders are engaging in a self-destructive process.

More markedly than any other private economic association, trade-unions are engaged in a blunt and naked pursuit of self-interest. Their conduct is, in fact, animated by a public-be-damned attitude. Strikes have been timed more and more of recent years to impose a maximum of inconvenience to the public. Strike records during time of war have been shameful, if not treasonous. So reserved a man as Senator John L. McClellan has recently referred to union practices at missile bases as "damnable." Attempts by government officials to induce moderation in the wage demands made by union officials have been met repeatedly with scorn and abuse.

This kind of selfishness will go unchecked by government only in a laissez-faire society, which depends upon competition to punish such arrogant stupidity. In the total state, whether of the socialist or advanced interventionist type, it will simply not be permitted.

It may be possible in the total state for trade-unions to have a formal existence, although even that is doubtful. What is not doubtful at all is that associations of wage earners will not be permitted to embarrass or hamper the planners of the total state by throwing cost and production schedules into confusion. When Peter Wiles wrote his interesting article, "Are Trade Unions Necessary?" (*Encounter*, September, 1956) he was operating within the assumptions of the British welfare state. There is nothing surprising, that being the case, in the fact that his answer was, "No."

There is already plenty of evidence that free trade-unionism cannot survive advanced welfare-state conditions, even in the United States, where the political influence of the leaders of the large trade-unions is so great.

While trade-unions continue to be the beneficiaries of special legal privilege, the course of regulatory development over the last twenty years in the United States has all been in a single direction, even so far as trade-unions are concerned. Governments at all levels have limited more and more the kinds of action permitted to trade-unions. As early as 1940, some states began passing laws prohibiting to unions conduct that the common law would permit, such as stranger picketing and secondary boycotts. After the Second World War a number of states adopted statutes or constitutional amendments prohibiting the closed shop. The Taft-Hartley Act of 1947 was by no means the "slave labor law" that unions called it; nevertheless, it too constituted a genuine restriction of the scope of union action. Between 1947 and the present, the movement toward greater and greater restrictions upon unions has continued, culminating in the Landrum-Griffin Law of 1959. That law in some ways only made definite the restrictions that the Taft-Hartley Act had intended, but in other ways it introduced new types of regulation, as for example in defining relationships between unions and their members. Those union leaders who clamor for greater governmental activity may not realize it, but the habit of governmental intervention that they encourage will necessarily affect their own operations.

They may hope that the advanced welfare state will intimately affect the operations of all other segments of society, while leaving them alone, but this is almost certainly doomed to frustration. Before the interventionist developments that began in the twenties and thirties of this century, injunctions were never issued against peaceful strikes for higher wages.[3] In the last thirty years, however, such injunctions have become more and more frequent. Indeed, it is no longer clear that there is a basic right to strike, even in a peaceful way for legitimate objectives. The Taft-Hartley Act specifically empowers the federal courts to issue injunctions against all strikes imperiling the national health and safety, even though such strikes are carried on in a lawful way for lawful objectives. The Railway Labor Act severely limits the right to strike. Many states have laws prohibiting strikes by employees of public utilities. When railroad employees refused to terminate a strike despite exhortations from President Truman, he demanded from Congress a law drafting them into the military. His intention was to force the railroad employees to work because their strike interfered with the government's notion of the needs of the nation.

These examples have all been drawn from cases of private employment. When one turns to public employment, the point emerges much more clearly. The Taft-Hartley Act expressly prohibits strikes by public employees. Several states, including the advanced welfare state of New York, have similar, express prohibitions. Thus the Condon-Wadlin statute in New York contains the following language:

It shall be unlawful for any public employees to strike or to engage in any attempt to change working conditions where such effort would interfere with the full and proper performance of their duties of employment. The Act applies to all employees of the state, cities, towns, villages, public schools, public or special districts, authorities, boards of commissions, and any other political or civil subdivision of the state. No person having authority or supervision over public employees shall have power to authorize or consent to any strike.

Taking existing court decisions as a guide, one may conclude that the same rule will be applied even in states that do not have specific prohibitions of strikes by public employees. The courts in a number of states have ruled that strikes by civil servants of all kinds are unlawful even with no express statutory prohibition.

Intelligent and responsible union leadership would presumably be informed of these developments, and being informed, would tend to resist expansion of both the public sector and the habit of interventionist regulation. This expectation is strengthened when one considers the large stake that unions have in a prosperous and flourishing "private sector."

C. *The Trade-Union Stake in the Private Sector*

Of the total membership of the large trade-unions in the United States, well over ninety per cent is in private employment. Most of the large unions exclusively represent workers employed by private business. For the steelworkers, the automobile workers, the machinists, and any number of other union members, the health and prosperity of the "private sector" are really all that count.

This is true not only from the point of view of the working man as producer; it is equally true of the working man and his family as consumers. All the goods they consume and a large part of the services they use are produced and provided by private industry.

Real wages are ultimately determined by productivity. As society advances technologically, productivity increases become almost exclusively a function of capital investment in ever more efficient factories and machinery. But capital accretions and investments in a free-enterprise, private-property system will flourish only in an environment of strictly limited government. Heightened taxation and regulation, necessarily associated with expansion of the public sector, drastically restrict profits and therefore capital investment. Although the national product has grown over forty per cent in the last twelve years in the United States, profits after taxes remain the same today that they were ten years ago. Politicians today complain of the poor growth record of the economy in the last few years. Portents for the future are even more ominous, if present taxes and regulations continue. The long-run prospects for real wages are necessarily the same.

While depressing profits, expansion of the public sector tends substantially to raise the prices of all goods and services, with devastating consequences for the union member as a consumer. The prodigious construction activities in the public sector— roads, bridges, tunnels, schools, and other public buildings— have pushed up prices significantly in the building and construction industry. The effect has been magnified by the notorious waste of both manpower and materials that all government construction entails. The costs of private housing have therefore risen greatly, so much so that the private part of the construction industry is in a depressed condition. Providing an excellent example of the self-energizing character of the "public sector," the high costs of housing directly attributable to government are seized upon as a justification for expansion of government's role in the private housing field.

To some extent expansion of the public sector is financed by inflation rather than by taxation, but the effect on prices is similar in either case. Prices go up universally, and the union member is, of course, affected in largely the same way as all other consumers, although, if his union is powerful enough and unscrupulous enough to exact monopoly wages, he is not hurt as badly—at least, not in the short run—as those consumers who have more or less fixed incomes. Even for the beneficiary of monopoly wages, however, the inflationary consequences of expansion of the public sector are damaging. One often hears members of the steelworkers' union or of the construction unions complain about the high cost of repairs to their washing machines or television sets. At the same time their union leaders are insisting that the trouble with President John F. Kennedy's program is that it does not go far enough in expanding minimum wages and other governmental activities.

Expansion of the public sector in the long run depresses wages on the whole and raises prices on the whole. Yet union leaders are among the most active proponents of such expansion. Why?

D. *In Bondage to the Welfare State*

The leaders of the large trade-unions in the United States work against the long-run interests of both the membership and trade-unionism itself for three reasons. First, there is a strong socialist bias in the thinking of many union leaders, reinforced by an abysmal ignorance of the basic truths of political economy. Second, to many trade-unions, interventionism provides great opportunities for lucrative short-run returns. Third, the extreme power that many union leaders now possess stems from special governmental privileges that can be maintained only by alliance with advocates of the welfare state who either formally or informally exact co-operation as a condition of the maintenance or enlargement of the special privileges.

The socialist inclinations of a large number of important union leaders are a matter of public record and need little elaboration here. Men such as David Dubinsky, of the International Ladies Garment Workers' Union, and Walter Reuther, of the United Automobile Workers, seem to be animated by socialist principles and convictions. While they consider themselves deadly enemies of the Communists, the Communists do not consider them enemies at all, but rather instruments in the inevitable socialist triumph. The United States Communist Party Convention had this to say of them:

To a degree the co-operation of labor reformists [trade-union leaders who stand for capitalism and with no socialist background or traditions], social reformists [those labor leaders like Dubinsky, Reuther, Randolph, et cetera, who have a socialist background], and bourgeois reformists [liberal wing of the Democratic Party] in such organizations as Americans for Democratic Action is, in the absence of a mass social democratic party in the United States, and under the conditions prevailing in our country, performing the function of social democracy." 4

The allegiance to the public sector of such men as Reuther and Dubinsky is perfectly natural. Their essential goal appears to be less the preservation of the free society and of such institutions as free trade-unionism than the advancement of socialism; and they are quite right in judging that the quickest way to socialism in the United States is by means of an ever expanding public sector.

Men such as George Meany, president of the AFL–CIO, and James Hoffa, president of the Teamsters, are in a different and more complicated position. Both these men are probably sincerely antisocialist, anticommunist; both probably feel a preponderant allegiance to the free-enterprise system and to trade-unionism. Their alliance with interventionism is accounted for in part by economic illiteracy, in part by the short-run gains that interventionism promises, and in part by the realization that they must co-operate with interventionists if they wish to retain the special privileges that law and inadequate law enforcement now provide them. What is true of such men as Meany and Hoffa is probably also true of the vast majority of union leaders in the country.

When men are unemployed, and especially when union members are unemployed, these union leaders never engage in a scholarly study of the basic causes of that unemployment. Least of all do they direct their attention to their own probably critical role in that unemployment. Publicly, at least, they deny that monopolistic wage levels are a cause of unemployment and of "distress areas." Moreover, no trade-union leader, to my knowledge, has ever admitted, let alone suggested, that excessive taxation of businessmen may be a cause of unemployment.

Instead, their uniform reaction is to seek political aid. They petition the government to embark upon vast construction projects, to raise the minimum wage, to give help to distressed areas, to increase the level of unemployment compensation, to bar imports to competitive nations, to "buy American," or in a myriad of other ways to expand public spending or to increase governmental direction and control of the economy.

The apparent effect in the short run is what interests them. Note that I have said the "apparent" short-run effect. I emphasize the point because most of the measures that such union leaders propose or support do not have any true value to working men even in the short run. If the government spends a billion dollars to bring industry to distressed areas in West Virginia and Tennessee, a harmful effect is felt immediately elsewhere in the economy. The billion dollars is taxed away from other citizens, for one thing; and the areas that do not receive governmental assistance are competitively injured by the recipients of government aid. Steelworkers in Cleveland, in short, will be harmed by the aid that government gives to miners in West Virginia. But the steelworkers themselves will not understand why they are on a short workweek; and David McDonald, president of the Steelworkers, is not likely to tell them that his advocacy of expansion of the public sector is responsible, if indeed he understands that it is.

I have a strong suspicion that quite often union leaders feel obliged to support statist programs that they would rather oppose, except for their political indebtedness. After all, many union leaders are hardheaded men who know the facts of life. They observe at first hand the wastefulness of government expenditures. They understand that, over the long run, employers can pay good wages only when they are making healthy profits.

Their consistent endorsement of all statist adventures is, I believe, often traceable to the debt that they owe the interventionists. To a very considerable degree, the power and prestige enjoyed by union leaders today are consequences of the special privileges that government has given them. On the one hand, the law gives them special privileges of compulsion denied to all other private associations; in the nature of things an exact figure cannot be ascertained, but I feel sure that hundreds of thousands of men belong to unions in the United States only because they have been forced to join if they wish to secure or to retain employment. On the other hand, the unions have benefited enormously from failures by government to enforce the laws against violence in labor disputes.

If union leaders wish to preserve or to expand these special privileges, they must go along with the objectives of the statists in government. The construction-industry unions, through the intercession of Senator John F. Kennedy, secured special exemptions from the regulations of the Landrum-Griffin Law. They are expecting still further special privileges in the current Congress. The price undoubtedly included acquiescence in the political plans of the politicians responsible for both the special privileges already granted and those expected in the future.

Mr. Kennedy would scarcely promise to deliver the construction industry to the tender mercies of the construction unions without firm assurance from the leaders of those unions that they would support him politically. Supporting Mr. Kennedy politically necessarily involves supporting the statist measures that Mr. Kennedy and his principal advisers advocate. The garment-industry unions were the beneficiaries of even more egregious special privileges added to the Landrum-Griffin Law at the then Senator Kennedy's insistence. The socialist convictions of the leaders of the garment-industry unions thus reflect themselves in two ways in the programs of the party presently in power. Not only do they coincide with the ideology prevailing in the present administration; there is also a political debt to pay.

E. *In Summary and Conclusion*

The trade-union leaders are the most active lobbyists to be found in Washington, D. C., today. Professional politicians have described their political activities as awesome. Many trade-union leaders consider themselves to be originators and founts of ideological doctrine.

All the prodigious political activities of union leaders in the United States today have a statist orientation. On the one hand, they support all proposals to increase expenditures in the public sector; on the other, they oppose all measures that would encourage the growth of the private sector. Of proposals to expand governmental expenditures, they have only one criticism: The administration is too modest. Of proposals to grant tax relief to the productive members of the community they say: This is a shameful give-away of public funds to greedy investors and businessmen.

As members themselves of the private sector, union leaders might be expected to favor measures designed to encourage the growth of private industry, for only then would real wages and real purchasing power be increased in a healthy way for their members. But partly through conviction and partly because of political commitment, they cast their lot with the statists. This alignment is bound to continue so long as union leaders owe their position and their power to special privileges granted by government. The kind of men who come to power in unions today can scarcely be expected to have the stature to renounce the system to which they owe their position.

The pre-eminence of the public sector today and the special privileges that governments have granted to trade unions are twin effects of a single cause: the prevalence of the statist ideology. Both effects will be removed when the cause is removed—and only then. Until the theory of the free society as expressed in laissez-faire doctrine prevails over the statist ideology, the public sector will expand at the expense of personal freedom; and for a while trade-unions and their leaders will possess enormous political influence and economic power. But in the end, if statism prevails, there will be no independent trade-unions at all.

NOTES

1. Pp. 320–23.
2. *Ibid.*
3. Contrary to the insinuations of (the then) Professor Felix Frankfurter's and Nathan Greene's well-known book, *The Labor Injunction* (1930), *passim.* For a fuller treatment of this interesting fact, *see* my *The Labor Policy of the Free Society* (1957), especially at pp. 276 *et seq.*
4. From the Convention of 1957, quoted by Senator Barry Goldwater at page 3706 of the McClellan Committee Hearings (officially: *Hearings Before the Select Committee on Improper Activities in the Labor or Management Field*).

10

The Unauthorized Growth of Bureaucratic Power

Lowell Blake Mason

This essay will deal with the present conflict between the public and private sectors in that area of polity generally referred to as trade regulation. Originally the public sector, following historically tested aims, proved its social value and its economic advantage to free enterprise by strengthening competition and protecting the consumer. This beneficial function of the public sector still operates; but right alongside there has developed what the biologists call a "sport"—a bureaucratic mutation from the norm. This "sport" is against competition. For example: The Federal Trade Commission has already put one phase of the Marxian mandate, "from each according to his abilities; to each according to his needs," into practice. Using the anti-price-discrimination statutes as a base, Federal Trade Commission decisions provide that every incompetent, sick, feeble, poor, bankrupt, lazy, careless or quarrelsome merchant with whom a producer does business must be let in on every promotion that is jointly worked out between the producer and his most competent, solvent, and co-operative distributor.

This "sport" is against the interests of the consumer: cease and desist orders are entered against small merchants if they secure business by saving a customer money. There are many orders like the Thomasville Chair case:

201

. . . . the savings . . . . was not retained by the respondent, but was passed on to the customer. . . . It is our conclusion, therefore, that the respondent has violated. . . . [the law].[1]

This "sport" is against the interests of the citizen. While in a free-enterprise market a citizen gets the best he can, the Federal Trade Commission has extended its supervisory authority over a certain kind of customer so that he may be sued for shopping around too much. If his friend, the storekeeper, saves him money once and gets caught doing it again, both of them can be liable for a $5,000 penalty.

My paper will contend that this "sport" is not only gorging itself on the private sector, but, like a wasp anesthetizing a torpid caterpillar for the future consumption of its progeny, this muta-tion, once it has sunk the teeth of its cease and desist order into the back of a single private entrepreneur, uses the decision as a precedent on which to feed future powers.

We now can document new facts and recent citations to sup-port what I forecast in 1959:

Mason's Law is concerned with the proliferation of powers. . . . . The most effective way peaceful totalitarianism can be achieved in the United States is through complete government control of the common everyday acts of all people, ... business, trade, and commerce. . . . .

Today a series of administrative court decisions are being quietly built up in the world of commerce which may provide future prece-dents for tyranny in any phase of a man's life. . . . .

Are these agency precedents which shortcut the Bill of Rights dan-gerous? The late Mr. Justice Jackson thought they were: "A court having in mind only the civil sanctions will approve lax policies, which later are imported into original proceedings. . . . ."

Mason's Law holds that bureaucracy will arrogate to itself all power available under a statute in spite of the limitations against tyranny in the Constitution.[2]

While I will mention the government's curtailment of competition, with its adverse effect on the prices of consumers' goods, I shall *not* deal with the tremendous impact of public buying on the private sector—expenditures to maintain farm parity prices, appropriations to supply our own and our purported friends' military demands, government outlays for public ownership of the means of production (TVA, etc.), or foreign economic aid.

As a critic of the growing public sector in trade regulation, I claim experience in this field. But not content with a broad approach to what Professor Stigler calls "the dense network of public controls over private economic activity," I have limited my *expertise* even more. For the past dozen years, I have centered attention on a fascinating phenomenon in the life of government bureaus, which burgeons for want of a better name under what I call Mason's Law. It is a law concerning the unauthorized growth of authority. I mean the constant tendency of government agencies to aggrandize their coercive powers far beyond what Congress gave them and often beyond what was permitted by our Constitution, as the words and language of that basic law were understood and accepted when it was adopted.

Whatever views my colleagues have regarding the outcome of a social order based on a gorged public sector, all have assumed that the growth was created by an outside source, the legislative. My paper deals with a growth that is generally spontaneous within the agency itself. It is not a growth of function, but a growth of power. Let me give three simple examples to illustrate:

The *function* of a city sanitary commission is to collect garbage, sweep the streets, and condemn unsanitary or unsafe buildings. It should not have the *power* to run a press gang for recruiting street sweepers or garbage collectors or to break into a man's home without a warrant. The Sanitary Department of the City of Baltimore carries out the functions enumerated. But it has assumed the prerogative of forcing its way into a man's home without a warrant. This aggrandizement of authority was certainly not contemplated by the drafters of our Constitution.[3]

The *function* of a fire marshal is to put out fires and to ascertain when possible the causes of the fire. He should not have the *power* to seize and hold incommunicado for grilling any citizen, not even if charged with a crime. In Ohio, after a fire occurred on the premises of a corporation, a deputy fire marshal committed an officer of the company to the county jail because he refused to talk without his counsel being present. A secret inquisition is not the function of a fire department; it is an assumption of tyrannical power. (*Groban,* 352 U. S. 338.)

The *function* of the Federal Trade Commission is to stop unfair acts and practices in commerce and to compile corporate statistics. This beneficial function of the public sector operates with the complete support of the private sector. Since the birth of the Federal Trade Commission in 1914, good government and honest business have maintained a fixed common goal with no shifting of the concept: protect the consumer against restraints of trade and deception. This is so because intelligent self-interest on the part of both business and the Federal Trade Commission dictates a joint adherence to a stable policy.

Business supports this policy because price-fixing, fraud, and deceit in the market place deprive the honest merchant of millions of dollars of patronage and destroy the confidence of consumers.

The Federal Trade Commission supports this policy because its aid in suppressing business venality gives it the proudest kind of justification for the existence of one more alphabet agency in the federal network. During my eleven years on the Commission, I often inveighed against the thoughtless, stupid, and sometimes tyrannous procedures it used in controlling advertising. But in spite of these bureaucratic aberrations, one must express admiration for the unity of purpose between the Commission and private enterprise in this field. Better Business Bureaus, supported by private funds, and Federal Trade Practice Conferences, supported by public taxes, work in close harmony. While less spectacular than litigated cases, here is the core in maintaining honest standards of sales promotion. Even in recalcitrant cases, or where the truth of factual statements is in dispute, Federal Trade Commission litigation to carry out its legitimate function accords with established judicial procedures.

But under the guise of carrying out this function, the Commission now assumes the power to presume a man guilty unless he can prove his innocence; it assumes the right to ignore statutes of limitations: a man can be charged with offenses dating so far back that he would never be able to marshal testimony in his defense; it assumes the power to prosecute a man for doing something that was not declared wrong until after he did it; it assumes the right to ignore facts and infer guilt; and it assumes inquisitional powers. Because there is no such material entity as "the state"—only a horde of little human beings running around behind a great big fictitious label—personal power feeds on public authority. One set of administrative officers, calling themselves "the state," subjects another set of humans called private citizens to inquisition, penalties, and even imprisonment without recourse to the courts. When a prosecutor is authorized by statute to sit in judgment on his own case, it is impossible to stop the growth of personal power never originally contemplated by Congress when it created his function.

Much of this tyranny in trade regulation stems from the bureaucratic notion that the public sector can force the market place to protect the dreamy, the ill-favored, the incompetent, and even the just plain lazy. Even with a bloated public sector and all the tyrannous powers outlined above, this will never be accomplished.

You and I might look down our noses because "a man of business knows that trade depends on people's desire for products they could easily live without. The desire, the taste, establishes the utility of all man-made things, a fifth of whiskey or a Fifth of Beethoven." But it is a fact, and being a man of catholic tastes, I find good in both and am glad the free market furnishes me a reasonable supply of each. But there are zealots who love one and reject the other. Their sense of values rises above the "common herd." This is why they want to nationalize everything. At an afternoon tea in Ann Arbor the other day, a sweet young lady took me to task for opposing the principle of a state theatre. Equipped with only a general aversion against anyone in government telling me what I must like, I decided to stand mute. She ended her diatribe against private enterprise by saying: "Commissioner Mason, do you know that because we do not have state-supported theatres, there are thousands of people in the backwoods of Northern Michigan who have never seen the modern dance?" This telling indictment of the private sector is unanswerable. It is true. I think it would be a good thing if thousands of people in the backwoods of Northern Michigan could see the modern dance; I would like to see it myself. If the day comes when we have in our Cabinet a Secretary of Terpsichore, I hope he will be so imbued with dedication that he will not sleep until every backwoodsman in Northern Michigan has seen how a swan dies in pink tights.

As a student of tyranny, I do not fear too big a public sector in the modern dance. If we are to have a Secretary of Terpsichore, he will not have to resort to writs of assistance (such as James Otis fought against prior to the Revolutionary War), *lettres de cachet* (used by the Louises of France before the French Revolution), or the imposition of sanctions without trials (*see* Hitler, *et al.*) in order to get the backwoodsman into the state theatre. If there are girls in the cast, the government will not have to call the wagon; he'll be glad to walk. Of course, if the Secretary of Terpsichore moves down into Southern Michigan and the other forty-nine States, it's going to cost a pretty penny. But this paper does not deal directly wtih profligacy, only with its aftermath—tyranny. Whether the government puts on girlie shows or buys up eight billion dollars worth of products that a farmer cannot sell in the open market, there is no occasion for the aggrandizement of unauthorized authority. Mason's Law is inoperative here because those who are directly affected need no coercion. They think that they are getting something for nothing. As the late Al Smith once said, "Nobody shoots Santa Claus." But dignified free riding is only one bait in the trap to lure the unwary toward a total public sector.

Fear has persuaded some of the great minds of this country to question the value of the private sector. Walter Lippman has written:

The national power, which we must have in order to hold our place in the world, is expensive, inconvenient, irritating, and dangerous. But though we must be acutely vigilant, we must not delude ourselves into thinking that we can do without it.[4]

Adlai Stevenson puts these questions:

Can our American system prevail in competition with the central planning, control, and direction of the Soviet system?

Can we mobilize, organize, and utilize our human and natural resources as effectively as they can?

Can we do so without imposing controls that imperil the very freedom and values we in the United States are trying to preserve?

Are our institutions adequate to conduct foreign policy in competition with the speed, secrecy, and certainty of the Kremlin?

German and Russian comparisons can offer no hope for those who are against our total public sector. It still thrives in Russia with no outward signs of decadence. The German total state was never cured. It was killed at the cost of millions of lives. And to top it all, the greatest obstacle to the glorious millennium of sociological universalism, the Supreme Court's former view that the Constitution was an absolute law instead of a relative postulate, has now been removed. There are other factors, of course, such as the indifference of people to liberty; the attractiveness of universal largesse; and the operation of Mason's Law, enhanced as it is by the appetite for power of the governing elite and the fact that the great mass of bureaucrats under them are like the vendors of college pennants outside the university stadium. When they go home at night, they are not concerned with the great principles for which the university stands or even with the question of who won the game, but solely with such questions as how many souvenirs they sold, how many inquisitions were inaugurated, how many complaints they filed, how many injunctions were granted, how many fines were assessed, how many cease and desist orders were issued.

Past a certain point, the growth of the public sector spells tyranny.

When the state has become omnicompetent, omnivorous of independent social forces, when it engages endlessly in warlike activity, in an increasingly complicated regulation of trivial economic behavior, and when it engages in vast propaganda and publishing enterprises—the stakes of politics and the perquisites of office are great indeed. Finally, they tend to become too high to let power be won and lost in the accidents of free elections and secret ballots. Gradually many things short of military tyranny are done to insure the proper outcome of elections, chiefly through controlling the flow of propaganda and the necessary corruption of voting procedures.[5]

Tyranny is never trivial. Those who would fight it effectively should bear two things in mind. First, its identification. The old tyrannies, at least in the United States, are long gone. Nobody quarters troops in our homes in times of peace. In fact, today's tyrannies cannot be identified by any of the outward earmarks that made yesterday's tyrannies so easy to recognize, and there are many false tracks to mislead us. Tyranny lurks in the changed attitude in America regarding the absolute and relative in law.

In human relations, and that is all trade regulation is, of course, there are absolutes. All wise men know them; all wise men also know that the minute we define an absolute, we limit it. Human definitions, being finite, contaminate the absolute with man's finitude. But the fact that we cannot define this does not mean we should live "as if" there were no absolutes. The surgeon knows he cannot attain perfect asepsis, but this does not persuade him to abandon all its techniques—white gowns, scrubbed hands, rubber gloves. He operates "as if" he could attain the absolute.

If we argue that there are no absolutes in law, because finite man using a finite language cannot verbalize an infinite aim, we are doomed. The wagon of the law, having lost its star, is hitched to nothing but the tendentious balancing of one evil against another, one good against another. This relativism (or "balancing" as it is called in the Supreme Court) denies the need to live "as if" there were absolutes. Our Constitution is no longer a leasehold in perpetuity, with only those changes allowed that are mutually agreed to by the landlord state and the citizen tenant. We are mere day-to-day occupants—tenants at the will of the landlord. The big-print covenants protecting the liberty of the individual on the front page of the Constitution are all modified by fine print inserted on the back page one hundred and fifty years after the document was executed. The denial that the Constitution is an absolute in law or that it must be lived up to as if it were an absolute has loosed the floodgates of tyranny. Already it has set aside these established protections to liberty.

I am talking about the protections to liberty—not liberty itself. Liberty is an abstract concept. How can it be measured? Shall we say that because twenty million Kulaks and White Russians died or were put into concentration camps or were shot in Siberia, Russia has suffered a twenty per cent decrease in liberty? Ridiculous! The number of people shot, sued, or exiled has nothing to do with the increase or decrease of legal precedents maintaining or destroying our protections to liberty.

Of the forty protections we have in our Constitution, some of which I shall enumerate for you, the loss of just one (the right of habeas corpus) would empower bureaucracy to put everybody in jail. Fortunately, this protection has not been lost. On the other hand, the ones we have lost have not led (so far) to such an increase in fines, penalties, or imprisonments as would alarm the public. Those who want total government have no intention (and, indeed, they would not have the power now) of applying their present authority against everyone at this time. This comes later. For the present, it is only a whip over every man or business in interstate commerce. Because of the losses in our protections to liberty suffered to date, we now have a situation in which not one businessman could successfully defend himself against some governmental accusation that could be brought against him.

But liberty cannot be expressed in the same terms as GNP, population increase, or profit and loss. Liberty is a moral evalua- tion incapable of measurement except in the scales of our shifting cultures. To the slave, liberty may mean only the privilege of dying. To me it means the right to make my own mistakes, not someone else's—not even the government's.

We are talking about the protections to liberty when we say that we have lost nearly a third of them in the last decade. A protection to liberty is not an abstract idea; it is a rule of conduct for government in its relations with individual men. The protections we are talking about are put down in black and white in that seldom quoted and much abused document known as the Constitution of the United States. Besides these protections, there are other fundamental concepts of fair play so ingrained in our present-day mores that it is unthinkable that anyone does not know what they are or that any arm of government would dare to defy them. You can count these pro- tections on your fingers and, as I tick off the ones we have lost and cite the precedents where we lost them, arrive at your own profit-and-loss statement or take mine after you check my addi- tion and subtraction.

Article I of the Bill of Rights gives us our freedom of expression—the protections to our right of free speech, to assem- ble, to read newspapers, to go to the church of our choice or to none at all, to petition Congress. Of course we have these rights. If we did not, I would not be openly writing this article.

Let us go on to the other protections to liberty which our ancestors most certainly had, and which a good many people today labor under the delusion they still have.

In fact, if I were to ask you the following questions, wouldn't you answer yes?

Is every man presumed innocent until proved guilty?

Are there statutes of limitations that prevent a man from being charged with offenses dating so far back that he would be unable to marshal testimony in his defense?

Are there prohibitions against *ex post facto* trials?—that is, can government punish a man for doing something that was not declared wrong until after he did it?

Are there rules against conviction by hearsay—that findings of facts against a man must be based on legally acceptable evidence?

Do you think only a judge can sentence you to jail? If someone who was not a judge did sentence you to jail, do you think you would at least be allowed to have your lawyer present?

Does everyone have the right to his day in court?

Are there prohibitions against prosecutors acting as judges in their own cases?

If you are accused, do you have a right to trial by jury?

Are you protected from punishment for something someone else did?

Must everyone be treated alike under the law?

Is your home your castle, which no official may violate except with a search warrant issued by a court?

You would undoubtedly tell me these and many other fundamental concepts of Anglo-American jurisprudence are the breath of life in the United States. But you are forty years behind the times, and you should be brought up to date.

From 1914 on, our legal code has gradually been split into two parts: One is enforced by the courts, most of which observe the letter and spirit of our Bill of Rights. The other part is enforced by administrative commissions and minor officials of state and city bureaus who operate in what they call "the public interest." This part of our legal code grows quietly and unobtrusively ever more powerful through an ever increasing assumption of authority. How?

We are following the Russians, not to Communism, but we are "shortening the punch" between the policeman and the punishment in those matters that do not appear important in the public eye.

Russia, during her period of militant Communism, treated those charged with crimes of violence and offenses involving moral turpitude with tolerance and circumspection. On the other hand, those accused of violating the state's political and economic demands were sentenced to death or exiled to Siberia without any semblance of trial as we know the word here in America.

In the United States we can see a growing acceptance of this same thesis: that violation of the economic commands of the state is more dangerous to our material welfare than criminal offenses and therefore can be punished without due process.

In the case I described earlier, where an administrative officer in Ohio (not a judge, but a deputy fire marshal) sentenced a man to jail after holding a secret inquisitorial proceeding, the Supreme Court upheld the sentence because the inquisition "was an administrative investigation of incidents damaging to the economy. . . . ." But Mr. Justice Black, the Chief Justice, Justices Douglas and Brennan jointly protested that the due-process provision of the Fourteenth Amendment was an absolute, and "for a state to compel a person to appear alone before any law enforcement officer and answer questions in secret against his will was a secret inquisition, justly feared by free men every-where . . . . a breeding place for the arbitrary use of official power and the beginning of tyranny as well as the indispensable instrument for its survival."

In the second example of administrative tyranny, a man was fined because he would not let an officer into his house without a warrant. The Supreme Court, weighing the rights of an individual who was not accused of any crime, on the one hand, against the convenience of the government, on the other, sustained the conviction because the officer who demanded entry into the home without a warrant could not take the time to get a warrant. "He had to be in his office at 3:30 P.M. every day to take care of his reports."

This theory, that the protections to liberty in the Constitution are absolute only when applied to criminals and mere relative protections when applied to owners of property, was caustically commented on by Mr. Justice Douglas in a dissent joined in by the Chief Justice and Justices Black and Brennan.

The fallacy in maintaining that the Fourth Amendment was designed to protect criminals only was emphasized by Judge Prettyman in

District of Columbia v. *Little*, 85 U. S. App. D. C. 242. The basic premise of the prohibition against searches was not protection against self-incrimination; it was the common-law right of a man to privacy in his home, a right which is one of the indispensable ultimate essentials of our concept of civilization. It was firmly established in the common law as one of the bright features of the Anglo-Saxon contributions to human progress. It was not related to crime or to suspicion of crime. It belonged to all men, not merely to criminals, real or suspected. So much is clear from any examination of history, whether slight or exhaustive. The argument made to us has not the slightest basis in history. It has no greater justification in reason. To say that a man suspected of crime has a right to protection against search of his home without a warrant, but that a man not suspected of crime has no such protection, is a fantastic absurdity.

It is true there is a general uneasiness among practicing attorneys over the loss of our protections to liberty through balancing the convenience of the government against an individual's rights. And lawyers often write learned articles in legal journals and talk before professional societies on the subject, and all too often that is all they do. But who besides the lawyers cares about due process? Most people think due process (the right to confront your accusers, etc.) applies only to those charged with crime. The constant association of due process with alleged communists, thieves, kidnapers, and bank robbers degrades the high regard that this basic concept of liberty and justice once commanded. This denigration occurs simply because these protections to liberty are seldom dramatized except when called into play by the arrest, indictment, or trial of those charged with crime.

People do not realize that the Bill of Rights and due process deal only collaterally with accused persons. Their major function is to protect democracy (using the word in its broadest sense), not persons. Such protection is the only way people can insure themselves against the blunders, tyrannies, and officiousness of their servants in government from the President on down, who, with what they consider the best of intentions, if exempted from the restrictions of our Constitution, will ultimately destroy it.

Every hour of the day and night due process should guard the liberties of those in the private sector against the tyrannies of those in the public sector.

Just where is the proper balance between the public and private sectors? Already,

> . . . . the Federal Government operates over one hundred business-type activities. It is, among other things, the largest electric-power producer in the country, the largest insurer, the largest lender and the largest borrower, the largest landlord and the largest tenant, the largest holder of grazing land, the largest holder of timber land, the largest owner of grain, the largest warehouse operator, the largest shipowner, and the largest truck-fleet operator.

Mr. Roland R. Hughes, former Director of the Budget, is responsible for this glowing picture of the American public sector, but Mr. Hughes ends on this sour note: "For a country which is a citadel and the world's principal exponent of private enterprise and individual initiative, this is rather an amazing list."

Nevertheless, the "do-gooders" cry, "Our society has reached a level of private wealth never seen before on this earth. Yet at the same time there is poverty in the public sector of the economy." We are spending 31 per cent of our GNP now in the public sector; England, 36 per cent. Is either too much or too little? The answer must be drawn to fit the ideals of our nation.

Advocates of a greater public sector have deplored the passing of a handicraft economy and the population explosion. To them, technology has relegated the sanctity of the individual— what Russell Davenport calls "the dignity of man"—to a minor part in life. We must forget self. Man has no status as a single person; only his communal effort is significant. Our national ideal is that the mass is greater than the sum total of individuals. Hence, the old fetish of personal liberty so feverishly expounded in our Constitution and Declaration of Independence must be reinterpreted in terms of present sociological and technological conditions.

If this be so, then the Federal Trade Commission and all

administrative officials are on the right track. There should be more inquisition, more breaking into homes, more orders to cease and desist, more incarceration without trial. The more quickly the commands of the public sector are made known and obeyed, the stronger the state. Is this our national ideal? Strangely enough, its advocates have no stomach for submitting the question to the people. They will not attack the sanctity of the individual by a direct request to the Congress; they will only betray it.

NOTES

1. F. T. C. Docket No. 7273.
2. *The Language of Dissent* (Cleveland, Ohio: The World Publishing Company, 1959).
3. *Franks* v. *Baltimore*, 359 U.S. 374.
4. *Washington Post,* June 27, 1961.
5. *National Review,* Francis G. Wilson, February 25, 1961.

11

Art and the Artist's "Citizenship"

ELISEO VIVAS

> To have turned down the Legion
> d'Honneur is not enough. One
> should never have deserved it.
> Erik Satie

I

One of the defects of our society is its failure to take art seriously. Americans do not believe art has the power to influence either thought or conduct. And yet, in a vague way, it is regarded as valuable. It is considered to be part of culture, though of culture, not in any of the sociological senses of this polysemic term, but in the honorific sense according to which one is cultured if one has a number of adornments that one can put on or not without essentially changing one's true being. Among us, quite often, art is confused with education. Because it is also considered valuable, although not taken seriously, just as every member of society is thought to have a birthright to as much education as "society" can possibly put into him, people are felt to be in need of a certain amount of "art." Thus, art, it seems, must be produced, fostered, and distributed by ever more public action very much in the way education is. But art and education are not the same, nor is the artist as likely to be benefited from intensified benevolence on the part of the public

216

sector as the teacher is supposed to be—and even in the latter's case, it is a matter of doubt.

In contradiction to this generalization, it may be urged that some artists, numerous critics, and even some aestheticians who ought to know better, write eloquently about the truths art conveys. "We go to the great writers for the truth. Or for whatever reason we go to them, it is for the truth we return to them again and again." [1] No great effort would be required to cull endless quantities of such rhetoric from critics, poets, and even aestheticians. The same claim has been made, not only for imaginative writers, as regards whose work the statement is not completely hermetic, but even for composers, as regards whose work the meaning of the statement, to put it moderately, is somewhat inaccessible. Let me give but one bit of evidence that I have used on a previous occasion—apologizing in passing for my fondness for a statement too useful to let lie idle. A well-known historian of music, Cecil Grey, quotes Schweitzer with approval as saying of Bach "that the dogma of the Trinity 'can be expressed more clearly and satisfactorily in music than in verbal formulae,' and consequently that music is capable of being a vehicle for the presentation of religious truth or philosophic concepts." [2] It is also true that the efforts of the Comstocks, nearly always bungling and unintelligent, to censor the arts seem to constitute evidence of the public's implicit belief in the power of art.

But neither the systematic confusion of knowledge with art nor the endemic nature of Comstockery constitutes evidence that, when examined, invalidates the generalization offered in the first paragraph of these notes. As for the confusion, it is cherished by a minority of a minority—a minority among artists, critics and aestheticians; and they are as ineffectual as they are wrong. Indeed, as should be evident from the thesis developed in this paper, while trying to save art from the trivialities of aestheticism, those who confuse art with knowledge fail to do justice to the unique role art plays in human life. The influence of art is much more radical and much more subtle, because indirect, than its capacity to convey conceptually formulable statements. As for the meddling Comstocks, a number of considerations are pertinent: The first is the fact that in the last decades they have been put to flight by the same forces that are helping to disintegrate the morale of our society. The second is that they represent only a minority that makes up for the lack of influence by the noise it manages to make. And the third is that they constitute evidence, not of the censor's intelligent grasp of the influence of art on life, but of something totally different. For the Comstocks, the term "morality" refers only to sexual conduct. It follows that one achieves perfection—irrespective of what kind of man one is—when one conforms to the censor's sexual mores. What Comstockery furnishes evidence of, then, is the narrowness of its conception of the good life and of the erosion to which language is subject by a kind of Lyellian uniformitarianism.

Let me say, in passing, that my disapproval of the censors does not entail an always favorable judgment of the works they censor.

But why do we fail to take art seriously? There are many answers to this question, and no doubt the social historian could furnish us with some of them. But one of them, for our purposes the most important, is that we simply do not know what art is and what effects it has on our lives.[3] If we did, we would not feel as superior as we do to Plato for planning the expulsion of the poets from his city.

What, then, is art? Let me attempt to answer as succinctly as I can a difficult question that would call for protracted effort. Art is a development into refined and deliberate activity of two capacities we human beings have that seem to be unique possessions of ours: the capacity to grasp the objective and the inner world in an identifiable manner and the capacity to embody in a system of symbolic forms the objects we identify perceptually. Whether these activities are only one or two we need not inquire. The capacity to grasp the furniture of the world by means of symbols, to be able to identify its objects in an ordered manner, is the *aesthetic* capacity—employing the term "aesthetic" in its etymological sense. As a condition of this capacity, we have the power of disengaging ourselves from the objects we identify, of retarding or even altogether suspending the satisfaction of our urges. We can suspend activity, but we suspend it without falling into a phantasmagoric reverie, into the booming, buzzing confusion of indistinct images into which animals fall when not bent on the fulfillment of a biologic urge —into which we also fall, perhaps more frequently than our vanity would allow us to acknowledge. But often we step back, so to speak, merely to look, to hear or touch, to sense discriminatively in any of the modes that are given to us to sense, identifying the objects of our sensing more or less accurately and in relation to an implicit and more or less ordered field of perception to which we turn explicitly when the identification is for some reason not satisfactory. I am suggesting that originally the animal that was later to become human responded as all animals do. Action in answer to biologic needs, phantasmagoric reverie, and physical play was all he was capable of. Having killed and eaten, having satisfied his sexual drive, he returned to the chaos of images and affective confusion that was his mental life, until need drove him to action once more. But something happened to his physiology—his brain, his hands: there is much speculation about this point—and when it happened, or perhaps, as it happened, a new activity intruded itself between action and chaotic reverie: in a confused way at first, things began to stand out by themselves when they were neither wanted nor eschewed, and the world—a world of objects and events that until then had functioned only as a source of stimuli—stood off and, with the aid of a developing power of symbolization, became more or less distinctly recognizable as populous with objects of intermittent attention.

The upshot of the physiological modifications that made possible the appearance of a symbolic process was that the animal that was becoming man as a result of such an appearance began to perceive, to distinguish, to grasp, at first vaguely and in confusion, and gradually more distinctly, an objective or outer and a subjective or inner world in which he could identify numerous fixities because he could lift them from the flux and

detain them symbolically. And at first he must have been un-
aware of the strange effect that his use of symbols had on his
companions: it produced on them an act of aesthesis similar
to that which things produced in him, leading them to make
the same discriminations that the user of the symbols made. In
other words, the time came when signals became symbols, and
to the capacity to communicate by means that were mere stimuli
was added the act of communion—if I may borrow Allen Tate's
profound and pregnant distinction, reinterpreting it for my
purposes, perhaps beyond recognition.[4] The human group was
no longer an animal pack.

In so far as this holds, it follows that perception is not the
mere passive response Locke took it to be, but a searching that
is an inventing, a receiving of sensa that goes *pari passu* with an
addition and creative elaboration of what is received. In idealistic jargon, *mind is constitutive of the world.* But not wholly so,
not entirely out of its own unaided resources. The world furnishes it with its data, with that which it gives the mind and
which only up to a point the mind can shape creatively. But
to leave the creative element out of account is to miss the role
art plays in the formation of culture and to lack solid ground
for what ought to be our proper high esteem of art.

For man was not satisfied to symbolize in an unsystematic
manner, doing so as the occasion offered itself for the use of
his new faculty, and solely for utilitarian reasons. Perhaps from
the very beginning of his use of his new virtue, he began to
refine his symbolic product, to elaborate it, to complicate it
and burden it, in response to the exigencies of form, unity,
and comprehensive intelligibility. And the result of his activity
is art as we know it today. Hence the role art plays in our life.
It is the means of our central grasp of the inner and outer
world of our experience. As Jaspers puts it, almost in passing,
in his essay "On the Tragic," we see things in the manner in
which the artist teaches us to see. This is not a discovery of
Jaspers or Cassirer, or Elijah Jordan, each of whom assigns to
the constitutive activity of the mind a basic role in his aesthetic.
It is the idealistic minimum that modern philosophy traces to

Kant and back of him to Leibniz. But whatever its source, it is true that the world in which we live, the world of reality, as we tend to think of it, has the modicum of order and the identifiable concreteness it has because the artist has taught us to see. Note, however, that in so far as the ordering of the world constitutes a process that puts at our disposal a concrete dramatic world, it is both a creative and an arresting, a conservative force. It is the artist, then, who first discovers and presents through his creative gifts the values and the meanings by which men live. And it is he who maintains them in their freshness. The paradox involved in asserting that the artist both creates and discovers I have sought to elucidate elsewhere.[5] Here it is desirable to emphasize that the creative activity not only involves the introduction into culture of new values and meanings, but the maintenance, in a viable, quick condition, of those values and meanings that already make up the substance of the culture.

To the extent that the symbolic capacity has begun to be exercised by the animal, he has begun to create culture: he has begun to develop, however rudimentarily, knowledge, morality, and religion, and whatever other procedures and institutions he requires for a distinctly human life. Back of culture we find, then, as a necessary, but far from sufficient, condition the symbolic ordering and fixing of the stream of experience that is the fruit of our aesthetic capacity.

II

We have now laid the groundwork for examining the private versus the public sector in art.

If the role art plays in human society depends on the creativity of the artist, it follows that any action on the part of society that interferes with the artist's creativity, any imposition of external control, any effort to guide the artist against his inner needs, may be expected to have adverse consequences for his work. And the consequences are not only adverse for the artist's work, but, through it, for the society in which he functions. It is, of course, a question of degree: the artist will always be restrained to some extent in some way that is pernicious to the extent that it is effective. But only to the extent that he is free from external restraints is he capable of functioning as an artist. Other factors are involved in his activity, but this one is a *sine qua non,* and for our purpose the most important.

An essay several thousand words in length would be required to state the qualifications that this statement, though true in general, calls for in order to make it adequate to the complexities of the actual facts. Only two observations can be made here and, even so, only in a very sketchy manner.

The first is that the artist, alas, is a man, as human as any other man, no more and no less; which is to say that he is as burdened as the rest of us with the ills the flesh and the spirit— if I may be allowed the archaic word—are heirs to. But we do not know enough about the way the human psyche responds to external and internal forces to decide with confidence whether what seems to help the proper development of the artist does indeed help, what seems to hinder does indeed hinder. I hope it is not because of the limitations of my reading that I have come *malgré moi* to a discouraging conclusion: the assured knowledge that depth psychology gives us adds up to the important but very limited insight that the human psyche, in its complexity, is subject to malforming forces from the moment of birth on. But we are still very much in the dark as to what these forces actually are. If we ask a member of one school, we get a categorical answer. Here, we sigh in relief, is a man who knows. But if, on turning the corner, we run into a member of another school and ask him for confirmation, we get an equally categorical answer contradictory of the first and a contemptuous dismissal of the first expert. These answers are of great interest—to those who, like the writer, are interested in such subjects.

The second observation is that thinking Americans incline to the belief—a comforting one, it must be acknowledged— that the creative mind functions best in a politically free society and cannot function at all under conditions of despotism. We seem to have what appears to be two decisive pieces of evidence for our opinion. The arts did not flourish under the Nazi heel, and Russian painting, the "socialist realism" for which the Russians must be grateful to Comrade Stalin and his successors, and the Pasternak affair and what it is a sample of—do not these two cases constitute evidence for the opinion that the lack of political freedom is fatal to the arts?

Not at all. We are indulging in an extreme oversimplification. All these two cases prove is that the commissar's loving kiss to the muses is as deadly as was Hitler's hatred of *Kultur-Bolshevismus*.[6]

But if we cannot say anything with confidence about the psychological factors that maintain the artist's creativity, and if he can flourish under political despotism, what will endanger his power? I have never come across a satisfactory discussion of this puzzling problem, and the large number of variables that are involved in an account of the emergence of cultures in which art has flourished, and the heterogeneity of these cultures, make general answers suspect. Let us therefore narrow the question to manageable terms. Many unanswered questions within the narrowed area will remain even then. But let us turn to our own day. And let us not ask what factors account for the burst of artistic activity in the nation in the last fifty years. Let us ask, rather, "What ominous factors threaten the continued creativity of the artist in the United States today?"

Two prefatory remarks are called for. The first is that a discussion that pretends to be more than an extremely tentative, hesitant opinion, instinct with dubiety is, for obvious reasons, inadmissible. The second is that I know of no time in the history of American art that was less propitious than the present for asking what factors are inimical to its blossoming. Whatever our attitude toward contemporary art, ours is an age of tremendous creativity in the arts. I write these lines two days after Hemingway's death and less than a week after reading in *Time* the account of the collection of the Chase Manhattan Bank. I cannot review the evidence, but anyone acquainted with American art today can hardly be expected to take seriously a pessimistic attitude toward it. Whether we like what the artists are making or not, the assertion cannot be denied. Just about fifteen years ago it was still possible to argue that there was no such thing as American painting, although many Americans were painting—French paintings with American subjects. This is no longer true. American painting, sculpture, and literature are exercising a powerful influence on artists and writers outside the United States, and the reason for their impact is their daring creative vitality. As regards the other arts there may be room for honest disagreement. But it is not possible to deny that, whatever their quality compared to the European product, they are active and vigorous. True, in literature we must go back a couple of decades to encounter the masters—to the generation of Hemingway. *Les jeunes,* alas, are feeble, rachitic epigoni. But the old ones are not all dead, and what is more important, their art is not dead—not yet.

To those aware of this fact, a discussion of threats to the continued flourishing of contemporary art must appear to be a purely academic exercise. Let it be. The question is still worth discussing, even if at the moment there is not much of a present danger. I shall take up two negative factors in the remainder of this section.

The first of these is represented by the proposal of federal aid to the arts. For the data, I refer to a transcript of a television discussion that took place February 11, 1961, in an NBC program entitled "The Nation's Future." Engaged in the discussion were Russell Lynes, managing editor of *Harper's* magazine, and Professor John Kenneth Galbraith.

I need not remind my readers that on the etymological meaning of the word "economics," Professor Galbraith can hardly be called an "economist," for what he preaches is mismanagement: he is a propagandist for increased federal aid to all that flies, walks, crawls, or creeps, above the surface of the earth, on it, or under it. As for federal aid to the arts, he is, of course, all for it. And he reminded his audience, the night of his discussion with Mr. Lynes, that the Federal Government already aids the arts, since it is "involved" with them in "a dozen different ways." What he is for is "the final step," by which he means the recognition that the artist is a "first-class citizen," and that

art is "one of the great and respectable resources of our society."
He is therefore for another government bureau—although the
word "bureau," I need hardly remind the reader, is no more
mentioned among proponents of federal aid than, as Spaniards
say, the word "rope" in the home of the man who was hanged.
This bureau—or, as the emancipator of the artist prefers to
call it, "council"—would fully exploit—and I follow the transcript *au pied de la lettre*—the opportunities of the Federal
Government to help the artist and to make the best possible use
of our artistic resources. Professor Galbraith assures us that the
cost in money would be very small.

It is worth while to stop a moment to notice the language
Professor Galbraith uses to speak of the arts, because it does
not lead one to believe that he is seriously concerned with art.
For Galbraith, the arts are one of the *resources* of our society,
and a new bureau needs to be created—I beg your pardon, a
council—"to bring the artist to the highest level of government."
I have pondered this euphemism, and regretfully have come to
the decision that a translation of it, uncouth but exact, is "to
give the artist a place at the trough." My reason is that we are
told that this "council" would "see that the opportunities of
the Federal Government to help the artist and to make the best
possible use of our artistic resources would be fully exploited."
While the language betrays the philistinism of the man who
would make "free loading" the basic principle of national
government, it would be unfair to him to overlook the superiority of his expression to the famous formula used by the social
worker who once controlled the systematic plundering of our
affluence. Harry Hopkins would spend and spend and spend—
for reasons given and with money from sources stated. Our
academic liberal will do the same thing, but he is at least free,
let us be thankful, from the cynicism of his nonacademic arche-
type. He does not propose that we spend. He would merely
"exploit to the full the opportunities of the Federal Government
There is a difference. Or is there?

It is reassuring to be told that the cost in money to bring the
artist to the highest level of government would not be large.

For this means that Professor Galbraith does not intend to turn Blair House into an asylum for artists. I am not interested, however, in the economic aspects of the problem, nor in the place of the artist's citizenship in the order of rank. I do not even know what the critic of our affluence means by this generous rhetorical flourish. It probably has to do with the frequency of haircuts. But is Professor Galbraith altogether certain that the artist is dissatisfied with his citizenship? I have been in intimate relationship with artists since the early, my own early, twenties. I claim firsthand knowledge of this subject. The great majority of artists, painters, sculptors, writers, and little-magazine critics I have known and now know—at least until the academic migration began—did not and do not yet make a living by their work. I heard Merce Cunningham some time ago state in a lecture that his audiences are very small. But I never noticed that artists suffered from an inferiority complex because of their citizenship. Indeed, the very contrary was and still is the case: the artist is afraid of what Professor Galbraith means by "first-class citizenship"—affluence *cum* what for the artist is the effluence of respectability. He would not mind a place at the trough. He remembers the halcyon days of WPA with deep nostalgia. And rightly so. Most of my friends, who starved through the twenties, did pretty well through the thirties on twenty-three dollars a week. But "first-class citizenship," bless his incorruptible bohemian soul, the artist is deeply afraid of. And I think he is right in being afraid of it.

But why the concern with the artist at a time when art is doing as well as it is now? The answer, I think, is obvious: Bureaucracy is on the march. It seeks new areas of national activity to conquer. Under the guise of emancipating the artist, it will rule him in the same way it is ruling so much of our national life. Even if the bureaucrat could make room at the trough for the artist without endangering the quality of his work, there would be reasons enough for objecting to the move: the reasons against the enlargement of statism. But the person concerned with art has his own worries. And these Mr. Lynes put beyond improvement when he said in his opening statement that he was not afraid of creeping socialism, but of creeping philistinism, creeping mediocrity in the arts. This is my central concern.

Mr. Lynes' fears cannot be disposed of by calling attention to the fact that so far as we know, the arts have always been the object of patronage: in Greece, by the city; in Rome, by the emperors and aristocratic families like that of Maecenas; in the Middle Ages, by bishops and nobility; in the Renaissance, by despots, popes, bishops, merchant princes; and since, and until our own day, by the moneyed bourgeoisie. These patrons were individualists, to some extent at least, and some of them were extreme individualists. Under the old patronage, the artist, by and large, could count on the acceptance of his talent, if not by one patron then by another, if not here then there. There was competition for artistic talent among patrons. Take only one instance: Benvenuto Cellini is a good example because he was not one of the very greatest of artists in his day. Yet two popes patronized him and a number of cardinals. He was patronized by Francis I, and he could have gone to England to work for Henry the-many-wived, but he would not take residence among "devils" and "beasts," whom he thought the English to be. Once, when he had to flee because of one of the many murders he committed, two cardinals—who had then the right of sanctuary—disputed the privilege of protecting so talented a criminal. In short, while the artist might have been treated as Mozart or Dr. Johnson was—and I do not know whether he was —the patronage of which he was the object brought him something infinitely more valuable to him than the effluence of Professor Galbraith's citizenship. It brought him freedom to be himself. Of Washington the same can be said that Prokofiev said of Russia, where the most tone-deaf commissar unhesitatingly calls the tune. Federal aid means federal control of anything the federal bureaucrat puts his power-greedy paw on. This is a coarser, but I suspect a more adequate, formulation of Mason's Law than Commissioner Mason's own.[7] Give the Washington bureaucrat power over the artist, and he may give the artist a first-class citizenship. That kind of citizenship is entirely in his power to give or to withhold. But the artist will produce what is called "art" because words have an unlimited coefficient of elasticity. What he will produce will have as much resemblance in quality to what the murderous Italian braggart left us—the saltcellar in the Metropolitan, the Perseus—as a Washington bureaucrat has to a statesman.[8]

The second negative factor to be considered is a relatively recent development in our society. I refer to the symbiotic relationship that has developed in the last two decades—give or take ten years—between artists and universities: versifiers, novelists, painters in residence, higher degrees in creative writing and finger painting, and, for all I know, doctoral degrees on the hula hula in the University of Hawaii and the cha cha at Rio Piedras, P. R. And last, because to me most astonishing, the successful beachheads gained by the *soi-disant* "new critics" in some of the universities of the land. It is usually taken for granted that the *rapprochement* between creative artists and critics, on the one hand, and the universities, on the other, is a good thing for both. I recently heard a speech by Harlan Hatcher, president of the University of Michigan, on the development of the arts in the United States in the last century—remembering that, as Gertrude Stein defined it, a century is one hundred years more or less. The speech was based on the assumption that the recognition of the creative artist by the universities was one of the desirable features of the development.

Let us put aside the problems stemming from the fact that this development is possible because the function of the university has gradually been corrupted, or, if you prefer, has changed without our being aware of what has been taking place. Academic institutions could lay claim once upon a time to being *uni-versities*. But they have gradually become *pluri-versities*, where anything that can be taught, as well as much that cannot or ought not to be, has become a legitimate—which is to say, an entrenched—part of the curriculum. Let us rather focus on the assumption that the symbiosis is a desirable state of affairs.

Now, I am perfectly certain that this development is a good thing for the university community, by which I mean, for us teachers and for our lords and masters. But is it necessarily a good thing for the work that is done or ought to be done in the institution? And is it a good thing for the artist? And is it good for art? Above all, is it good for art? For what it may be worth, let me offer my answer to this question in the form of a report of an encounter told me by my friend, De Bossu, professor of romance languages, at the moment doing time at Midwest University. The meeting took place just before the last national conventions. De Bossu was introduced to a newly appointed painter, coming to Midwest as assistant professor. After the pleasantries of the introduction, De Bossu told me, the young man, for a reason he could not recall, said defiantly:

"I'll be damned if I am going to glorify General Motors or Nixon."

Amused by the naïveté of the fellow, De Bossu answered, "Oh no, no one is going to ask you to do *that*. You'll be able to paint what you like, as you like. What's more, all but four of your colleagues will think all the better of you if you do a vitriolic caricature of Nixon." [9]

"Well," reiterated the painter with an edge in his voice, "I'm not going to become a whore."

"Look," said De Bossu, "your colleagues are all liberals—except four. They'll fight to the death for your right to paint what you like and as you like—so long as you do *not* glorify General Motors, Nixon, or J. Edgar Hoover."

"I won't do it." Clearly the fellow seemed to be girding himself for a battle with the giants of reaction.

But De Bossu is a bit of a ham and not altogether free from a touch of sadism. In his most dramatic, Ancient Mariner manner, he held the painter with his glittering eye, and let him have it:

"No, that's not the way we are going to get you."

Panic turned to bewilderment. "How are they going to get me?" the other asked weakly.

The incorrigible old ham, pretending to feel very sad for the poor fellow, said slowly, *"We,* not they. But *we* won't do a thing

to you, nary a thing. Before long, however, you'll be wanting a
haircut every four weeks. They say in Spanish that criminals
begin by killing flies. Just think of it, thirteen haircuts a year!
And before you know it, it'll be every three weeks. That's only
the flies. Before long, your wife will want a new stove, like the
one she saw at the home of Mrs. Nachbar. She's tired of the old
one. It's no longer flies, see? And by and by, you'll want a new
station wagon. The professor of art history has one. You need
one much more than he does—to take your pictures to the open-
air show next summer. It's not even insects any more. You're
killing heap big animals already. *That's* how we are going to
get you. . . . ."

Diminuendo, now, since his Wedding Guest was standing still,
listening like a three years' child, Mariner de Bossu went on:

"But don't worry. The treatment is painless. And it has its
rewards. A salary all year round; tenure in seven years if you
don't pinch the wrong coeds; steaks Saturdays in the back yard
from late spring to early fall. True, you won't make as much as
a plumber. But what do you want, breakfast in bed? So you see,
it is much more deadly than if we were to ask you to glorify
Nixon, which no one here but three of the four conservatives
would care to see you do. Because I would never ask you to
glorify Nixon."

De Bossu is likely to let himself be carried away by what he
takes to be his humor, for which he has unconcealed admiration.
"Come to think of it," he added, "you may be asked to glamorize
Eleanor, although the job. . . ." His voice trailed off in a cloud of
doubt. "No, I don't think so. Your colleagues are *reasonable*
liberals."

"I wouldn't even do that. I won't paint to order." You could
almost see the stamping foot.

"Don't worry," said my friend, reassuringly. "You'll never
know what's happening to you. And neither will your wife notice that your voice will be going up in pitch—the change will
be so gradual that she won't notice it."

De Bossu is certain that he failed to convey his intention to the young painter; as they parted he was still worrying about Nixon. And I suspect that were these notes to enjoy the undeserved honor of falling under the eyes of the great critic of our affluence, that eminent man would not understand the danger either.

NOTES

1. John F. Danby, *Shakespeare's Doctrine of Nature: A Study of King Lear* (London, n.d.; originally published in 1956), p. 15.
2. Cecil Grey, *The History of Music* (New York, 1931), p. 270.
3. I shall have to let this statement stand without support. The evidence for it consists of citations from the work of critics, aestheticians, and artists, with appropriate analysis and commentary. This task is outside the scope of this paper.
4. Allen Tate, *The Forlorn Demon* (Chicago, 1953), "The Man of Letters in the Modern World," particularly pp. 11 ff.
5. *Creation and Discovery: Essays in Literary Criticism and Aesthetics* (New York, 1955), particularly Pt. II.
6. This is not true of the old Bolsheviks. Trotsky, Litvinov, and others of their generation were neither ignorant nor uncouth in matters of art. Whether the same qualification must be made for some of the Nazis, I do not know. Goering, perhaps?
7. See the brilliant formulation of Mason's Law in *The Language of Dissent* (Cleveland and New York, 1959), pp. 31–61.
8. Can we take the same attitude toward state backing of the arts in Europe? What of state museums, subsidized theatre, the dance? I would answer this question with the statement that, in my opinion, Erik Satie's devastating dictum, used as the epigraph of this essay, sufficiently disposes of the problem. But, of course, Satie and I are speaking of the arts, not of what goes by the name of art in official and dominant circles.
9. It should be explained that De Bossu and three other members of the faculty of the College of Arts and Sciences were named as the only conservatives at Midwest in an article that appeared in a local newspaper. Search for other members of the species reveals that they are even more rare and in a more serious danger of extinction than the whooping crane.

12

The Public Sector versus
the Private Sector in Britain

A. A. Shenfield

It is now ten years since Britain was ruled by an avowedly socialist government.* The decade of the fifties was in many ways one of liberation beyond the nation's hopes. Rationing was brought to an end, the planning of the economy by physical controls was almost wholly given up, the process of nationalization was halted, and private enterprise was given sufficient freedom to display a fair measure of its natural vigor. It was a period of significant economic growth, even though the growth was disturbingly slower than that of the other industrial countries of Western Europe and ran a halting and checkered course, owing to the need to deal with repeated balance-of-payments crises.[1]

Ten years of Conservative government, however, have hardly lessened the relative importance of the public sector. Its dead weight remains substantially unchanged. Indeed, since 1957 the part under direct government control, as distinct from that of the boards of the nationalized industries, has been slowly growing. The Conservatives have removed most of the shackles fastened on the private sector by war and Labor *dirigisme*. They have failed—indeed they have not seriously tried[2]—to reverse the measures that made the public sector so large. When they intervene in the private sector, they do so by methods that are,

* This essay was written in October, 1961.

232

for the most part,[3] consistent with the needs of private enterprise (e.g., by the manipulation of interest rates). Thus, they have not merely restored the freedom of the private sector; they have also respected it and tried to maintain it. But equally they have judged it to be politic, or necessary, to maintain the public sector substantially as it was bequeathed to them by their opponents.

Tables I, II, III and IV (see Appendix) present a selection of figures to give a statistical image of the public sector. They show that we have an economy in which government directly disposes of over one-third of the national income; in which more than one person in five of the employed population (not including the armed forces) is in the service of government or the nationalized industries; and in which more than a quarter of gross fixed investment has gone into the economic activities of the state. Clearly the public sector is of formidable proportions for a country that is governed by a party of private enterprise and economic freedom, as the Conservative Party represents and believes itself to be. It is interesting to see that the proportion of public expenditure attributable to defense, which has never been conspicuously the first love of Labor, has actually fallen under government by Labor's opponents; while that attributable to the social services, which even more than the nationalized industries are Labor's pride and joy, has risen. Clearly, the forces that favor and sustain the public sector must be as deeply entrenched as they are powerful.

Yet so too are the forces on the side of the private sector. If Labor were returned to power, the relative size of the public sector would indeed grow, but not by spectacular proportions. Steel and road haulage would certainly be renationalized. Expenditure on the national health service, education, and pensions would grow.[4] And the shadow of the state in all economic matters would lengthen and widen. But Labor's nationalization program would be unlikely to go beyond steel and road haulage,[5] for its leaders have lost their faith in nationalization and retain it as a major plank in their platform only to appease their followers. Their program for the expansion of the social services would quickly run into the barrier of taxation, for not even the most "swingeing" and discriminatory taxation of the better-off could yield the money that an ambitious program would require, and when it comes to taxing their own supporters, the Labor leaders become wonderfully conscious of the due limits of government. As for intervention in the private sector, this would, of course, be niggling, self-contradictory, hampering to the efficient and forward-looking, and favorable to the backward and out-of-date. But it is unlikely to be far-reaching or deep-searching, though it might be made to appear as such; for the deep unpopularity of physical controls must alone prevent this. And the Labor Party has no more thought out what it would do if it really received a mandate for socialism than the German Social-Democrats had in 1919 or than its own leaders had in 1945.[6] No doubt the economic decay that Labor policies would promote would call forth cries for truly radical remedies. But the kind of "remedy" that made the public sector grow like a cancer cell at the expense of the private sector would be applied by those on the extreme Left or Right who might succeed Labor after a debacle, not by Labor itself.

Thus, we appear to have reached a state of rough stability in the relative dimensions of the public and the private sectors. The Conservatives are unlikely to reduce the public sector significantly. Labor would increase it significantly but not explosively. As the Conservatives appear to have a permanent electoral edge over Labor,[7] except at times of balance-of-payments crisis, the outlook is probably one of no great change. How has this come about? Can the stability be lasting? And what ought to be done about it?

This is not the place to recount the story of the development of socialist thought in Britain. It is enough to say that though it was very late in taking root in Britain, as compared with the Continent, it has succeeded in so deeply impregnating the nation's attitudes that only the rarest minds are wholly free from its influence. It constitutes the unspoken assumptions that are the real determinants of public debate; and though they are by no means clearly or consistently socialist, they long ago ceased to be liberal.[8]

In such a climate a luxuriant growth of state economic activity can hardly surprise one.

However, there are some special reasons why the Conservatives have found it not unpalatable to run an economy with a large public sector. As practitioners of the pure art of retaining power, they outshine, after all, the conservatives of all other democratic countries; and their success arises from certain attitudes that hinder them from effectively reversing the etatism of our times. These attitudes display themselves in a variety of facets of two broad characteristics. The Conservatives are men of common sense; and they are men of national unity.

As a man of common sense, the Conservative is intensely suspicious of the theorist[9] and the doctrinaire. Since most far-reaching changes are initiated by men who are moved by some theory of society, the Conservative is reluctant to attempt to reverse the trend of the times where such reversal itself requires far-reaching changes. Once it is entrenched, etatism can be dislodged only by those who have deep convictions about the rights of man that hang together in some coherent theoretical form. Such men appear to be as doctrinaire to the Conservative as do the Socialists themselves. It is, of course, a commonplace that this attachment to common sense is an enormous source of political strength, first because of its appeal to an essentially commonsensical nation, and secondly because, though it prevents the Conservative from pursuing truth very far, it also prevents him from doing likewise with error.[10] And as most theories have more error than truth in them, a nation that is ruled by the British type of conservative is in broad terms not unblessed by Fortune. Nevertheless, if a nation has somehow got itself on to a disastrously wrong road, he is not the man to save it, except in the sense that, by slowing the pace of movement down, he gives time and opportunity for new ideas to arise and unseat the ideas for the time being in the saddle.

As a man of national unity, the Conservative must avoid deep, irreconcilable conflicts with his opponents. At the level of day-to-day politics this may be merely an expression of the need to avoid offense to the middle-of-the-road, floating voter; but at a higher level it is without doubt an expression of outstanding political wisdom. The Conservative knows instinctively that safe and sure progress upon the road that he wishes to travel is possible only if he carries many more than his own supporters with him; and he knows also that his opponents are less likely to seek once-for-all, cataclysmic changes when in power if milder changes are unlikely to be quickly reversed when they are out of power.

Supremely wise though this is at its best, it can easily degenerate into mere caution, timidity, or allegiance to safe (i.e., mediocre) men. On the other hand, brilliant men may easily be tempted to make more of national unity than it deserves. After all, etatism knows very well how to pitch its appeal cunningly to deep and worthy feelings of national pride.[11] Modern British Conservatism has suffered grievously from both of these faults. In a nation that is at least three-quarters working class, it is a great achievement for the party with a middle-class image to defeat at the polls the party with a working-class image, but this is perhaps as much the result of the Conservatives' faults as of their virtues.

The Conservatives' attachment to what they believe to be common sense, in which they have more often than not been joined by most of the nation, used often to be attributed to stupidity. Their opponents do not often nowadays call them "the stupid party," as the radicals loved to do in the nineteenth century. Nevertheless, an echo of the taunt still lingers in the charges made by our socialists except when, baffled by their failure at the polls, they profess to see a masterly cunning in the Conservatives' handling of the electorate. The Socialists thus tend to give the Conservatives the very attributes that some foreigners used to give Albion itself—perfidious and cunning, yet impregnably unintellectual. It need hardly be said that there is nothing in this. In the nineteenth century the Conservatives probably did generally have more, and more conspicuously, stupid men in Parliament than their opponents, but, if anything, the boot is nowadays on the other foot. If to be unintellectual is to be stupid, one need go no further than the trade-union section of the Labor Party to find a mountain of stupidity. But if a mere capacity to repeat slogans in the language of intellectuals is not accepted as a certificate of intelligence, then a most dismal array of stupid men can be found in Labor's non-trade-union ranks. Stick-in-the-muds, impervious to argument, are nowadays far more numerous on the Labor benches in the House of Commons than on the Conservative benches, if indeed there are any at all on the latter.[12]

Since the Conservatives' attachment to national unity appears to be a permanent strand of such philosophy as they have, it is often regarded as a foundation for a conscious and fully understood etatism. Were not the Tories the pioneers of factory legislation in the nineteenth century? Did they not always recoil from the "extreme" belief in freedom of enterprise of the Manchester men? Did not Mr. Macmillan himself write a book in the 1930's entitled *The Middle Way*, which put forward some kind of blueprint, hazy though it was, for a planned economy? The belief in this is widespread, both among the Conservatives and their opponents, but on examination it proves to be elusive and insubstantial. It has never been more than a superficial reaction to the ideas of their opponents. No British Conservative thinker of the past two centuries has worked out a policy of etatism that merited the respect, or even the notice, of scholars. The opposition to the Manchester School in the nineteenth century was always superficial, and often cranky and perverse (which does not mean, of course, that a sounder opposition could not have been, or was not, mounted). The approach to economic planning in the 1930's, as exemplified by *The Middle Way*, was equally superficial, though not, of course, cranky. The belief in freedom is, in fact, a much stronger strand in the Conservative philosophy than any kind of etatism, and the Conservatives' readiness to preserve a large measure of state economic activity in our system is far more the result of political strategy and instinct than of philosophy.

In addition to all this, there have been practical difficulties in the way of reducing Labor's legacy of public economic activity. First, from 1951 to 1955, the Conservatives' Parliamentary majority was too slender for large, bold measures. Secondly, since 1955 they have been beset by grave economic difficulties from time to time and preoccupied especially with the problem of the instability of the position of sterling. Thirdly, at first sight the denationalization of the major nationalized industries and the dismantling of the welfare state appear to present tasks of such Herculean proportions as to dismay all but the most resolute of politicians.

In the case of the welfare state, as distinct from the nationalized industries, there is a special influence at work that supports and sustains the expansion of the public sector. It is the continual pressure for more expenditure coming from the "expert" in social services. Combined with the pressure of the vested interests that are created by social services, this becomes a force of extraordinary power. It is one that is peculiarly difficult for the Conservatives to overcome, because the "expert" who constantly preaches the need for more state provision for health or education or pensions can be effectively confuted only on his own ground of theory and analysis, and this is an arena that few Conservatives are equipped to enter.

Experience of the strength of the forces that cause social expenditure to expand shows how ill conceived is the so-called Theory of Social Balance [13] which Professor Galbraith has announced to the world and which has received so much acclaim. This is not the place to examine the theory of wants on which it is founded, which is that as affluence increases, the wants of the consumer become more and more the creations of the producer. Under dissection it turns out to be both empty and pretentious. There is, of course, no way of distinguishing between wants that are the result of persuasion or example from those that have other origins; or between wants that result from the persuasion of producers and those that result from the persuasion of parents, guardians, teachers, or preachers. The motive of the persuader cannot be set up as a test of the substantiality or insubstantiality of the want.

What concerns us here is not Professor Galbraith's theory of wants as such, but his contention that the structure and institutions of our society favor the expansion of private expenditure and hinder that of public expenditure. The truth is the reverse. Of course, there is a large and powerful apparatus for the stimulation of private expenditure. Madison Avenue does indeed influence people. No doubt it sells goods on a very large scale. But consider the character of its appeal and the resistances that it must meet. Apart from the provision of genuine information, which is the greater part of its work, its weapon of persuasion is the selected fact, the partial analysis, at worst the half-lie, not the outright lie. Now the half-lie must meet two powerful resistances; first, the continual assessment of satisfaction against expenditure by the consumer who has to meet the expenditure from his own pocket and knows better than anyone else what the satisfaction means to him; [14] and secondly, the supply of expert information on advertised products by consumers' organizations.

Compare this with the strength of the appeal of the champions of the expansion of public expenditure and the character of the resistances that they must meet. Their half-lies are much more unashamed and effective than those of Madison Avenue. Not even the noblest politician conceives it his duty to present both sides of a case; it is enough that he honestly believes in his own case, which may then be better described as a half-truth rather than a half-lie. What is even more important is that he is not regarded as blameworthy if he deliberately presents his argument in a manner calculated to arouse the emotions of his audience and thus clouds their judgment. No advertiser of soap or toothpaste can hope to match this in persuasive effect. As for the average politician, exaggeration and the biased selection of evidence are notoriously part of his stock-in-trade. At the very least he uses slogans that blunt the edge of reason and analysis. There is no more preposterous picture than that of the politician who attacks Madison Avenue for a mendacity of which he himself is far more guilty.

Thus it is that, since to be for public expenditure on, say, education appears to be for education itself, and to be against public expenditure on education appears to be against education itself, the half-truths or half-lies of the politician who wishes to spend more and more public money are outstandingly persuasive.

But the modern expert in social services is much more persuasive than the politician. He has the enormous advantage of appearing both impartial and scientific. He is thought to have no axe to grind, and he has the prestige of academic training or standing. In fact, he is both biased and, more often than not, unscientific. The expert in health or education is trained to seek improvement in his specialty. To push out the frontiers of practice and knowledge means to increase expenditure. As the government disposes of larger funds than any individual or group of individuals likely to be interested, he is in favor of public expenditure even if he gives a thought to the possibility of private expenditure. If the government is already the principal supplier in his field, he is unlikely even to think of any other possible support for the improvements that he advocates. His training gives him no inkling of the larger effects on society of increased government expenditure. It is likely only to make him contemptuous of those who appear to wish to save the taxpayer's money at the expense of the lives he thinks he can save or the minds he thinks he can improve or the new knowledge he thinks he can discover. As for his scientific approach, he is notoriously as prone to fads and fashions as is the man in the street; the difference is mainly one of sophistication.

There is another type of "expert" whose influence is much more often than not on the side of public expenditure. It is the academic teacher and research worker in the field of social administration. The social sciences have developed an academic fringe that is heavily populated by persons who deal with matters of economic importance but who are ill-equipped with powers of economic analysis. This is a field in which it is possible to erect an academic reputation on a foundation of snippets of descriptive work, law, statistics, and general guesswork. Thus it is, for example, that a race of so-called "labor economists" has arisen the principal result of whose work is to promote the received opinions of our time, which are, of course, heavily biased in favor of the views of organized labor, by means of tattered and threadbare economic analysis. Similarly, many who expound the subject of social administration do little more than give a sophisticated dress to popular opinion, which is heavily in favor of the virtue of public expenditure even when it may reluctantly concede that it is beyond the people's pocket. Hence, the preponderant weight of what is called academic opinion in this field is thrown on the side of the expansion of public expenditure, and it too is clothed with the prestige of what is believed to be impartial scholarship.

Now consider the resistances to the expansion of public expenditure. They are mainly two: the limits of taxation, and the vested interests of private provision for the wants concerned. Of course, resistance to taxation is powerful. But under a system of progressive taxation it cannot supply a discipline as strong as the constant attention to his pocket by which the private consumer checks his own expenditure. That millions of citizens can vote for expenditure which will not, or which they think will not, come from their own pockets must produce a built-in factor of expansion. Thus it is that, despite all the resistance to taxation, the percentage of the national income spent on the social services has steadily increased during the past decade. As for the vested interests of private provision, there is none now of any consequence in Britain. The medical profession was defeated and dragooned into the National Health Service, and is now for the most part a champion of increased public expenditure. The public schools [15] and the private preparatory schools have retained their own special market and seek no other. The life assurance companies and societies have shied away from a fight with the state on the question of graduated pensions and have refrained from exposing the weaknesses of the new state scheme, which offends all actuarial principles.

But is it not true that we have inadequate schools, hospitals, roads, police forces, and the like? Inadequate for the demand, of course; for the supply is mainly free to the consumer. On this footing the supply will and must always be inadequate. Is it not inadequate in some more absolute sense? Perhaps. But, in the first place, we must remember that much of the supply must come in very large units. For this reason there must always be cases where supply falls short even of recognized demand, for it may not be economic to provide the large unit until there is already some unsatisfied demand. In the second place, if there is an absolute sense in which public provision may be said to be inadequate, the same is true of private provision. Does no one ever go hungry? Is everyone well clothed? Are all houses roomy and sound? It would be tedious to elaborate this.

Let us now examine the problems that the public sector has forced upon the government and the measures it has taken to deal with them. We shall then be in a position to consider the possibilities of finding solutions for them in the future.

In the case of the welfare state, the greatest problem has been the strength of the tendency of expenditure to run ahead of expectations. When Mr. Aneurin Bevan initiated the National Health Service in 1948, he estimated the cost to the Exchequer at £250 million. Within two years it had reached £490 million. At present it is running at about £850 million, despite successive vigorous measures to reduce its cost by introducing, and then increasing, charges for drugs. Even the Labor Government was forced to do this,[16] and the Conservatives have been unable to avoid taking it further. This great increase in cost has been only partly due to the fall in the value of money. It represents a substantial increase in real terms, and, of course, it would have been far greater if restrictive measures had not been applied. The folly of the original scheme is thrown into sharp relief by the fact, which is now usually glossed over, that restrictive measures were not contemplated. If the original scheme had been allowed to run its course unhampered by later financial considerations, it would have grown like Alice and thus displayed the wonderland character of the thought behind it.

Once it became clear even to its champions that health, and indeed other welfare, expenditure was bound to keep rising, its defense shifted to the new proposition that what mattered was the proportion that it took of the national income. As long as this did not increase, the argument ran, not only was there nothing to complain about, but also there was no "real" increase at all. This is what may be called the Theory of Perpetual Poverty: however affluent a society becomes, there must always be enough poverty to call for a constant proportion of the national income to be applied by the state to its relief. It is, of course, true that there cannot be an absolute standard of poverty. Some relativity is inescapable. Hence a rich society will reasonably take a more generous view of the definition of poverty than a poor one and will accordingly provide assistance at a higher level. This is the germ of truth that gives some persuasiveness to this theory. The relativity of poverty, however, cannot justify the expenditure of a constant proportion of the national income on its relief. As the national income rises, the increase in the ability of the people to provide essential services for themselves must be greater than the rise in what is popularly accepted as the desirable minimum level of supply. Thus, though the proportion of the national income that will need to be applied to the relief of poverty will fall less than the national income itself rises, fall it must. If the actual proportion ostensibly applied to the relief of poverty does not fall, influences have entered into policy that purport to be concerned with the relief of poverty but are, in fact, shaped for other purposes.

We shall return to this when we consider the requirements of future welfare policy, but we may note here that even the easy test of the proportion of the national income has been sadly failed in the case of the great and growing cost of pension provision. This is now firmly set on a fast-rising curve and is likely to present the welfare state with its most refractory problem. The chief reason is the decision taken by Labor, and accepted and endorsed by the Conservatives, to provide pensions at prevailing rates for those already too old to make a full, or any, contribution by way of national insurance levies. Even Beveridge was not guilty of advocating this; indeed, he warned the nation of the dangers that would arise from it in the shape of insuperable financial burdens. His warnings were ignored because pensions became a football of politics. The Conservatives have felt obliged to swim with the tide, even though at a cautious distance behind Labor. Sooner or later the system will break down, and the expectations of many of those now looking forward to the enjoyment of state pensions of a certain real, as distinct from monetary, magnitude will be disappointed. A nonactuarial scheme can be sustained only by taxation or by inflation. If the pension liability under such a scheme expands faster than the national income, it must in due course run up against the limits of tolerable taxation or inflation. By one device or another the liability will then, at least in part, be repudiated.

The problems of the nationalized industries have been more varied than those of welfare expenditure but equally, or even more, refractory. They principally concern questions of pricing, investment, and public control.

The nationalization acts of Parliament enjoined the newly created boards to pay their way "taking one year with another" or "on the balance of good and bad years." This was a vague injunction from the beginning, and it has never been made precise. In practice the prices charged by the National Coal Board and the British Transport Commission have fallen far short of the level required to meet their full costs, including depreciation at replacement cost. The other boards have generally fared better, especially in the case of electric power supply, but even there it is doubtful whether costs have been consistently covered in full. Coal and transport have accumulated large losses. In the case of transport, a part of the loss has ben written off by the creditor, i.e., the government, and it seems most unlikely that even the balance will ever be made good.

The failure of prices to cover costs has been due partly to the mistaken belief that the national interest is served by the supply of what is called "essential services" at low prices, and partly to the reluctance of the government from time to time to face the political unpopularity of sharply raised prices. Looked at from this point of view, the nationalized industries' prices have clearly been too low; but they may not have been too low if the true cause of the trouble has been that their costs

have been too high. The remote control of an overlarge scale
of operation; the weakness of control over labor; the reluctance,
induced by politics, to charge particular classes of customers
(e.g., the user of domestic coal, the domestic consumer of
electricity at peak periods, and the railroad commuter) a proper
differential price—all these have undoubtedly made operations
inefficient, with obvious effects on their costs.

The same sorry business record is displayed by the story of
investment. Table V (see Appendix) gives a comparison between
the returns on investment in private industry and in the nationalized industries. If the disparity between the rate of return on
capital in the nationalized industries and that of private industry
were due solely to a policy of charging below-market prices, costs
being held down as successfully as in private industry, the absence
of an adequate business return could not be criticized. The true
return on the nationalized industries' capital would take the
form of the cheapness of the products purchased by the consumers, including private industry. In any case there is no
reason to expect the same rate of return in industries that differ
in important economic characteristics. Nevertheless, on the evidence of control of costs, there can be little doubt that the
nation has wasted an enormous amount of scarce capital by
pouring it into the nationalized industries. It is one of the
principal reasons for the failure of the British economy to grow
as fast as some others have done.

The investment problem that has bemused the government
has been not so much the inadequacy of the return, for that
is in part the result of pricing policies, but the difficulty of
controlling the quantum of investment and the burden imposed
on the national budget by the absence of a free-market source
for the capital required. For some years funds were raised from
the banks, but with a Treasury guarantee, except in the case of
coal and the airlines, which were financed directly from the
Treasury. Since 1956, all the boards have been fed directly by
the Treasury in order that, as Mr. Macmillan, then Chancellor
of the Exchequer, put it, he who paid the piper might call
the tune. But, of course, this has in no way solved the problem

of finding some rational criteria for the control of investment. The piper, in fact, does not know what tune to call.

Painfully slowly the government has begun to tackle these problems of pricing and investment. More and more it has tried to make the boards simulate the practice of private enterprise. Uneconomic coal mines and railroad lines and services are being abandoned at an accelerated rate. And, in April, 1961, it announced a new pricing policy under which the boards are to plan to "break even" over five years and to pitch their prices at a level not only to cover depreciation at replacement cost but also to produce a surplus as a contribution to further capital development.[17] Undoubtedly the changes will improve the efficiency of the nationalized industries. But they have not gone very far. There will still be plenty of uneconomic coal mines and railroad services in operation, and the National Coal Board, for example, will still refrain from working its most profitable units to the full, namely, its open-cast units, in deference to the National Union of Mineworkers, whose members do not produce open-cast coal. As for pricing, nobody knows what sort of surplus is to be aimed at or is possible; nor is there any valid reason why present customers should be forced to pay for future capital development.

The problem of public control has proved impossible to solve. Those who preached nationalization always presented it as a means of making industry accountable to the people, private industry being alleged to be accountable only to its managers, shareholders, or financiers (all, of course, being greedy and antisocial in the myths of the nationalizers). As far as accountability is concerned, nationalization has proved to be a fiasco. This was very easily predictable. Parliament is not a body equipped to control the operation of business, and not all the consumer consultation in the world (by means, for example, of the various consumer councils set up under the acts) can possibly replace or even simulate the constant and pervasive control that the consumer enjoys in a free market.

What can we now do? Must the British people be forever saddled with this large, unmanageable public sector? The answer is, in principle, clear, though its application is beset with difficulty.

Take first the welfare state. It is essential to begin by recognizing that the largest element in its foundations is humbug. In a nation that tends to run to humbug in its less admirable moods, this is perhaps not surprising. The welfare state rests on humbug because it was ostensibly established to relieve poverty, while what it in fact does is something else. Beveridge's four giants—Want, Disease, Squalor, and Ignorance—were to be banished from the land, and minimum standards were to be secured for everybody. In fact, the true purpose of the welfare state is to socialize the provision of certain services, whereby it actually reduces standards below what they might be. Yet so captivating is the name "welfare state" that millions of citizens think that it gives them or their fellow citizens welfare that they would not otherwise enjoy.

The method of the welfare state is to require that everyone must pay for and be free to take state-provided services in order that those who cannot provide them for themselves shall have them. Thus, it raises taxation to a level which reduces the nation's wealth by weakening the incentive to produce and save, and which holds over our heads the constant threat of inflation (even though at any given moment an increase in taxation can, for the time being, have a counterinflationary effect). It undermines both the personal responsibilities that are the warp and woof of freedom and the family responsibilities on which the wholesomeness of society rests. It teaches the electorate to vote for things that most of them do not intend to pay for. Above all, by providing services for all, it fails to provide fully effective services for those that are really in need.

In place of the welfare state, we need a state whose citizens are both free and humane. If they are free, the great majority will be able to provide for themselves—and at an ever rising level, owing to the wealth-creating power of freedom. If they are humane, they will vote the state sufficient resources to provide at an ample level for those (who will be an ever-dwindling proportion of the population) who cannot provide for themselves. Against the Theory of Perpetual Poverty that imbues the welfare state, we must set the aim of emancipation from poverty, which enables the state to act as a provider as long as it is necessary, but to wither away when it ceases to be necessary.

Policy for Britain thus requires the following fundamental changes:

1. The institution and progressive application of tests of need for state social services. This should begin with the general-practitioner part of the health service, provision for old age, and the higher educational services. All are feasible, and the transfer to private provision of those above the level of need would be a powerful stimulus to experiment and improvement.

2. The development and promotion of the private supply of these services. Here the state could properly assume the function of providing information on available or prospective supplies, and it could stimulate the organization of group purchasing.

3. In the interim, the wide extension of the principle, already adopted minimally in the case of National Health Service drugs, of charging fees for state services. The charges should progressively be brought up to full cost level until there is competition on equal terms between state supply and private supply.

Let us now turn to the nationalized industries. The comparison between their part and the welfare state's part of the public sector reveals a paradox. While the idea of the welfare state is widely popular, many people have begun to see the need for dismantling it by changes such as those suggested above. On the other hand, the nationalized industries are widely unpopular (even among Labor voters); yet very few indeed would seriously propose to denationalize them. Nevertheless, there is no complete solution for their problems short of denationalization.

It is true that great progress can be made by simulating as far as possible the aims and methods of private enterprise. But this cannot go the whole way. First, the problem of pricing cannot be solved by leaving it wholly to the free-market mechanism as long as large elements of monopoly power remain with the nationalized industries. Secondly, the investment problem cannot be dealt with in the manner of private industry because only the state can hold the equity in the nationalized industries. A monopolistic supplier of risk capital is in a different position from free-market suppliers. Thirdly, as long as these industries are large and important (and not marginal state investments like, say, the British Government's holding in the British Petroleum Company), it will be impossible to prevent political interference with their managerial policies.

Yet denationalization is almost universally rejected, partly because it appears to be too doctrinaire, partly because it is too easily dismissed as merely turning the clock back. But the main reason given is that it is impossible, and this on two grounds. First, it is said, you cannot unscramble eggs. These industries have been so fully integrated that it would not be possible to split them up without doing great harm to their efficiency, and the market would not take any of the major ones, at least, without very considerable splitting. Secondly, it is said, the market neither could nor would supply the quantity of risk capital necessary to buy up these industries.

The first objection does not survive examination. There are no insuperable technical or managerial difficulties in splitting even the largest of these organizations. Indeed, in the case of coal, individual mines or groups of mines form natural units, the splitting off of which would present no difficulty, despite the present provision of certain essential services from the national or regional centers of the Coal Board.

The second objection is at present admittedly an insuperable one, but for one reason only, namely, that as a Labor Government would renationalize any industries sold, there would be no buyers except at give-away prices. In this way, and to this extent, the Labor opposition still rules the country. If the Labor Party wins the next election, there will, in any case, be no question of denationalization for a long time. But if the Conservatives win it, the victory will be their fourth one in succession. It is quite likely that then the Labor Party will abandon nationalization, as the German Social-Democrats have done, or cease to be an effective opposition. The question will then be whether the market will be able to supply the necessary risk capital.

Now in this respect the situation has recently been transformed. The immense growth of private and institutional savings, the rise of the cult of the equity, and the new-found legal freedom of trustees to invest in equities have together produced so abundant a supply of risk capital that, taken gradually over a period of years, denationalization would meet no insuperable difficulty on at least this score. The test would be the prospect of profitability.

Rough stability between the relative proportions of the public and private sectors may well be our lot for the foreseeable future. It will not serve our need for economic growth and personal freedom, and if we accept it, the fault will be in ourselves, not in our stars.

APPENDIX

TABLE 1

PERCENTAGE OF GNP SPENT BY CENTRAL GOVERNMENT AND LOCAL AUTHORITIES

YEAR	ON CURRENT ACCOUNT ONLY	ON CURRENT AND CAPITAL ACCOUNT
1938	25.8	n.a.
1946	55.9	59.0
1950	34.6	39.2
1951	34.4	41.0
1952	35.8	41.5
1953	35.2	40.25
1954	33.9	38.0
1955	33.1	36.8
1956	32.8	37.0
1957	32.0	36.0
1958	32.7	36.6
1959	33.6	37.4
1960	34.0	37.8

TABLE 2

PERCENTAGE OF POPULATION IN CIVIL EMPLOYMENT

YEAR	EMPLOYED BY CENTRAL GOVERNMENT AND LOCAL AUTHORITIES	EMPLOYED BY NATIONALIZED INDUSTRIES
1939	7.7	—
1946	11.5	—
1950	11.6	11.2
1951	10.5	12.0
1952	11.7	12.8
1953	11.6	12.7
1954	11.5	12.2
1955	11.3	11.5
1956	11.4	11.2
1957	11.4	11.2
1958	11.5	11.2
1959	11.6	10.9

TABLE 3

PERCENTAGE OF GROSS FIXED INVESTMENT
AND OF GROSS DOMESTIC PRODUCT
ACCOUNTED FOR BY GOVERNMENT ENTERPRISES

YEAR	PERCENTAGE OF GROSS FIXED INVESTMENT	PERCENTAGE OF GROSS DOMESTIC PRODUCT
1955	25.1	14.1
1956	25.1	14.6
1957	26.6	14.5
1958	27.1	14.0
1959	28.2	13.8

TABLE 4
ANALYSIS OF CENTRAL GOVERNMENT'S AND LOCAL AUTHORITIES' EXPENDITURE

PERCENTAGE ATTRIBUTABLE TO	1950	1951	1952	1953	1954	1955	1956	1957	1958	1959
DEFENSE	18.8	25.0	28.4	28.3	28.3	26.0	25.1	23.1	21.6	20.5
SOCIAL SERVICES	42.2	39.4	39.9	41.2	42.3	43.2	43.2	44.8	46.0	46.7
HOUSING	7.4	6.9	7.5	8.1	7.8	6.7	6.1	5.8	5.0	4.7
EDUCATION	9.7	9.5	9.5	9.5	10.3	10.8	11.5	12.6	12.5	12.9
HEALTH	10.4	9.5	8.8	8.6	9.0	9.4	9.5	10.0	10.0	10.2
NATIONAL INSURANCE	14.7	13.5	14.1	15.0	15.2	16.3	16.1	16.4	18.5	18.9
OTHER	39.0	35.6	31.7	30.5	29.4	30.8	31.7	32.1	32.4	32.8

TABLE 5

NET RETURNS ON CAPITAL

(PER CENT)

	1955	1956	1957	1958	1959
MANUFACTURING AND DISTRIBUTION	17.4	16.3	15.5	14.3	14.9
IRON AND STEEL	19.0	16.8	16.4	14.1	13.3
NATIONAL COAL BOARD	0.4	6.8	3.6	2.8	1.6
ELECTRICITY COUNCIL AND BOARDS	5.1	4.7	5.0	5.7	5.6
GAS COUNCIL AND BOARDS	4.0	4.4	4.5	3.4	3.3
BRITISH TRANSPORT COMMISSION	1.9	0.2	—0.6	—2.1	—1.3
BRITISH OVERSEAS AIRWAYS	4.2	3.4	—0.2	—0.7	3.9
BRITISH EUROPEAN AIRWAYS	7.0	4.1	7.8	4.7	8.6
POST OFFICE	4.4	6.9	7.5	8.0	8.6

NOTES

1. We have had an almost complete biennial series of crises since the War; viz., in 1947, 1949, 1951, 1955, 1957 and 1961.
2. They denationalized most of the steel industry and a goodly part of the road haulage (i.e., trucking) industry. Steel and road haulage were nationalized by the Labor Government shortly before it lost power, and their new nationalized organizations had hardly got under way when the Conservatives rode in again. One large steel company remains in public hands, and the government intends to dispose of it when the private capital market appears ready to take it on reasonable terms. There appears to be no serious intention now to get rid of the remaining public part of road haulage (i.e., "British Road Services").

   As the government has missed the opportunities when the private market was ready to take up the steel company on terms that in retrospect can now be seen to have been reasonable, a not excessively jaundiced observer may conclude that the Conservatives are unlikely to dispose of it at all.
3. But not wholly. Directives to the banks to limit loans, for example, are of a different character from raising the rate of interest and are akin to physical controls. Subsidies to private enterprise (e.g., to agriculture and some industrial companies) are, of course, in the last analysis poison to the free-enterprise system.

4. Partly by design, but largely also as a simple result of greater laxity in control.

5. And probably also water supply; but there is not much party controversy in this because water supply is already largely in public hands, and where it is not, the suppliers are closely controlled by statute.

6. Consider, for example, the almost fantastically naive confession of Mr. Emmanuel Shinwell, who, after nationalizing the great coal and electric power industries, stated that on assuming office he expected to find that his party would have ready a blueprint for nationalization, for after all it had preached it for two generations. He was astonished to find nothing in the locker. That he himself had spent a long life preaching nationalization without knowing, and obviously without caring to know, whether there was a blueprint or not, appeared in no way to abash him. Consider also the current password amongst the designers of Labor's program: control over "the commanding heights of the economy." This is brilliantly fashioned for Labor's needs; for it gives the impression of strategic mastery without necessarily meaning anything at all (other than the sense in which central banks already exercise control). The use of a military metaphor is unconsciously revealing of the mind of the economic planner.

Of course, to draw attention to the absence of a blueprint for nationalization is in no way to suggest that Labor's policy would have been better with a blueprint than without one. It might have been worse.

7. There is little doubt that this is correct, even though at the time of writing (October, 1961) the Conservatives' popularity appears to be crumbling.

8. In the European, not the American, sense, of course. I am referring here to debate on economic and social matters only, and among the general public, not among professional economists. There are still some fields in which Britain is splendidly liberal.

I know, of course, that some American libertarians speak in similarly gloomy terms of their country, but illiberal notions have won a far deeper and more pervasive influence over the unconscious attitudes of men in Britain than in America. The mean animus against the economically successful (masquerading under notions of fairness and morality); the tenderness to those who resist economic change; the almost automatic tendency to think that if anything appears to be wrong, the state must put it right; the widespread assumption that the incomes of rich taxpayers (and only of rich taxpayers) belong to the state, in the sense that a reduction in their taxation is a "handout" of the people's money—these are the distinguishing marks of the attitudes of millions of Britons of all classes.

9. That is to say, the openly declared theorist. Men of common sense also act on theory, of course, but are not conscious of it.

10. The great exception to this is the tariff reform campaign of the early years of the century, culminating in the protectionism of the thirties. When the Conservatives, in a regrettable aberration, allowed themselves

to be captured by the Radical, Joseph Chamberlain, they adopted and tried to expound German theories that were, in fact, through and through etatist. But it was poorly done. Mostly their protectionism was on a man-in-the-street level even in the Cabinet chamber. Their philosopher-satesman and leader, Balfour, could hardly conceal his disdain for the level at which some of his colleagues pitched their appeal.

11. There are some things in Britain that the people love to tell themselves are the best of their kind in the world. British justice is an example; but the very fact that the popular belief in the superiority of British justice is mainly well founded is an unfortunate cause of our failure to notice that there may be a few features of the organization of justice in which we have something to learn from other countries. Now this tendency to pat ourselves on the back (we even pat ourselves on the back for not blowing our own trumpet!) can have a powerful political influence. Thus the Left has propagated the preposterous myth that we have a National Health Service that is the envy of the world. Described in this way, the National Health Service comes to excite pride even in the Conservative's heart, despite his awareness of its many defects.

12. Similarly the hard-faced men who had done well for themselves out of the First World War and who were once alleged to throng the Conservative benches have disappeared without trace and without successors. On the other hand, the Labor Party has always had, and still has, a contingent, corroded with self-righteousness and envy, even more unpleasant than any hard-faced men.

13. John Kenneth Galbraith, *The Affluent Society* (Cambridge, Boston: 1958), chap. 18.

14. Except in the eyes of the self-styled champions of the common man. Their contempt for his common sense and intelligence is as baseless as their flattery of his probity and integrity.

15. I.e., *Anglice,* private schools.

16. In protest against which Mr. Bevan, who regarded a completely free health service as his own pet child, resigned.

17. See Command Paper 1337, Her Majesty's Stationery Office, April, 1961.

Index of Names

ALBRECHT, KARL, 25
Arze, Walter Guevara, 147 f., 153, 180
Ayres, E., 85, 104

BARLOWE, RALEIGH, 104
Barnett, Harold J., 81, 83, 102, 104
Bator, Francis M., 105
Becker, Gary S., 105
Bedregal, Guillermo, 181 ff.
Beltrán, Fausto, 181 ff.
Bevan, Aneurin, 242
Boorstein, Edward, 81 ff., 102, 104
Brown, Harrison, 75, 103
Buchanan, James M., 104 ff.

CALLAHAN, J. C., 103
Cellini, Benvenuto, 227
Christy, Francis T., 83, 102 ff.
Clark, Colin, 26, 53
Clawson, Marion, 83, 103 f.
Coase Ronald A., 106
Colberg, Marshall R., 101
Cook, Robert C., 75, 103

DAHL, R. A., 105
Darwin, Charles Galton, 75, 103
Denison, Edward F., 102
Dorfman, Robert, 104
Dowhurst, J. Frederic, 103
Downs, Anthony, 105
Dubinsky, David, 195 f.
Dunn, Edgar S., 103

EGGER, ROWLAND, 177
Estenssoro, Victor Paz, 148 ff., 153

FERNÁNDEZ, JOSÉ, 181 ff.
Ferry, W. H., 10
Fisher, Joseph L., 81 ff., 101 f., 104
Ford, Bacon, and Davis, Inc., 182 ff.
Frankfurter, Felix, 200

GALBRAITH, JOHN KENNETH, 10, 51 f.,
   72, 189 f., 224 ff., 238 f.
Garner, Robert L., 142
Graaff, J. de, 105
Greene, Nathan, 200
Gutiérrez, Ostria, 180 f.

HAND, LEARNED, 123
Haven, James C. de, 104 f.
Hayek, F. A., 105
Held, Burnell, 83, 103
Herfindahl Orris, 81, 83, 103
Hirshleifer Jack, 101, 104 f.
Hitler, Adolf, 30
Hoffa, James, 196
Hoover, Calvin B., 143
Huff, Darrell, 4
Hughes Roland R., 214

JEFFERSON, THOMAS, 12

KNOWLES, JAMES W., 102

LAMPARD, ERIC E., 103
LaPiere, Richard, 35
Lindblom, C. E., 105
Lippmann, Walter, 207
Lynes, Russell, 224

257

McDONALD, DAVID, 197
McKean, Roland N., 106

MÁRQUEZ, MARTINEZ, 158, 181
Marx, Karl, 12
Mason, Edward S., 86, 102, 104
Meany, George, 196
Milliman, J. W., 11, 102, 104 f.
Mills, C. Wright, 10
Musgrave, Richard A., 105
Muth, Richard F., 103

NETSCHERT, BRUCE C., 83, 85, 103
Nourse, Edwin G., 46 f.

ORDWAY, SAMUEL H., 75, 103
Osborn, Fairfield, 75, 103

PACKARD, VANCE, 10
Perloff, Harvey S., 103
Pigou, A. C., 72
Potter, Neal, 83, 102 ff.
Putnam, Palmer, 75, 85, 103 f.

RADIN, ALEX, 143
Renshaw, Edward F., 102
Reuther, Walter, 195
Rickover, Hyman, 75, 103
Robertson, Ross M., 104
Rousseau, J. J., 87 f., 104

Rusk, Dean, 149
Ruttan, Vernon W., 101, 103 106

SCARLOTT, C. A., 85, 104
Schurr, Sam H., 83, 85, 103
Scott, Anthony, 102
Shinwell, Emmanuel, 254
Smith, Adam, 22
Stark, Harry, 143
Stevenson, Adlai, 207
Stigler, George J., 105
Stoddard, Charles H., 83, 103

TAFT, W. H., 72
Toqueville, Alexis de, 5 f., 8
Twain, Mark, 10

VELARDE, JOSÉ FELLMAN, 147 f., 180
Villarroel, Gualberto, 146
Vogt, William, 75, 103

WAGNER, ADOLPH, 13
Wiles, Peter, 191
Wollman, Nathaniel, 102

ZIMMERMANN, ERICH W., 102
Zondag, Cornelius H., 181 ff.
Zuazo, Hernán Siles, 148 f., 151 f.,
    157, 159, 163 f., 173, 180 f., 104

Index of Subjects

absenteeism, 45
absentee landlords, 45
abundance, 10
academic freedom, 3
administrative
 commissions, 211
 tyranny, 212
advertising, 59 f.
 agencies, 61
 demand contrived by, 58
affluence, 56
The Affluent Society, 51, 56, 189
agrarian reform, 154, 156 f.
agricultural policy, 29, 46
agriculture, 40
Alianza para el Progreso, 121, 178
allocation, 51 f.
antidemocratic element
 in critics of individual competence,
  20
art, 216
 contemporary, 223
artist's citizenship, 216, 226
assistance programs, 138
authority
 aggrandizement of, 203
 unauthorized growth of, 203

balance-of-payments, 119
 deficit, 113
balancing, 209
benefit-sharing, 24
 separation of cost-bearing from, 39
big government
 unintended consequences of, 134

Bill of Rights, 210 f., 213
Bolivia, 146, 154
 as a dumping ground, 174
 United States aid to, 176
Bolivian
 planners, 167
 tin industry, 166
bread grain, 30
Britain, 232
 socialist thought in, 234
British Conservatism, 236
bureaucracies
 expansionist forces inside, 27
bureaucracy, 209
bureaucratic
 administrations, 46
 power, unauthorized growth of, 201
Buy American Act, 110 f.

campesinos, 155
capital, 76
 marginal productivity of, 79
 markets, 78, 95
 total base, 76
Catholic centrist party, 30
central
 government, 7
 power, 7
churches, 3
class revolution, 152
classroom shortage, 65
collective
 goods, 99
 wants, 88
collective action, 6

growth of, **7**
collectivistic movements, 178
collectivization, 44
Commodity Credit Corporation, 32 f.
Communist China, 42
competence, 20
competitive enterprise system, 122
complexity
  argument, 19
  of social life, 16
compulsory
  cartels, 31
  methods, cost of, 22
  school laws, 21
Condon-Wadlin statute, 192
conservation literature, 89
Conservatives, 235
consumer, 55
  demand, 13
  purchasing power of, 58
consumer-oriented allocation of
    resources, 25
contraproducente consequences, 145
corporative state, 31
cost-bearing, 24
cost of substitution, 78
creativity of the artist
  in the United States today, 222
creeping philistinism, 227
crop insurance, 38
culture is contrivance, 58

denationalization, 248 f.
depressed areas, 8
discriminatory taxation, 234
diseconomies of small-scale operation,
    94
distressed areas, 196 f.
domestic procurement, 118
due process, 213

economic actitvity, decentralized
    organization of, 47
economic
  commands of the state, 212
  growth, 24
  monopoly, 132
  progress, 13

economics
  academic discipline of, 47
  of scale, 14, 93
economy
  mixed, 5, 131, 140
  planned, 31
Edsel, 59
education, 64
  higher, 46
Employment Act, 25
energy-bearing materials, 37
equality, 7
equal opportunities, 38
equilibrium, 53
escape clause, 122
etatism, 235 ff.
European Economic Community, 33
evidence of injury, 124
expropriation, 168
externalities, 94 f.

farm
  decision-making on a, 43
  enterprises, cooperative, 43
  prices, 62
  program, 63
farmers, 34
  low-income, 62
fascism, 30
federal aid to the arts, 224
Federal Trade Commission, 201 f.
  function of, 204
flood-control protection, 99
foreign aid, 118 f., 177
  in Bolivia, 145, 169, 173
  program, 116, 136, 168
  and trade, 119
foreign
  commerce of the United States, 107
  -exchange control, 44
  policy, 131
  sector, 107
Foreign Operations Administration,
    117
fossil fuels, 85
Fourteenth Amendment, 212
Fourth Amendment, 212
fringe protection, 121 f., 127

future generations, 73
future needs, 79

garment-industry unions, 198
general
    resource shortage, 80
    sales tax, 58
    will, 87, 90
General Services Administration, 112
government
    convenience of the, 213
    expansion, proponents of, 186
    monopoly corporations, 31
    technology of, 15
governmental
    agencies, operational efficiency of,
        27
    controls, criteria of efficiency or
        success, 15 f.
    decisions, 5
    intervention, 97
Great Depression, 7

health service, 248
historical force, defined, 13
hydroelectric power, 37, 97
human needs, 190

imbalance, 52, 190
imperialistic enterprises, 159
Indian railway case, 118
individual
    action, 6
    choice, 91
    decisions, 73
    failures, 22
    incompetence of the, 18, 20
industry
    concept of, 124
    domestic, 124
inequality, 5 f.
inflation, 152 f., 155, 168
intellectual leadership, 48
intellectuals, 28
interdependence, 17
interoccupational mobility, 68
interventionism, 195

Japanese textiles, 127 f.
Japan's agrarian reform, 44

kolkhozes, 40 f.
kolkhoz statutes, 43
Korean War, 7

Labor Party, 237
labor's nationalization program, 233
labor unions, 17, 31
laissez-faire, 187
    theory, 190
landowner, 45
    Landrum-Griffin Law, 192, 198
latifundismo, 154
Latin America, 44, 121, 178
    agriculture in, 175
left-wing revolutions, 178
lobbying, 29
long-run consequences, 8

Madison Avenue, 57, 239
management elected by political pro-
        cedures, 44
marginal analysis, 5
market
    allocation process, 86
    economy, 48
    imperfections, 94
    process, 91
    system, 73
Marxians, 52
Mason's Law, 202 f., 206, 227
medical care for the aged, 6 f., 189
medical research, 2
mercantilism, 10
middle class, 152
minifundismo, 154
Ministry of Mines, 164
Missouri River Basin Project, 77
monopolistic wage levels, 196
monopoly, 17, 35
Movimiento Nacionalista Revolu-
        cionario, 146 ff., 150 ff., 166

national
    defense, 29
    income, 53

security, 109, 127
National Coal Board, 246
National Institutes of Health, 2
nationalization, 159, 233, 246
  of agricultural land, 45
  blueprint for, 254
nationalized
  industries, 244 f., 248
  mines, 159, 166
  tin mines, 160
National Socialists, 31
natural resources, 8, 39, 72, 74
  base, 80
  investment, 88
  policy, 73
  scarcity, 101
neighborhood effects, 95
neomercantilism, 1
neosocialist criticism of the private
  economy, 28
New York Times, 67

oil imports, 126
  restriction program, 127

Papal Encyclical *Quadragesimo
  Anno,* 30
paternalistic decision-maker, 91
pension liability, 244
persuasion, 238
political
  allocation process, 86
  arena, 93
  processes, 91
  technology, 15
political parties, 93
  public financing of, 3
pork-barrel system, 98
poverty, 51, 243, 247
pragmatic, 5
pressure groups, 9
  tactics of, 38
price-fixing, 24
  compulsory cartel, 30
pricing, 249
private enterprise, 248
  system, 26
private property in land, 40

private provision, 242
private sector, 1
  of the economy, distortions in, 29
  and imbalance between public
    sector, 51
  trade-union stake in the, 193
private service, 2
private versus public sector in art,
  221
problems of ignorance, 94
procurement policy, 112
productivity, 193
profit motive, 28, 74
profits, 194
progressive income taxes, 40
public
  controls, 18, 20, 246
  education, 14
  interest, 23
  opinion, 47
  provision, 242
  -resource projects, 97
  sanitation, 36
  service, 2
public and private, division between,
  2
public and private enterprise, differential performance of, 37
public enterprises, 36
  decisive weaknesses of, 35
  preference for, 28
public expenditures, 53, 233
  on education, 64
  expansion of, 241
  growth of, 2
public sector, 1, 26, 34, 40, 47, 56,
  131, 139, 205
  definition of, 3
  increase in as a side effect of legis-
    lation, 33
  protagonists in the U.S. of the, 188
  self-energizing character of the, 194
  statistical image of the, 233
public squalor argument, 3

quota, 127
  -peddling, 125
  voluntary, 3

Realpolitik, 47
real wages, 193
redistribution of income, 90, 92, 97
relativism, 209
resource
  base, 82
  depletion, 94
  owners, 94
Resources for the Future, Inc., 80
Revolución National, 146, 175, 179
ritualistic liberalism, 57
roads, 54
role of the state in economic life, 12
rural communes, 42
Rural Electrification Administration, 36

scarcity, 51 f.
  economic, 79
  physical, 79
social
  action, 23
  administration, 241
  benefits, 90
  costs, 95
  justice, 38
  rate of interest, 90
  spending, 6
  unmet needs, 8
Social Democrats, 30
socialism, 3, 9, 165 f., 188
social rate of time preference, 90
social security, 18, 31, 163
  program, 7
social services, 233, 238
  expert in, 240
society
  coercive, 30
  noncoercive, 25
Soviet Russia, 4, 40, 43
Soviet Union's agricultural
  experiment, 44
  production, 41
sovkhozes, 40 f.
state
  activity, 13
  enterprises, 140
  farms, 41

pensions, 244
remedies, 29
role of the, 185
state-supported theatres, 206
statism, 187
statistical misrepresentation, 2
statistics, 20
  how to lie with, 4
statutes of limitations, 205, 210
strikes by public employes, 193
subsidies, 62
sugar, 30
sugar-beet output, 78
sumptuary and political freedom, 59
surplus
  agricultural products, 115
  food, 175
symbols, 220
symptoms, temporary relief of, 8

Taft-Hartley Act, 191 f.
tariff
  barriers, 121
  policy, 109
  reductions, 122
tariffs, 120
tastes, minority, 56
taxation, 26
teachers, 68
  licensing of, 21
tests of need, 248
Texas Railway Commission, 97
Theory of Perpetual Poverty, 243, 248
theory of wants, 238 f.
Thomasville Chair case, 201
tin interests, 158
trade
  regulation, 201, 203, 205
  restrictions, 109
trade-union leaders, 186, 197
  engaging in self-destructive process, 190
trade-unions, 185 ff.
  and advanced welfare-state conditions, 191
  stake in the private sector, 193

transportation, 54
trivialities, 55 f.

uncontrived demand, 58
underdeveloped world, 139
unemployment, 196
United States Constitution, 209 f.
United States Tariff Commission, 121, 123

violence in labor disputes, 198
voter ignorance, 93
vulgarities, 56

waste-makers, 93
water resources, 78
watershed management, 85
wealth of nations, their control over economic life, 13
Weimar Republic, 30
welfare
  economists, 91 f.
  policy, 243
welfare state, 185, 187 f., 238, 242, 247
West Germany, 25
worker control, 162